LIFE
ON THE
CUTTING EDGE

SAL RACHELE

Life on the Cutting Edge
Personal Growth and Spiritual Development

Published by Living Awareness Productions
P.O. Box 73,
Sedona, AZ 86336

First Printing January 1994

ISBN: 0-9640535-0-0

Printed in the United States of America by
Mission Possible Commercial Printing
P.O. Box 1495,
Sedona, AZ 86339
(602) 282-6523

LIFE ON
THE CUTTING EDGE

SAL RACHELE

This book is dedicated to all people who are in service to Earth's awakening and to those who supported me in the writing and production of this work.

LIFE ON THE CUTTING EDGE

Table of Contents

Chapter 4 (continued)

TABLE OF CONTENTS

Chapter 21 (continued)

TABLE OF CONTENTS

LIST OF FIGURES AND TABLES

Figures and Tables (continued)

PREFACE

This book attempts to do the impossible. If it even partially succeeds in meeting its objectives, the effort will have been worth it. Since I became involved in personal growth activities in my early 20's, I have read countless books, attended numerous workshops and seminars and met many remarkable people. I have looked at several versions of the Creation story, the scientific process, psychology and spiritual awareness. I have come to the conclusion that no teaching contains 100% of the truth, and certainly this book is no exception. What this book does do, however, is explore most of the significant questions of our time in a logical, straightforward manner.

Part I contains material from various classes I taught in the 70's and 80's on personal growth. It explores aspects of the self and the methods I've found most effective for increasing self-awareness. Unless we are able to expand our limited perception of inner and outer reality, there is no way we can know for sure the validity of many of the subjects explored in Part II.

Part II takes a fresh look at many of the most basic and thought-provoking issues of our time, from the story of Creation and the real history of Earth, to the inner workings of secret societies and their mystical knowledge.

As you can see, there are very few bibliographical references in this book. Second-hand knowledge is of limited value. Hence, this book is based primarily on my direct experience. By direct experience, I'm including information given by my own higher mind (also known as higher self), mystical revelations, spiritual visions, contacts with human potential teachers, telepathic communication with spirit guides, and common sense. However, no amount of direct experience automatically guarantees the accuracy of the information. This is particularly true of dates and times of events from ancient mythology. Although I have received very specific information regarding chronology, this information differs considerably with some scientific and archeological data.

In most cases, I have verified the information presented here through more than one source, and where I have uncertainty as to the validity of a statement, it is usually prefaced with some form of "I believe..." Because there is no way to objectively prove much of the material, I leave you to draw your own conclusions.

To get the most out of this book, I highly recommend you read the Glossary and refer to it every time you run across a term you don't understand. Words in the English language are used in various contexts, depending on the background of the author. For example, to one author, "knowledge" can mean an experience of facts stored in memory, and to another, it can mean supreme enlightenment. Obviously, these are very different definitions for the same word.

One of the difficulties in writing a book of this nature is the fact that new information continues to pour in pertaining to the subjects presented here. By the time this book goes to print, some sections could already be obsolete. Reality is not static. It is continually evolving and mutating. And since it is different for each person perceiving it, to define it completely in a book is not possible. Notwithstanding, most of the stories and experiences described here are of a universal nature; issues that are common to most, if not all mankind. I'm sure you will find many of these issues of interest in your own path of personal growth.

FOREWORD

The purpose of this book is to share with you my perceptions of reality as I see it. If this helps you in your ability to understand what you perceive, then my time has been well spent. Part of my intrinsic nature is to share my experiences with others. While I love to do this spontaneously, it is better, in written format, to begin with the basics and gradually introduce new topics. I have attempted to do this, and although it is not easy to find a pace that suits everyone, I encourage you to read the information in this book in the order presented.

Much of the material given here can only be understood from a deeper level of the self than the intellect. Although many chapters deal with the mind, mental understanding will be inadequate to grasp the full meaning of what I am trying to communicate.

I have one basic requirement for my readers. It may sound simple, but it is often difficult to put into practice. *I want you to keep an open mind at all times.* Do not flatly accept or reject anything I say here. A healthy response, if you encounter new information, might be to say *"That sounds interesting. I don't know whether it's true or not, but I'd like to find out."* The truth regarding most of the material given here can be discovered through personal exploration. If something sounds incredible, check it out. Go inside yourself and find out why you are reacting to it. If it clearly feels wrong to you, reject it. However, more than likely, the information has triggered an old belief system you have that is not in accord with what I am saying.

If you have problems in any area of your life, you may find the information in this book of particular value to you. But please don't feel I'm going to solve your problems for you. Rather, I'm going to give you some tools that I have found valuable in dealing with my own issues.

In our society, personal growth is often difficult to find time for. Many people, even if they do have the time, still find it difficult to achieve the goals they set for themselves. Before making the commitment to exploring your inner nature, you may be asking yourself:

(1)　Is this practical? Is it compatible with my lifestyle?

(2)　How can I find the time to work on myself and still maintain my livelihood, social life and multitude of daily obligations?

In order to reconcile self-exploration with the rest of life, we must understand the importance of such an undertaking and the need to give daily attention to it. If it were possible to see in advance all the benefits of self-exploration, then I believe everyone would make time for it.

For many, there is a degree of skepticism. We have been sold all sorts of things, from high-priced seminars and get-rich-quick schemes to products with magical claims. There are a lot of paths and a lot of teachers. Some are complete frauds, others are questionable at best, and many are genuine. I can't tell you which ones will work for you, but I can make suggestions. I can also make a few general observations.

When contemplating a new method of self-exploration, ask yourself the following: *"Does this path allow me the freedom to discover the truth for myself, or does it dictate a rigid system or theology I must follow in order to be saved?"* Unless there is respect for individuality and diversity within a group, it becomes a cult.

Most true teachers aim to empower their students to become as knowledgeable as they are about the subject matter. Be wary of anyone who encourages dependence on a leader for all the answers. Jesus, through His teachings, provided direction and insight for His disciples and did urge them to follow Him, but He did not try to force compliance; He left it to them to make their own decisions.

Within each of us are the answers we are seeking. My intent here is to trigger your own growth process and give you tools for discovering your own answers.

Several hundred years ago, one person had the idea that the Earth was round. To the general populace at the time, this thought was incredible. My point is obvious. In this book I will be challenging beliefs held by almost every single human being on Earth. Unless you have direct experience of something, it remains a belief system. Your task, if you desire the truth, is to seek out the direct experience necessary to know what is truth. This may mean abandoning some very cherished ideas that no longer serve you.

With this in mind, I invite you to go on a journey with me into the nature of the self and the universe. I hope your experience of this book brings you increased understanding and personal fulfillment.

The Way I See It

This is the way I see it.
It is different from the way you see it.
So why write about it?

This is a time of great awakening.
Many believe they have no one to share
Their experiences with.
The world has believed in separation
For so long.

There is a new world being born,
Rising from the ashes of the old.
We are the explorers, you and I,
And we meet on common ground.
I have a piece of the puzzle -
So do you.

This is my way of sharing my piece with you.
Take what you like; leave the rest.
And do not be concerned
If it's right or wrong.
How does it feel?

Does it make sense to your heart?

Let us begin the journey.

INTRODUCTION

My Story in a Nutshell

There are several sections of this book that are controversial. Much of the material is difficult to prove because it is subjective. Perhaps this brief biography will give you a glimpse into my own process and help you discover the truth behind my words.

I was born in Salt Lake City in 1955 to parents of modest means. No, they weren't Mormon. In fact, they weren't even Christians. Having come from a Roman Catholic lineage, my father was one of 11 children growing up during the Depression. Although he was the third born, he carried the family name, Salvatore, which means "savior" in Latin. As the oldest of four children, I continued the family name. My childhood was turbulent and somewhat traumatic. We moved around a lot, and I found it difficult to make friends in school. My father had a hard time with my mother and four children, and since I was the oldest, he frequently took out his frustrations on me. Later, he felt guilty for the way he had treated me, which didn't help.

Although I received a generous portion of guilt, shame and poverty growing up, I was also introduced to progressive religion - my parents were Unitarians, a non-sectarian church with no dogma or creed.

My mother was a classical music fan and I began piano lessons at the age of six. I became quite good, competing in concerts and recitals in Oregon, where we moved in 1963.

I was a rather shy child, and not very happy, so I escaped into the world of the intellect. I read voraciously, got mostly A's and B's in school, and had little or no social skills. I was incredibly intelligent, according to the aptitude tests, which I didn't give much credence to.

In my teen years, I discovered alcohol, drugs, rock and roll and sex. In my senior year of high school, I skipped out and moved to California to live with a Native American woman I had met during the summer of 1972. During the five years she and I were together, we went through a multitude of emotional roller-coasters, constantly breaking up and then coming back together. Although my mind was in a fog at the time, I later realized we were enmeshed in a classic codependent/alcoholic relationship.

In 1976, we separated and I began my spiritual quest. I hitchhiked to San Francisco near the end of the hippie days, dropped LSD and hung out with the counterculture. After a couple of years, I got tired of this and went back to school, majoring in electronics at a community college.

I graduated in 1976 with an AA degree and promptly went to work in Silicon Valley (California) as an electronics technician.

It was in 1976, in San Jose, that I met a psychic who proceeded to describe, in detail, people in my life whom she had never met. I knew then that psychic phenomena was real. The woman encouraged me to take Silva Mind Control, which opened up my higher mind and got me moving quickly on my path. My Silva teacher was an extraordinary man who taught meditation and enlightenment in addition to the basic course. After one particularly engrossing class, we took a break and I went outside on the lawn and sat under a tree, gazing up into the summer sky. As I watched the leaves rustling in the breeze, the unknown entered my consciousness. Suddenly the past was gone and the present moment extended into infinity. I was reborn--new again--eternal. I had just discovered how much greater the universe was than my little, intellectual version of it.

After my initial awakening, I took several personal growth seminars at night while continuing my daytime electronics job. One evening I went to a lecture by a group who called themselves "Solar Cross." I had no idea what to expect, and when I received the written materials, I thought it was some sort of science fiction group. They claimed to be in telepathic contact with a group of extraterrestrials, or "space brothers" who served "the Radiant One."

I was not a religious person. I had always had great difficulty with the concept of God and Christ, but I had an open mind, so I continued to go to the classes which met every week.

Several weeks later I was sitting on my balcony looking out over the city when I began to get telepathic transmissions of my own. It was as though the whole universe had opened up and poured itself into my brain. Suddenly I knew things I had never known before; volumes and volumes of things. In that moment, I realized my "science fiction" class was based on truth. I began to put the pieces of the puzzle together.

Later that fall, I had another experience, this one on a more spiritual note. I was listening to Wagner's "Prelude to Lohengrin" when suddenly Christ and the angels entered my consciousness and I merged with them. There was a brilliant white light permeating my being and an instantaneous comprehension of my spiritual path. I knew then that I would become a healer and teacher and eventually leave the world of electronics behind.

Within a couple of years, I grew tired of the "rat race" and moved to Santa Cruz where I joined a spiritual community and began practicing Rebirthing, a conscious breathing yoga. I travelled around the west, living the life of a spiritual vagabond, giving Tarot readings and breathing sessions for ten dollars or whatever people were willing to give. I was happy and free, up to a point.

After relaxing at a hot springs for several months, I decided to move back to Oregon and teach at an experimental college. I taught Rebirthing and psychic awareness classes off and on for two years until I once again grew tired of my routine.

I then moved to California and "re-entered" the mainstream, taking a job in computer graphics. I wasn't really sure why I went back to a regular job, but it seemed the right thing to do at the time.

I lived in San Francisco for two years with a woman I had met in Oregon, then moved to Marin County, just north of San Francisco. I continued Rebirthing during that time and took a One Year Seminar from my friends Jim Leonard and Phil Laut, who were nationally-known seminar leaders. Several months into the seminar, I decided to begin recording my piano music. For many years I had been improvising and composing my own music, but until now, I had never thought to record it. Well, that was the beginning of my career as a recording artist.

I found that my original music was inspired from another dimension and that it was highly relaxing to most people. I produced four tapes in about six years, some of which had modest success in the marketplace.

In 1991, I moved to Sedona, Arizona, acting on guidance I had received over a year prior while living in the Bay Area. I gave up a good-paying job and decided to devote myself full-time to healing work.

My spiritual growth accelerated dramatically when I moved to Sedona. I began remembering levels and dimensions of myself that had been veiled since returning to embodiment. I realized that my previous lifetime had been in another dimension, on another world, a place of great beauty and evolvement. I began to understand why it was so easy for me to detach from the world, and why so many of the so-called important things in life had so little meaning for me.

In the fall of 1991, I took another quantum jump by joining a theatre group. We wrote, produced and directed our own material, a blend of drama, dance and sacred ritual. The company focused on bringing spiritual transformation to the stage, healing the ancient pain of our "fall from grace" and celebrating the fullness of life.

As I played out the light and dark sides on stage, I began to truly integrate those polarities in my life. I realized I had denied my shadow side for lifetimes, opting for a path of religious supremacy and monastic detachment. I realized the importance of embracing the physical and emotional components of the self, and as I did so, I felt a new sense of power and security coming from within.

I began writing this book in the fall of 1991, as ideas were pouring into my consciousness daily. Some of the material was from a book I had started 15 years earlier on the nature of the mind, but most of it was new - material I had not seen in the hundreds of books I had read.

In the spring of 1992, I neared completion of the book. But it was not until almost a year later that I had grasped the teachings in a way that made the project feel complete.

I realized that I could not directly impart my experiences to another human being, but I knew that through this book I could be a wayshower for many that I could not otherwise reach. So, dear reader, I hope you are one of those who can receive my gift.

We live on the cutting edge - the most exciting time in all of history. In the next 20 years, we will either achieve our wildest dreams, or destroy ourselves. The choice is up to us. I have made my choice, now it's your turn.

Sal Rachele

Sal Rachele

****

PART I
MODELS OF
REALITY

****

CHAPTER 1
WHAT IS REALITY?

Reality and Truth

Truth is different from reality. Reality is dependent upon the perceiver, while truth is what's actually so about a given reality. Another way to say this is that reality can have many levels and dimensions of experience, while truth involves all the levels and dimensions simultaneously. Reality is perceived while truth is known.

Outer Reality

Outer, or "objective" reality, is commonly believed to be that which is perceived through the body's senses. My definition of outer reality will be a bit broader than that because I am aware that we have many more senses than the five basic ones. Also, we have scientific instruments that are capable of measuring aspects of the universe that our senses cannot perceive. We know about atoms, molecules, cells, etc., yet we cannot see them physically with the naked eye.

We also hear of the larger "spiritual" universe that exists beyond the physical one. One definition of "spiritual" is *"That which exists in the invisible."* Both science and religion acknowledge the existence of this vast realm. For example, if you've ever seen a chart of the light spectrum (Figure 1.1), you know that the visible part is only a tiny line between infrared and ultraviolet. All the beauty of this world, as well as the billions of stars in the night sky, are represented by this tiny line on the light spectrum. Although we can measure some of the frequencies beyond our physical senses, these frequencies are invisible to us and hence, by definition, are part of the infinitely larger spiritual universe.

Many religions teach that the physical world is an illusion. This is partially true in the sense that what we see with the body's eyes is only an image of what is actually there. All we see is the reflected light from an object as it hits the retina of the eye, is recorded by the brain, and is then transmitted via nerve impulse back to the optical faculties. Also, when we look at the physical world with our conventional senses, we see only the past. We do not see what is occurring now. Even this printed page is viewed in the past. It takes light reflected from this page approximately one-billionth of a second to reach the retina of the eye.

Figure 1.1 - The Light Spectrum

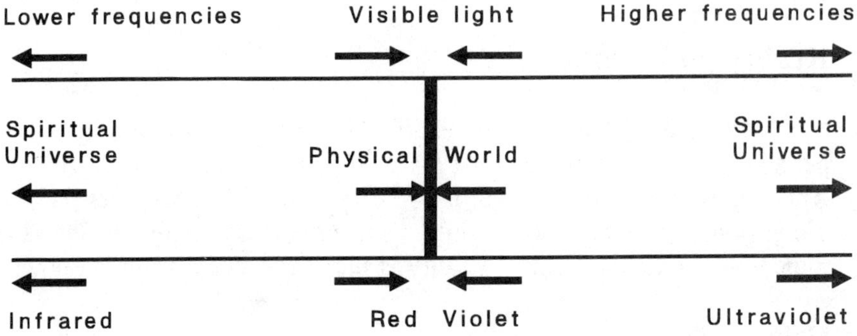

Lower frequencies   Visible light   Higher frequencies

⟵   ⟶   ⟵   ⟶

Spiritual
Universe   Physical World   Spiritual
                                                        Universe
⟵   ⟶⟵   ⟶

⟵   ⟶   ⟵   ⟶

Infrared   Red   Violet   Ultraviolet

The further away an object is, the further into the past you are looking. Distant galaxies may be billions of light years away, and as a result, it may take billions of years for the light from these galaxies to reach the retina of the eye as it peers through a telescope. If we assume that the measurements are accurate by not taking into account curvatures and distortions in the space-time continuum, it would seem that we are actually witnessing what took place billions of years ago in a faraway galaxy. It is theorized by some astronomers that if they could create a powerful enough telescope, they might be able to look far enough back in time to see the beginning of the physical universe.

In addition to the time lag involved in physical perception, there is also the illusion of solidity in material objects. The atoms that make up physical matter are like tiny solar systems floating in a vast space. The speed at which the electrons orbit the atomic nucleus gives the appearance of solidity. The sheer number of atoms in an object also make the object seem solid. Actually, there is far more space than atomic substance. Most objects are more than 99% empty space. It is the energy fields within the atomic structure that hold objects together enough to form solidity. If this energy field were not present, we would walk through walls and be unable to sit on a chair.

This rudimentary discussion of physics is simply to point out the validity of the statement "the world is an illusion." However, it is not that the world does not exist, it is just that we do not perceive it as it actually is. The world is very real. It has an objective reality involving the interaction of billions of atomic particles, and it has a contrived reality given it by the collective consciousness of humanity (more on this later).

Inner Reality

The fascinating outer universe is small potatoes compared to the inner universe. What do we mean by "inner?" Certainly not the inside of the body, although the body and brain are a whole, complex universe unto themselves. Generally, the inner universe consists of the emotional, mental and subtle levels of experience.

The key to understanding the outer world is to understand the inner, because in many ways, the outer is a reflection of the inner. The inner world is so vast and complex that it often does not appear to create the outer. In fact, most people believe they are at the effect of the outer world; mere pawns in a chess game created by some outer deity. These beliefs arise from misunderstandings about the nature of the self.

Beliefs

Beliefs create reality. For example, let's suppose two people each have $1,000. The first person believes he is in poverty and feels his $1,000 is woefully inadequate to meet what he perceives to be his needs. The second person feels wealthy and sees his $1,000 as a lot of money that can bring a lot of things to him.

The first person's reality is one of poverty while the second person's reality is one of wealth. The truth is they both have the same amount of money and are simply perceiving it differently based on their belief systems about their needs.

A related idea is that reality is largely dependent on the culture we live in. In many parts of the world, people have very little in the way of material comforts, yet seem relatively happy. In the United States, many with far greater material wealth are not as happy. Obviously, the belief that material wealth brings happiness is not entirely true. It is also obvious that there is a wide variance of beliefs about what one needs in order to be happy.

Beliefs create reality. It sounds so simple. But the monkey wrench here is that beliefs and their resulting realities occur on many levels and dimensions simultaneously, with one level of belief often conflicting with another level or canceling it out. In addition, most of us can only see the "tip of the iceberg" of our belief systems. Most belief systems are deeply embedded in the subconscious mind. Our conscious mind is like the part of the iceberg above water. The real power of belief lies in the vast chunk under the surface.

If we have a conscious belief that we are wealthy, for example, but a subconscious belief that we are poor, the subconscious belief will probably have a greater influence on our overall experience of reality. In later chapters we will explore ways to uncover and reprogram the subconscious mind to bring our subconscious beliefs in line with our conscious ones.

There are many layers to the subconscious. For example, think of the unhappy millionaire who believes that money brings happiness. If that were the only belief he had on the subject, he would probably be happy. (Actually, in this case, it would not be the money that brings the happiness, but the belief itself.) But suppose underneath that belief is another one that says "No matter how much money I have, I'll never be good enough." This belief may have power over the first one and create a feeling of dissatisfaction for the millionaire.

Throughout history, there have been individuals who succeeded, against seemingly insurmountable odds, to accomplish their dreams. These are the individuals who broke out of the belief in victimhood. There are many books on the power of belief and positive thinking and I will not duplicate efforts here. My intent is to go deeper than that; to look at the most sacred of all beliefs and then go beyond these core beliefs to their origin.

In the following chapters, we will dive in and investigate the various levels and dimensions of the inner world, taking a look at some of our most commonly held belief systems. By understanding ourselves and our inner workings, we can then move into the mysteries of the Universe at large.

Individual and Collective Realities

Basically, there are two levels of reality on Earth: *individual reality* and *collective reality*. Your individual reality is yours alone; no other human being has the exact same set of beliefs and no other human being is perceiving the world from your body. Collective realities consist of those belief systems that are shared by two or more people. Collective realities often tend to have more power than individual realities. Since belief creates reality, the world of humanity is a reflection of the composite beliefs of each individual combined with the collective beliefs of humankind. In order for society to function efficiently, individuals enter into agreements as to which realities will be accepted and which will not. When enough people agree on a particular reality, it becomes known as a fact. Everyday facts are real in the sense that the human race has collectively agreed to perceive physical reality in a certain way. This is obviously necessary in order for humans to live together on this small planet. Imagine the chaos if everyone had a different interpretation of a red stoplight, for instance. Without collective belief, *red* is simply *red*. But we have all agreed that *red* means *stop* and so this becomes a fact. Someone can still disagree, and for that person, *red* may not mean *stop*, but it may be difficult for him or her to drive an automobile.

The realities with the most power are those that are believed by the most people. Death and taxes seem inevitable because the vast majority of people believe in them. It is possible for an individual to disagree with death and taxes, but due to the extreme pressure to conform to the mass consciousness, very few individuals have broken out of this collective reality.

Because there are many levels and dimensions of reality of which we are not always aware, it is often very difficult to tell reality from truth. There are many people, for instance, who would argue that death is an absolute truth. But unless it is true on every level and dimension, it is not absolute truth.

Later, when we talk about dimensions, we will see that the "higher" dimensions include the "lower" ones, but are not bound by them. In other words, the physical universe can be thought of as a lower dimension contained within the higher dimension of the spiritual universe. If death is not true in this larger universe, it cannot be true in the smaller one. And yet, it is certainly a reality for almost everyone on Earth.

I have seen very clearly that if you create a new set of beliefs that do not conform to what the mass consciousness believes, you are living a very different reality from the one we call "normal." Much of the information in Part II of this book would not have come to me if I had not broken out of many of the mass beliefs of humanity.

The Steps to Awareness

The primary purpose of life is to expand our awareness. We do this by learning from the experiences we have. At first, we do not consciously choose our experiences; they seem to just happen to us, often against our will. As we gain awareness, we begin to see how we caused the various events and circumstances in our lives. There are five main steps to becoming aware. They are as follows:

1. Desiring to become aware. This is the most fundamental desire of humankind: curiosity. We want to find out about things. We search for life's meaning. We want to experience life more fully.

2. Becoming aware of being unaware. This involves noticing our inattention and becoming aware of programming and conditioning that is not beneficial to our growth. We begin to notice our wandering thoughts without resisting, controlling or suppressing them, but rather, seeing the distortions in our perceptions and understanding the nature of illusions, discovering the causes of conflict within ourselves, and being aware of being caught up, emotionally and intellectually, in the past or future. We become aware of feeling tension, pressure and fatigue--bodily sensations that are signs of conflict or inharmony. We look at our responses to situations that arise, without analyzing or criticizing excessively.

3. Letting go of the old. This begins with dispelling ideas, concepts, past programming and belief systems that are no longer appropriate for expansion of awareness. Later, this includes letting go of techniques and methods for consciousness expansion; after all, they are only tools--a means and not an end.

4. Integration. This involves bringing all the parts of ourselves into alignment, reclaiming the aspects we judged against, and experiencing complete self-acceptance.

5. Freedom. Integration brings unity within the self, and unity brings true perception; the ability to perceive what's actually so. This is enlightenment.

In order to reach Step 4 of the awareness process we must go beyond ideas and concepts to the direct experience. But until we have a direct experience, we must start with ideas and concepts. If you have never experienced skydiving, you must start with basic instructions, viewing films, talking to those who have had the experience, etc. However, you can talk to thousands of people who have been skydiving and gain all the knowledge possible about it, but until you have the experience, you really know nothing at all.

To reach Steps 4 and 5 of the awareness process, we must first ask ourselves, *"What is awareness?"* Often this word and *consciousness* are used interchangeably. They are not the same. Consciousness is an intelligent energy; a state of being involving the awareness of existence. We all have consciousness to some extent, but not all of us are aware. Awareness is an active state of being. We may have consciousness in several different dimensions, but we may be aware of only two or three of those dimensions at any given time.

Expansion of awareness means the ability to become simultaneously aware of more and more of our consciousness. If we are normally aware of the first three dimensions of reality, our goal may be to become aware of the other dimensions as well.

There are two types of awareness: *selective awareness* and *choiceless awareness*. Selective awareness involves zeroing in on a specific level or dimension and discovering the truth about that reality. This is often done through concentration, exploration and mind control techniques. Choiceless awareness, or *simultaneous awareness*, is usually achieved through meditation and involves expanding the conscious mind to include the subconscious and superconscious levels.

Many people confuse choiceless awareness with selective awareness. Selective awareness always involves denying one level of reality in favor of another. This is necessary in order to perform certain tasks or communicate ideas about a certain reality. If I'm instructing someone in how to drive a car, I do not want to be exploring the more abstract realms; I want to concentrate on the mechanics of driving. However, if I've had a hard day dealing with practical issues and want to give myself a rest, I need to allow my mind to move into expansiveness and take in the whole picture of life. When I do this, my little third dimensional reality becomes nothing more than one frame in a cosmic movie; one tiny aspect of a glorious whole. All the issues and people in my earthly life become merely "actors on a stage," to quote a famous playwright. From this expanded state I can view all the different angles of a given problem and come up with creative solutions.

Models and Reality Constructs

In my experience with hundreds of personal growth students and teachers, I have discovered what I call "level confusion." Level confusion is a situation where one or both of the following takes place:

(1)   **An idea is conveyed from one person to another, but the language barrier causes misinterpretation.** This is

because not everyone has the same definition for the popular buzzwords in the human potential movement. For example, "God" and "Infinite Intelligence" may have the same meaning intrinsically, but a Christian might be better able to grasp "God", while a scientist might relate to "Infinite Intelligence."

(2) **An idea is communicated with the sender's intention that it be understood on one level, but the receiver interprets it on another level.** This confusion is deeper and more subtle than the language barrier. The most common manifestation of this kind of level confusion occurs when a seeker of truth has discovered a law or principle of life that he or she believes will apply to all of life, but in actuality applies only to a specific level of understanding.

An example of type (2) level confusion involves the law of karma. There is a realm (or level) of Creation where karma is real and valid. However, there are also levels of reality where the concept of karma is meaningless. If the student believes karma is an absolute, immutable law, he or she is in for confusion every time a level of reality is experienced that does not fall into the domain of karma.

In metaphysics I am constantly hearing about how we create our own reality. I have seen well-meaning people take this principle to its extreme and try to explain everything in Creation in terms of what thoughts are present in the thinker. The law of mind is indeed a powerful principle that affects many levels of Creation. However, in my experience, love and compassion are higher (more all-encompassing) principles than creative thought. No place is the dichotomy between creative thought and love/compassion more evident than in the scenario where metaphysicians detach from the woes of the world and close their hearts to those who are suffering by claiming "They created it. It's their karma. I'm not responsible."

To help alleviate level confusion, I've created, throughout this book, various figures and diagrams to illustrate the different realities. Keep in mind that **models are a symbolic representation of reality; they are not the reality itself.** The word is not the actuality. Models are only a means of communication. In truth, there are seldom discrete borders and lines between levels of reality; one aspect tends to blend into another without neat, convenient divisions.

From a truly wholistic perspective, levels, densities, and dimensions are meaningless. There is simply life, with its many facets and experiences. So I urge you to use the models to go beyond them. They may be helpful up to a point, like a teacher, but do not become stuck in them. While you are arguing about whether Jesus came from the seventh dimension or the eighth, you are missing the fragrance of life and the beauty of stillness.

Because there are so many teachings, each with its own specific set of models and constructs, I've borrowed from the ones that seem the most helpful for me, and then added many of my own ideas. One teaching I will mention briefly is "A Course In Miracles." The issue of level confusion is quite evident here. The course is a set of channeled books, purportedly from Jesus, and teaches how to awaken to your true Self. So-called "experts" of the course claim it is written on seven different levels, and after having studied it extensively, I am inclined to agree. To the uneducated, the course appears to contradict itself frequently, but to the trained observer, it simply vacillates between levels.

For example, in one section the course advocates the use of medication for the body when it is sick. In another section it says the body cannot get sick and that the cause of all illness is in the mind. Later, it says the body is an illusion; a meaningless idea. Then it goes on to say the body was created purposely to hide the truth. Further along, it says the body is real, but is only a "tiny fence around a glorious and complete idea." And finally, there is reference to the "incorruptibility" and immortality of the body. All these perceptions appear to be valid depending on what level of awareness you are operating in, but obviously, you can see the potential for confusion.

In the following chapters, we will explore the various aspects of ourselves and how we perceive reality. You will discover how to broaden your consciousness through alpha and theta brain wave functioning and how to increase your awareness greatly in a very short period of time. The exercises in the Appendix will also help you awaken the psychic and intuitive centers of your mind. Later, we will explore several models of reality, including aspects of Self, densities, and dimensions.

Now, I would like to define and describe some models and reality constructs pertaining to various levels of awareness.

Model #1: Levels of Awareness/Aspects of Self

"Levels of Awareness" and "Aspects of Self" refer to the way in which we perceive reality and the human faculties used to perceive that reality. In general, we are referring to inner states of being; i.e., aspects of the Self. Most of the levels of awareness described here will be familiar, some may not be, but all are within, or perceived by, the Self. A level of awareness is similar to a dimension, except that its boundaries are not so much defined by universal laws and principles, as by states of awareness. For example, the physical body and emotions are two different levels of awareness, but both exist in the third-dimensional world.

Levels of Awareness

Higher levels of awareness are not necessarily better than lower levels. Each level has its specific function. Sometimes it is better to focus on the mundane than the expanded states. Ideally, one should be able to shift focus easily from one level to the next or be simultaneously aware of many levels at once.

Levels of awareness can be inclusive or exclusive; that is, they can take in the totality of a given reality or they can select specific attributes of that reality and concentrate on those. For example, cosmic consciousness is inclusive and generally refers to a level of universal awareness, while true meditation is more exclusive and means an inner stillness beyond conscious awareness.

To read this book requires the intellectual level of awareness. But to truly understand it requires a higher level of awareness. Because reality depends on perception, two people can view the same reality from two different levels of awareness and have two completely different experiences. The intellectual person may get the impression that this book is extremely wordy and fails to address deeper issues, while the more spiritually-focused person may gain tremendous insight and energy from reading it.

To properly write, edit, proof, and publish this book required an intellectual awareness and knowledge of mundane details. However, from a higher perspective, the words are simply tools to help the reader go beyond the intellect. In nature, the gardener and botanist must look at a flower from a scientific, intellectual point of view; noting the germination times, proper amount of water, right amount of sunlight, etc. If you look at the same flower from a meditative mind, you may see the handiwork of God in all its splendor.

Aspects of Self

Closely related to levels of awareness are aspects of self. These are the qualities of being which are used to perceive the various densities and dimensions of the universe. For example, the body aspect sees the universe from a physical level of awareness while the soul views life from the soul level.

At the end of Part I, I've included several tables and charts that tie together all the models of reality used in this book: Levels of awareness, aspects of self, densities and dimensions. I've included a seven-dimensional model and a 12-dimensional one.

In the following chapters, we will look at some models of reality based on the following levels of awareness and aspects of self:

Table 1.1 - Levels of Awareness and Aspects of Self

Level of Awareness	Aspect of Self
1. Physical	BODY
2. Emotional; instinctual; sexual	WILL
3. Intellectual; rational; logical	EGO/LOWER MIND
4. Psychic; intuitive; imaginative	HIGHER MIND
5. Love; unity; oneness	HEART
6. Pure essence; higher Self	SOUL
7. Intelligence; wisdom; knowing	OVERSOUL
8. Universal/cosmic consciousness	SPIRIT
9. Nirvana; supreme enlightenment	GOD/GODDESS
10. Eternal newness; silence; timelessness	THE TAO
11. The unknown/the unknowable	THE VOID
12. The Great Mystery	? ? ?

Model #2: Densities

Densities are similar to levels of awareness and aspects of self, but refer to discrete vibratory states of life forms in the universe. I've devoted Chapter 9 to the study of densities. Densities are as follows:

Table 1.2 - Densities

Number/Level	Description
1.	The mineral kingdom
2.	The plant kingdom
3.	The animal kingdom
4.	Human beings
5.	The etheric light body
6.	The soul body
7.	The oversoul
8.	Angels
9.	Archangels
10.	Creator Gods
11.	Universal Gods
12.	The Godhead

Model #3: Dimensions

Dimensions are like worlds within worlds. I've differentiated between densities and dimensions because attaining higher states of consciousness involves making a density shift; i.e., evolving from a lower order life form to a higher one. However, my view is that we all exist simultaneously in at least 12 different dimensions and that our form is the result of where we put our attention. While densities represent specific frequencies, dimensions include entire space-time continuums within the Universe at large. The dimensions in our model are as follows:

Table 1.3 - Dimensions

Number/Level	Description
1.	Existence
2.	Location
3.	Depth; magnitude; physical plane
4.	Time; thought; astral plane
5.	Love; oneness; etheric plane
6.	Soul plane; essence
7.	Oversoul worlds; lower celestial heavens
8.	Celestial planes
9.	Paradise/mansion worlds
10.	Other universes
11.	The Godhead
12.	The void; the unknown

Let's begin our exploration of the models.

CHAPTER 2
THE PHYSICAL BODY

The body is the first level of awareness/aspect of self we will look at. It is a communications medium and vehicle for experiencing the physical universe. The body is controlled by the brain. You can think of the brain as a central computer system, the body as a building in which the system is housed, and the body's senses as input and output devices.

The body is capable of receiving a wide array of sensory input when it is functioning properly. Information from many other levels of awareness can be felt as physical sensations. Although it is obvious that emotions are felt in the body, many psychic, intuitive and other subtle energies are also filtered through the body's sensory input. The kundalini, for example, is an etheric energy field which activates certain aspects of the nervous system along the spinal column.

The body has a built-in survival mechanism and instinctual response which protects it from harm. If something feels unpleasant in the body, it is a sign of imbalance on some level. The imbalance may be physical or it may exist on another level of awareness, such as mental or astral. To determine the origin of problem areas, you must not only be tuned in to your body sufficiently to hear and feel its messages, but you must be able to shift levels until you find the cause of the imbalance.

Health and Illness

Health is the natural state of the body and occurs when all the levels of your being are in alignment. When illness or uncomfortable bodily sensations are experienced, one or more levels are out of alignment. To effect healing, the problem must be corrected on the level or levels where it occurs. Some problems, such as environmental contaminants, are relatively easy to isolate and correct because they occur on only one level. Most imbalances, however, occur on many levels simultaneously. Healing these problems requires going to the deepest level of causation and working back through the more superficial layers. After the deepest layers of imbalance are healed, the other layers usually heal quickly, and some superficial levels may require little or no correction. As we go through our exploration of each level of being, I will list some of the common imbalances found there.

The Brain

(NOTE: For our purposes, we will include our discussion of the brain under the category of the physical body. The mind refers to a non-physical aspect of consciousness and is considered a discrete level of its own which will be covered later.)

Scientists admit they only know about 20% of the brain. Of this 20%, only about half is in daily use by the average individual. In other words, we commonly use about 10% of our brain capacity during an average lifetime.

The brain is like a huge communications center - a biocomputer network similar to a mainframe computer network in a large office building. Like an electronic computer, the brain receives, processes and transmits information which travels in electrical impulses through its various regions. It is well known that the left side of the brain contains many of the analytical and logical functions, while the right side of the brain seems to house the intuitive, imaginative and psychic centers.

The brain receives information from many sources on many levels and dimensions. The most obvious source is from the body through the nervous system. Not so obvious are the impressions received from the electromagnetic field around the body (the aura) and the electromagnetic field surrounding virtually every object in the universe. Information (in the form of electrical impulses) travels through nerve endings called synapses and is imprinted in tiny receptors called neurones.

This is an overly simplified description of the brain. If you wish further detail on the subject, there are many good books available.

Brain Waves

The brain emits electromagnetic waves which can be measured using sensitive electronic equipment (EEG machines, etc.). Brain waves are categorized into four modes. Figure 2.1 below shows sample waveforms for these four states:

Figure 2.1 - Brain Waves

Type	Frequency (cycle/sec)	Waveform	Activity
BETA	15-35 cps		conscious waking state
ALPHA	7-14 cps		dreaming, meditation
THETA	4-7 cps		deep hypnosis, trance
DELTA	0-4 cps		unconscious-ness, deep sleep

Beta (14 - 35 cycles per second)

Beta waves are short and rapid and occur when the brain is busy processing analytical information. This is the state most of us are in when going about our daily tasks. Anything that requires calculating, frequent decision-making or active conversation usually generates Beta waves. Studies have shown that the brain does not function optimally in this state - it is much like spinning your wheels in thick mud. Worry and stress are symptoms of too much Beta activity.

Alpha (7 - 14 cycles per second)

Alpha waves are much slower than Beta waves, but have a greater amplitude. This means the thought forms generated during an Alpha cycle are more powerful and generally contain more energy, despite being slower. Alpha waves occur during periods of meditation, daydreaming, hypnotic repetition of tasks or light sleep. As you can see in Figure 2.2, the most easily remembered dreams occur just before waking and occur during the Alpha state.

Many people can consciously shift from Beta to Alpha merely by autosuggestion, hypnosis or meditation practice (See Figure 2.3). Some people function almost continuously from an Alpha state. On a job, these people tend to get more done than their Beta co-workers even though they are more relaxed. It has been reported that a person who works seven hours per day and meditates for one hour accomplishes far more than one who works eight hours per day. Many creative breakthroughs occur during the Alpha state. This may explain why great inventors often ponder a problem ceaselessly for days, and then the answer comes in a dream or moment of rest.

Theta (4 - 7 cycles per second)

Theta waves are very slow with a large amplitude. Like Alpha, people can be very creative in the Theta state; however, most people cannot remain awake in this state unless they have trained themselves through hypnosis (See Figure 2.4). Theta waves are generated during deep hypnosis and during the earlier portion of the sleep cycle (See Figure 2.2). They can also be induced by certain drugs (See Figure 2.5).

Theta dreams are often harder to remember than Alpha dreams, but may be just as creative or even more so. Those who are able to generate Theta waves consciously often have extraordinary control over normally involuntary bodily functions, and are able to still their minds to a gentle whisper. Some have reported feeling as rested after 30 minutes of Theta as if they had just gotten eight hours of sleep.

Delta (0 - 4 cycles per second)

Delta waves are the slowest form of brain activity and normally occur only during deep sleep and unconsciousness. I have heard reports of people being able to generate Delta waves while being awake and cognizant, but this is rare. Apparently, some trance channels go into Delta while another energy or entity is using the body. These trance mediums usually have no recall of their experience when they come out of trance.

Figure 2.2 - Normal Sleep Cycle

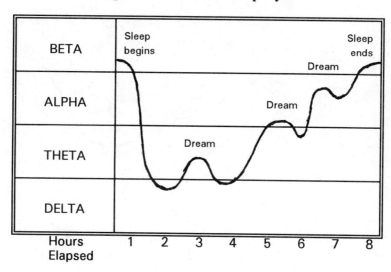

Figure 2.3 - Meditation or Deep Relaxation

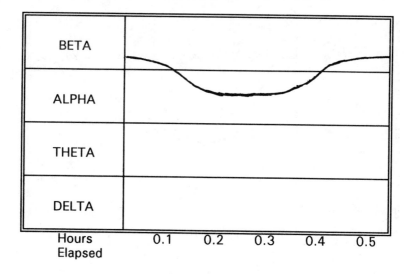

Figure 2.4 - Hypnosis

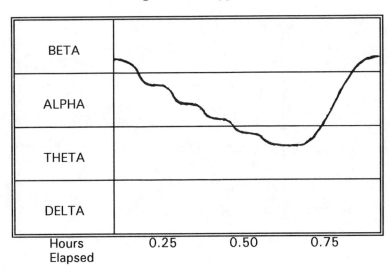

Figure 2.5 - Drug Induced

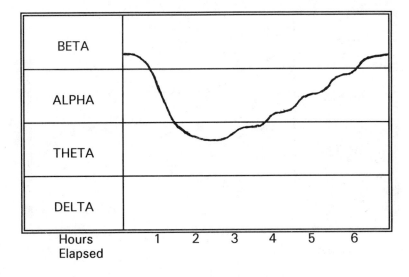

Magnitude of the Brain

The brain is the most complex object known to man. To give you an idea of the magnitude of complexity, consider the following:

Approximate number of brain cells = **10,000,000,000** (ten billion)

Number of neurones/synaptical junctions = **1,000,000,000,000,000,000,000,000,000,000,000** (one decillion)

Number of possible interconnections (paths for information flow) = **the number one followed by more than 1000 zeroes!!!**

The universe did not happen by accident. Obviously, there must be some purpose for the nearly infinite number of possible channels for information flow. The fact that there are trillions of times more connections in the b 'n than stars in the known universe ought to give us a clue as to who and what we are.

Memory and Association

In Chapter 4 we will talk about the rational mind and how it is programmed and conditioned with various belief systems. The brain, being the physical counterpart of the mind, sets up neuronic and synaptical pathways for the information given it by the mind. When something is learned by memory, the same pathways are utilized over and over in the brain until the signal is "etched" into the circuitry. If a particular stimulus enters the brain, any existing experience or beliefs around that stimulus will trigger the pathways that were previously activated by that stimulus. This process is called "memory by association."

For example, if you have a favorite song on the radio, you may notice that every time you hear it, you think of a certain place or feel a certain emotion. It may be that the first time you heard the song was during a drive along the coast, and so every time you hear it now, you remember that drive.

There are good things and bad things about memory by association. If you need to memorize a long list of facts, there are techniques that utilize association to help you remember. On the other hand, once a pathway becomes etched by a certain stimulus, it is very difficult to reroute the information along a different pathway. We will look more deeply at programming and conditioning when we talk about the rational mind.

Figure 2.6 below shows a sample map of synaptical pathways stimulated with memory by association. The single words represent a chain of ideas triggered by a stimulus:

Figure 2.6 - Memory by Association

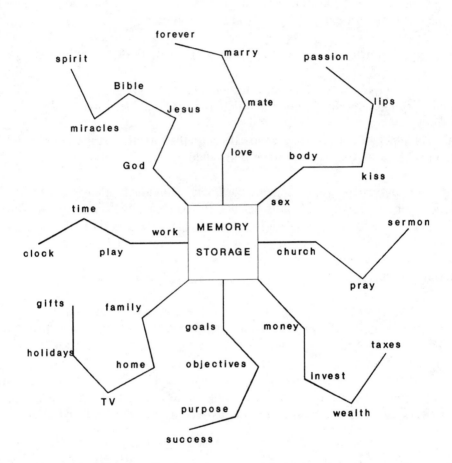

Now let's look at some other aspects of the physical body.

Breathing

One of the secrets of life is breath. Why is this a secret? Because most of us take breathing for granted. There are several breathing techniques that can enhance health and help eliminate illness. One of the forms I use is called "Rebirthing" (or "conscious breathing"). For more information on Rebirthing, see Appendix A.

Breathing properly increases oxygen in the blood, strengthens the immune system, restores chemical imbalances and helps integrate and heal other levels, such as emotional problems.

Exercise

The main benefit of exercise is improved blood circulation and increased oxygen, not only in the moving body parts, but in the brain and circulatory system as a whole. For relatively healthy people, I recommend yoga, dance, Ta'i Chi and nature walks. Massage and polarity bodywork are also highly recommended. Intensive activities, such as jogging and aerobics may work for some people, but are easily abused by overworking the body past the point of therapeutic value.

Diet

I will refrain from preaching about what you should or should not eat, although I will give some general guidelines. Different diets work for different people. Balance is the keyword here. Too much of anything can be a problem. Also, sudden changes in diet can cause shock to the body. If you are sensitive to your body, it will tell you what it needs. Most people are insensitive to their body because they have substance addictions. It is not the substance itself that is the problem; it is the addiction. Eating itself can be an addiction.

There has been much misinformation concerning diet. The meat and dairy industry once decided that the average human needs approximately 2500 calories per day. The latest estimate (by some holistic MDs) is 1000 calories (if there is a high nutritional content in the food). Most people eat way too much. We eat for social and psychological reasons as much as for hunger. If we only ate when our body was genuinely hungry, we would probably consume about one-fourth as much food as the average person in the U.S. consumes today.

Although red meat has a very dense vibration, there may be times when it is appropriate to eat dense food. The high level of fat and cholesterol in red meat makes it easy to overdo it, however. More than one ounce of red meat per day is probably overdoing it. There has been much misinformation given about a meat and dairy-based diet, so if you want the bigger picture, I recommend reading *"Diet for a New America"* by John Robbins.

Again, these are only guidelines, not dictates. By listening to your body, you will find the right diet for you.

Substance Addictions

A substance addiction involves a craving for certain foods (or drugs) for reasons other than genuine bodily hunger. The craving is almost always emotionally based and usually arises from not having emotional needs met in early childhood.

The most common substance addiction is sugar. Many of us were given sweets as children when we were good. As a result, we grew up equating sweets with parental love. Desperately craving love as we grew older, we tried to satisfy the craving by eating sweets. A small amount of simple sugar is usually beneficial to the body, but more than a teaspoon of sugar a day is probably too much.

Another addictive substance is salt. If you buy only products that contain no added salt, and you never salt your foods, you probably get enough salt in your diet.

Alcohol is obviously a big problem in our society. An occasional beer or glass of wine may work for some people; for others, total abstinence may be best.

There are many legal and illegal drugs that are physically and/or psychologically addictive. Often the legal ones are even more addictive than the illegal ones. Drugs are usually only appropriate during acute physical or psychological stress, or when there appears to be no other way of resolving an issue or relieving pain. Depending on any substance to alleviate pain or enhance life is an indication that you are on the path to addiction.

Pollution

There is no place on Earth where the soil, air and water are free from manmade pollutants. However, there is much you can do to minimize pollution. If possible, you should live far away from large cities, at an intermediate altitude (4000 - 7000 ft.) in a temperate climate where there are trees and flowing streams.

The two biggest sources of pollution are the automobile and the consumer. Minimize driving whenever possible. Carpool or ride the bus if you live and work in a large city. Get rid of that old gas hog. Its purchase price may be less than an economy car, but the daily operating expenses are much higher.

If you can afford to, shop at health food stores that carry organic produce. Ninety percent of the food in a normal supermarket is, in my opinion, not fit for human consumption. Additives such as monosodium glutamate (found in most soup and snacks) and sodium nitrite (found in hot dogs, bacon and processed foods) are toxic to the human body and should be banned from store shelves. Even if you stay away from chemical additives, you will find pesticide residues on virtually all non-organic foods. Chemicals such as dioxin (for which there appears to be no safe level) are found in many products.

Common Physical Level Problems

•   Environmental contamination and pollution (noisy machinery, industrial waste, toxins in food, overcrowded cities and social settings, etc.)

•   Poor diet (lack of nutrients, substance addictions)

•   Lack of exercise (lack of oxygen in the blood)

•   Excessive exercise or repetitive body movements (eye strain, heavy equipment operation, excessive manual labor, etc.)

•   Chemical imbalance (often caused by improper breathing and lack of oxygen in the blood)

•   Immune system imbalance (from improper breathing, pollution, excess carbon dioxide in the air, lack of blood oxygen, ozone depletion, etc.; also caused by emotional problems, and problems on other levels)

RNA and DNA

If the brain is the biocomputer, and the body the housing and frame for the biocomputer, the RNA and DNA are the actual program codes. These codes (comprised of molecular chain proteins) determine the size, shape and appearance of the body, among other things. They also control the body's ability to receive and transmit information from other levels of being. They are the actual blueprint for physical life.

The secret to genetic engineering is found in the RNA and DNA. It is possible to reprogram the genetic codes. Without the proper understanding, however, this can be very dangerous. Most attempts at reprogramming have been done by gene splicing and attaching foreign molecules to existing RNA and DNA. This is like pulling teeth with pliers. There are techniques using subtle technologies which are far more efficient and don't produce the dangerous side effects. The real problem with manipulating biological codes is that it usually fails to solve the root causes behind genetic defects. Genetic problems are rarely caused on the physical level. The real causes are found on the etheric, causal and soul levels, and in past lives. These are levels of reality not understood by most scientists and genetic engineers.

Tampering with the genetic makeup of an individual can also be interfering with that person's free will, since it can speed up or delay the process of evolution for that person's soul. With the proper knowledge, it is possible to reprogram the RNA and DNA for physical immortality. If the person receiving the alteration is not sufficiently evolved, it can kill instead. At the very least, it can deprive that soul of needed Earth experience. This is not to say there aren't instances where genetic manipulation is desirable. Many people on the leading edge of mankind's evolution are consciously mutating their cellular structure using natural techniques.

Evolution and Mutation

Mutation is a sudden shift from one level of genetic makeup to another. It can be caused by environmental factors, evolutionary quantum factors, or can be done consciously through certain spiritual techniques. Contrary to Darwinism and related scientific theories, evolution does not occur gradually in a linear fashion. In most life forms, there are stable periods followed by mutations. Evolution proceeds from one density (stage of evolution) to the next in a hop-skip path. The organism evolves through a given density until it reaches the uppermost part of that density; i.e., the highest possible frequency representative of that density. Then there is a mutation or quantum shift into the lowest frequency of the next density (See Figure 2.7). For more information on densities, see Chapter 9.

Figure 2.7 - The Evolutionary Spiral

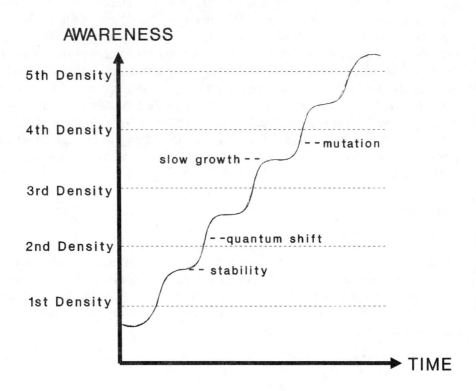

Mutation can be caused by cosmic radiation coming into the Earth during certain phases of the cosmic cycle, such as near the end of a master cycle of 26,000 years. According to the Mayan calendar, the current master cycle will end sometime around the year 2012.

Mutation can also be caused mentally by changing your thought forms, by meditation, prayer, emotional integration and a variety of other factors.

Reincarnation

Reincarnation is a rather complex subject. It is not as simple as just dropping a body and picking up a new one. There are many levels and dimensions to a soul. At physical death, some of the levels return to the spiritual realms and some do not. Chapter 20 partially explains the process of soul fragmentation during physical death.

From a purely physical perspective, most souls take on hundreds of embodiments during their evolution on Earth. Past lifetimes are remembered only when a person's consciousness is centered in the realms of the higher self (also known as the oversoul). From the vantage point of the higher self, one can view the entire timeline of incarnations and perceive information from any or all of them. The soul chooses when and where to incarnate, and determines what many of the circumstances of that life will be prior to incarnation. The oversoul engineers the RNA/DNA codes necessary to create the kind of body that the soul wishes to have. Most genetic diseases are the result of the soul taking on karma (life lessons) for the purpose of remedying imbalances from past lifetimes. Karma is not a punishment, but a learning device that eventually becomes unnecessary.

Ascension

Ascension occurs when a soul evolves beyond the cycle of reincarnation and increases the vibratory frequency of the physical body sufficiently to graduate from the fourth to the fifth density (level of evolution). This means the body's cellular structure is sped up to the point of becoming invisible to ordinary third dimensional consciousness. (A more complete explanation of densities and ascension is given in later chapters.)

CHAPTER 3
THE EMOTIONAL BODY

The second level of awareness is the emotional body. There is a link between the emotional body and the etheric body, but we will discuss the etheric body later. This section will deal with the basic issues of the emotional body: desire, will, power and sexuality.

The emotions are the bridge between mind and body. They are felt by both, but are controlled either by the mind or directly by the soul. The emotional body is the most misunderstood of all the levels of being. It is the experiencer, the feeler of life. Ninety percent of all physical illness originates in the emotional body.

"Negative" Emotions

Emotions are not really positive or negative. All the experiences of life are neutral. It is the mind which judges an experience to be either positive or negative. Every emotion is simply energy-in-motion. Emotions are energy experiences of varying intensity. If they feel uncomfortable in the body, it is a sign of imbalance somewhere. If, instead of judging the uncomfortable feeling, you explore it, it will contain a healing message.

We all have our ups and downs. This is true even with people who claim to be always in a state of bliss, although their ups and downs may not be as pronounced. Emotional swings become a problem when they dominate the consciousness. This means the person is stuck in the emotional body and is unable to balance with the other levels of being.

Some people seem to be continuously in a state of depression, anger, frustration, guilt or anxiety. Most of the methods taught to get rid of these feelings do not really get to the heart of the matter. This is because we are not seeing the total picture of what is happening.

Basically, a negative emotion is a reaction to something in our consciousness. It may be triggered by an event in our lives or it may rise to the surface from a layer of programming or conditioning in the subconscious mind. When we respond to something with uncomfortable emotions, it is usually because we have internal programming or beliefs that are not in harmony with the present situation.

If we feel negative, we can express the feeling or we can suppress it. If we express it, it usually reveals the layer of suppressed material directly beneath it and gives us an opportunity to understand and heal something from our past. If we suppress it, it adds to the existing layers of programming in the subconscious, or creates a new layer on top of the layers already present in our consciousness.

Emotions may be felt but not expressed when it is inappropriate to express them. This keeps them in awareness and they are not added to the subconscious layers, but it does not resolve them until they find an outlet for expression.

Suppression occurs when a feeling is judged as undesirable. By pushing an emotion into the subconscious, it leaves our awareness and we seem to avoid feeling uncomfortable. However, the real cost of doing this is enormous. During suppression, the part of the consciousness receiving the suppressed emotion becomes unavailable for anything else. Its full-time job is now holding the feeling in place until it can be brought to the surface and released.

The key to integrating emotions (aligning the emotional body with the rest of the self so that it is working in harmony) is to love and accept one's emotions at all times and to find appropriate means of expressing them. This is not easy in a society with strict moral rules and regulations. But it is usually better to risk inappropriate expression than to stuff the feelings.

Suppression of emotions creates energy blockages in the body. Life force energy cannot move in those areas of the body where the emotions are stuck. Eventually, the organs in those places begin to malfunction and decay. Aging and most chronic diseases are due largely to problems in the emotional body.

It has been discovered that emotional energy is stored in the cells, affecting the RNA/DNA structure and chemical makeup of the body. Through psychotherapy, Rebirthing, hypnotherapy, meditation and other disciplines, it is possible to liberate the emotions from the cells.

No healing is permanent unless the emotions are allowed free expression. However, expression alone does not integrate emotions. There must be acceptance and understanding as well.

Figure 3.1 shows the bubble analogy of how suppressed material builds up in the subconscious until it is completely filled. When there is no more room in the subconscious for additional suppressed material, unpredictable emotional outbursts can occur. This is the "boiling point" referred to in psychotherapy.

The totality of the conditioning and programming in the subconscious mind is referred to as "historical content." This historical mind is composed of frequently accessed programs (such as learned languages and vocabulary), suppressed experiences (events one is aware of, but consciously avoiding), and repressed experiences (events that one has no awareness or conscious memory of).

Figure 3.1 - The Bubble Analogy

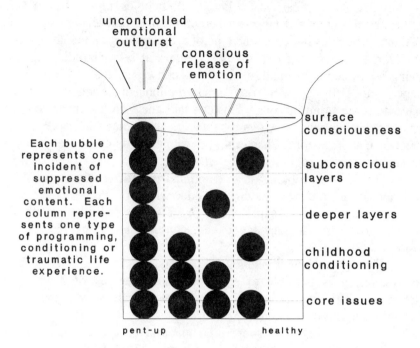

uncontrolled
emotional
outburst

conscious
release of
emotion

surface
consciousness

Each bubble
represents one
incident of
suppressed
emotional
content. Each
column repre-
sents one type
of programming,
conditioning or
traumatic life
experience.

subconscious
layers

deeper layers

childhood
conditioning

core issues

pent-up   healthy

Figure 3.2 - Positive Automated Responses

Positive
programming
for automated
responses when
beneficial for
soul growth.

This person has
released all
suppressed and
repressed emotional
material.

Let's take a closer look at Figures 3.1 and 3.2. The first container (Figure 3.1) shows a carbonated liquid with bubbles, representing layers of historical content and suppressed emotions in the consciousness. Each column of bubbles indicates one type of programming and conditioning. As long as the content remains unconscious, it keeps building up and being reinforced until finally it enters the conscious levels. If the entire subconscious fills up with suppressed emotional material, the bubbles have no place to go but out. This can take the form of uncontrollable emotional outbursts or violent behavior, depending on the type of emotional suppression. Chapter 4 goes into more depth on the origin of these destructive programs and belief systems.

Often, when looking at an emotional disorder, only the bubbles near the surface are seen, leaving a residue within the deeper layers. By being aware of this "pressure-cooker" process, it is possible to bring the bubbles to the surface and burst them consciously (by expressing the emotions constructively).

Through various psychological processes and modes of emotional expression, it is possible to empty the subconscious of destructive programs. This usually takes a considerable length of time and much commitment and dedication to personal healing.

When the layers of suppressed material have been successfully integrated, positive automated responses may be programmed into the layers of the subconscious previously taken up by the negative emotions. The second container shows how the subconscious can be used to benefit personal growth.

Desire

There is a commonly held religious belief that desire must be abolished. There is, in fact, a state of desirelessness which results in a still mind, timelessness and higher awareness. This is a very ecstatic state, but one that cannot be forced by trying to go beyond desire. To judge desire as being less desirable than desirelessness is to get caught in a very painful trap. Like everything else in life, desires need to be loved and accepted so you can learn from them. Desires are not bad. They are a necessary part of evolution. When desires are suppressed, they become cravings, which are destructive. Underneath virtually all cravings are sublimated desires. Usually the craving is simply a mask to hide the real desire, as in the case of craving sweets, where the underlying desire is for love.

Desire can be thought of as the means the will uses to ask for what it wants (see the next section for a definition of "will"). Unless you are already highly evolved, it is very difficult to simply will something into existence unless you first have desire. The will uses desire to spur us into action - if the desire is strong enough, the action will be more immediate. When all the levels of our being are balanced, desires will be normal and healthy. It is only when we are out of alignment that desires become destructive. Destructive desires always indicate there is some part of ourselves we are not accepting.

Suicide, for example, is a multilevel disease involving the will, mind and body. When desire is suppressed, the will becomes frustrated because the mind is ignoring will's means of communication. Eventually, it gives up and loses the will to live. If this is done consciously, the person may try to take his or her own life. If it is done subconsciously, the person may have a fatal accident or contract a fatal disease.

Desire is suppressed mostly because of societal and parental conditioning. If, for example, you always wanted to be a painter, but your parents discouraged you because they didn't believe you could earn a living from it, and you became a doctor instead, you may have lost some of your will to live by denying your artistic desires.

Will

Perhaps the best explanation of will I've found is in the channeled material *"Right Use of Will"* (Four Winds Publications). This set of books defines "will" as the feminine, or magnetic pole of Creation, and "spirit" as the masculine, or electric pole. In a sense, spirit *inspires,* and will *feels.* Spirit comes through the mind and will comes through the emotions. Spirit sees Creation and will experiences it. Spirit is the creative and will, the receptive. In our society, will and power are considered to be masculine traits, but this is based on the learned roles of a patriarchal system.

A healthy human being has spirit and will in balance. However, the patriarchal world we live in has heavily denied the will and this has manifested as emotional problems. While the spirit tends to move fast, the will tends to evolve more slowly. As a result, most people are impatient and try to force their wills to live up to their spiritual ideals.

Power

The will takes ideas from spirit and uses desire and emotion to spur the action needed to manifest the ideas in the world. Most of us feel powerless to change the world in any significant way. This sense of powerlessness comes from suppressing and denying the will. We have been taught that it is wrong to have power. Virtually all the world's religions have instilled this belief. We look at powerful figures in the political arena and see how they have abused their power and we start to think of power as something evil and corrupt.

Power is neutral. It is simply the potential or active energy behind a creative urge. If the will is not allowed to express itself, there will be very little energy behind your ideas. If you judge your power as bad or wrong, you withdraw life force from your emotional body and you no longer have the energy to manifest your desires.

Misuse of power stems from the belief that we must force ourselves on others in order to get what we need. This can occur if we did not get our needs met as a child or if we were shamed into believing our desires were wrong.

Sexuality

The most powerful energy in the emotional body is sexual energy. Because of the power inherent here, this has been one of the most heavily suppressed energies throughout most of history. Sexual feelings need to be loved and accepted no matter what society thinks. Inappropriate sexual expression arises, as you probably know, from suppressed sexual desire. If sexual feelings are accepted, they eventually evolve into a whole-body experience instead of a purely genital one. When the sexual energy is moved up through the body instead of out through the genitals, a totally different experience results. This is called Tantra yoga, or Kundalini yoga, depending on the technique used. Kundalini is actually feminine energy from Mother Earth ascending up the spine to reunite with spirit.

Emotions and Feelings

There is a difference between emotions and feelings. "Feelings" is a generic word used to describe sensations in the physical body, intuitive urges and other impressions, while emotions are specific energy patterns in the emotional body. Actually, there is no separation between body, emotions and mind, so the emotions I'm going to describe here also involve sensations felt in the body and ideas going through the mind.

There are primary and secondary emotions. Secondary emotions are combinations of primary ones. In addition, there are varying degrees of emotions. There are highly enhanced levels and partially denied or suppressed levels of a given emotion. For example, anger, a primary emotion, has a highly enhanced form called rage and a partially suppressed form called resentment.

Although guilt is a feeling, it is not an emotion. It is a state of being which generates the emotions of shame and fear. I have devoted Chapter 17 to guilt, which should clarify this definition. The following table lists the most common emotions and their various forms:

Table 3.1 - Primary and Secondary Emotions

Primary Emotion	Enhanced/ Aggravated Form	Suppressed Form
Anger	Rage	Resentment
Fear	Terror	Anxiety/worry
Sadness	Grief	Seriousness
Happiness	Ecstasy	Contentment

Secondary Emotion	Enhanced/ Aggravated Form	Suppressed Form
Frustration (Anger & Fear)	Impatience	Boredom
Jealousy (Anger & Fear)	Vindictiveness	Envy
Hurt (Anger & Sadness)	Rejection	Loneliness
Despair (Fear & Sadness)	Depression	Apathy
Shame (aka guilt) (Anger, Fear & Sadness)	Humiliation	Embarrassment
Excitement (Fear & Happiness)	Thrill	Anticipation

Common Emotional Level Health Problems

The following is a list of health conditions that usually originate from emotional problems. I could probably include over 90% of all known ailments, but for the sake of brevity, I've only included the most common ones.

Table 3.2 - Emotional-based Health Problems

Ailment	Suppressed or Denied Emotions
AIDS	Anger - rage and shame
Arthritis	Sadness - hurt and boredom
Asthma	Anger and sadness
Cancer	Anger - rage and rejection
Chronic Fatigue	Sadness - despair and apathy
Constipation	Fear - resentment
Digestive problems	Anger and fear
Headaches	Fear - anxiety
Heart problems	Sadness - grief and hurt
Lower back pain	Sadness - rejection and loneliness
Sexual impotency	Anger - frustration and rejection
Infections (internal)	Fear - anxiety and shame
Ulcers	Anger - rage, resentment and impatience
Nervous disorders	Fear - humiliation and excitement
Hepatitis; liver	Sadness - grief and apathy
Pneumonia; influenza	Sadness - despair

CHAPTER 4
THE EGO

(NOTE: Throughout this chapter, you will find several ideas repeated over and over. This is intentional due to the significance of this material.)

The third level of awareness is the intellectual, logical, rational mind. This is the ego; the sense of self, the personality, the worldly image of who you think you are. This is the "I" that judges feelings and thoughts and believes itself to be a separate entity from the rest of Creation.

In many popular spiritual paths, eliminating the ego is suggested as a way to free the self. In my opinion, this is erroneous, because the ego is necessary in order to function in the world and differentiate between the various levels and dimensions of time and space.

There are two selves to every person. The ego is the "false" or "image" self and the soul is the higher, or true Self. To help differentiate between the two, I will use a capital "S" when referring to the soul Self, and a small "s" when referring to the ego self.

The sense of self must encompass both linear and momentary time. The ego functions in linear time and uses a process of selective awareness. This means it tends to focus awareness on one thing at a time in sequential fashion. The ego creates its own version of time, which I will call psychological time. This sense of time comes into play every time you imagine an interval of time in the past or future. As you know, psychological time is a variable. If you are deeply engrossed in something, time seems to pass very quickly; if you are bored, a minute can seem like forever.

The higher Self (soul) functions in momentary time. It is aware of many levels and dimensions simultaneously, in a state of choiceless awareness. To the higher Self, the only time there is, is NOW. When the future comes, it will still be NOW. The higher mind is the bridge between the higher Self and the lower self. The next section will explore the many facets of the higher mind.

Separation and Fear

The ego is often defined as the belief in separation from God. What do we mean by separation from God? If God is all that is, then it is obviously impossible to be separate from all that is. Everything in

Creation is a part of the whole. However, it is possible to believe that the world outside yourself exists independently of your ability to be a part of it. Although modern physics has proven that the observer affects that which he observes, most of us live our lives as though we are simply a cog in a giant machine and that we really have little or no effect on the machine.

The belief that we are an insignificant part of the cosmos draws that experience to us. We then feel powerless to change the events and circumstances in our lives and, as a result, blame others for our misfortunes and so-called "accidents."

The belief in separation is the cause of fear. We become fearful because we believe something outside ourselves can harm or hurt us or cause us pain and suffering. In addition to feeling separate from the world at large, we feel separate from our own real Self. We find it incredibly difficult to listen to our own inner guidance. We fail to distinguish between the ego and soul, both of which are constantly speaking to us through our physical and emotional bodies. As a result, we become distrustful of our own ability to do what is in our best interests, and so we fear what is inside us.

Fear is both an emotion and a mental state; an energy that exists simultaneously on up to four levels of being. Ultimately, fear is an illusion, but the nature of illusions is that as long as you believe in them, they are real for you. Following are some models and concepts regarding the nature of fear, and a look at how to end fear.

As with any personal growth technique, the deeper you go into the subconscious, the greater the effects of healing. This is because you are approaching the problems at their source. You do not remove a tree by pruning its branches. You must uproot it. The closer you get to the roots, the harder it is for the tree to grow back. The diagram on the next page shows the tree of fear. The items along the main trunk represent deep layers of fear. In the leaves are many of the emotional and mental outcomes of fear, and above the leaves are the many manifestations in the outer world.

Figure 4.1 - The Tree of Fear

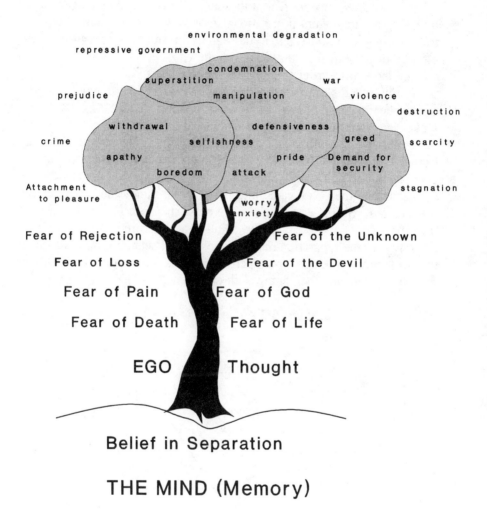

Before you can get rid of fear, you must embrace the emotional aspect of it and learn from its messages. Fear is not inherently bad; it is a learning device which is useful until you get the message. When you no longer need fear, it is then appropriate to lovingly release it by recognizing its illusory nature.

The Circle of Fear

How do we uproot fear at its source? It obviously cannot be done by trying to circumvent it or rationalize it away. In fact, any attempt at transcending fear must fail if the ego is in any way involved in the effort. Because fear is a product of the ego, we must be able to step outside the ego in order to integrate the fear.

Figure 4.2 shows what happens when we try traditional techniques for eradicating fear. This is the ever popular "Catch-22" that every seeker encounters on the path to wholeness. In order to eliminate fear there must be clarity and stillness. Yet as long as fear is present, there cannot be clarity. This is because fear generates thought and thought generates more fear. So which came first and where do we start? The answer is that they both came into being at the same time when the ego was created. So the ego is where we must start. In Figure 4.2 we see that the ego is the part of the mind that interprets life experience according to the separation model. This model sets into motion a chain of events within the ego which perpetuates the separation. Let's follow this chain of events, beginning with experience.

Figure 4.2 - The Circle of Fear

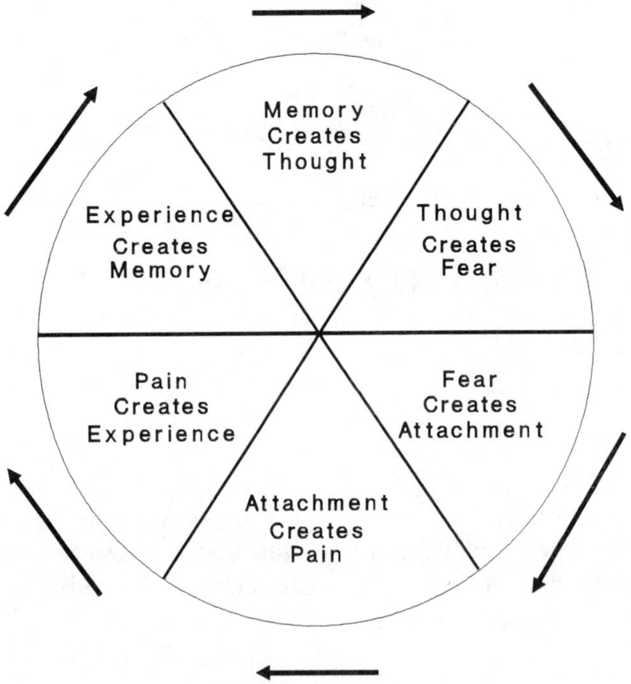

1.   Experience Creates Memory

Every moment of life we are experiencing. The physical and emotional bodies are the main agents of experience. Although we perceive events with the mind, it is the body and emotions which make these events real for us. Our body and emotions send signals to the brain which are recorded in memory. We are then able to "play back" the experience at any time and feel the emotions and physical sensations all over again. Every time a similar event happens, we re-experience the sensations and emotions associated with the original event. The aspect of self that re-experiences is often called the "reactive mind." The reactive mind is the part of the subconscious that gets triggered by life experience.

2.   Memory Creates Thought

Every time we have an experience that triggers memory, thought results. Thought is the movement of mind. Thought can come from the subconscious, conscious or superconscious regions of mind. Whenever memory is triggered, there is movement in the subconscious which triggers thought.   These thoughts can be conscious or remain subconscious depending on the level of denial or suppression involved. If the thoughts are pleasant, we often allow them to come to the surface. If they are unpleasant, we may deny and suppress them. Denying and suppressing thought forces it back into memory and creates energy blockages in the mind. Because the thoughts have not been resolved, they are still actively creating our reality but we are no longer aware of them or how our reality is being created.

3.   Thought Creates Fear

As long as we are operating from ego, we will be judging, comparing and analyzing our thoughts as they arise. This "selective awareness" process inevitably results in some thoughts being accepted as desirable and some rejected as undesirable. The rejected thoughts become denied or suppressed, returning to the subconscious. If a thought arising from the subconscious is not completely integrated (accepted and understood from a higher level of awareness), a division with the self happens. This division becomes a part of the separation. Thoughts of separation result, because we are then out of touch with the higher Self. All thoughts of separation generate fear. These thoughts are essentially based on feelings of insecurity resulting from the belief that we are separate. As long as we are stuck in the subconscious reactive process, we will have thoughts of fear.

4.   Fear Creates Attachment

Thoughts of fear are the ego's attempts to overcome its insecurity. This usually involves seeking an external remedy to alleviate the discomfort caused by the sense of insecurity. The train of thought can become quite elaborate at this point and often degenerates into worry and projected future outcomes. "What will the future bring?" "What if I starve?" "What will happen if I die?"

When the ego finds something or someone it believes will heal its feelings of insecurity it attaches itself to that something or someone, believing that this remedy will save it from its insecurities. Most religions are examples of ego attachment. We are afraid of life and so we seek a god that will come and save us. At the same time, we often believe we are unworthy (see the chapter on Guilt) and we project that belief on our deity, making Him into an angry, vengeful dictator. This breeds further attachment; this time to rules, regulations, sacrificial rites and other codes of ethics.

We may attach ourselves to loved ones, forming dysfunctional relationships. Feeling separate and alone, we seek union through intimate contact with another, forgetting that external bonding cannot, in itself, alleviate inner division within the self.

5.   Attachment Creates Pain

It is inevitable that if we attach ourselves to something or someone, that external "security blanket" will eventually fail us. Life, like a river, is always moving and changing. Attachment is like the stagnant, algae-filled ponds along the side of the river. We demand things to stay the way they are so we won't lose our object of attachment. So we resist the flow of life. Resistance causes pain. Now we are out of alignment with life, either fighting upstream while insisting the river should be flowing another way, or we decay and rot in the stagnant pond, wondering why life is passing us by. The pain of stagnation is unbearable because it negates life. At first, we may deny or suppress the pain but sooner or later, it forces itself to the surface, creating an unpleasant life experience. This unpleasant experience gets stored in memory and the circle of fear turns another cycle.

Breaking the Chains

To break the chain, we must be able to step outside the circle of fear and see it from a higher perspective. The easiest and most direct place to do this is on the step "thought creates fear." When you look directly at something with full awareness, there is no thought; only complete attention. J. Krishnamurti, in his many books on the subject, discusses at length the process of quieting the mind by giving complete attention to the movement of consciousness. This meditative, attentive mind has stopped thought. When there is no thought, there can be no fear because the circle has been broken.

Obviously, before you can get to this state, you must look directly at the fear. What happens when you give your complete attention to fear? Below is the proof that fear is transcended when it is seen completely and accurately.

Proof that Fear is an Illusion

In order to prove this fact, it is necessary to clarify some definitions: *Truth* is that which is actually so in any given moment. *Illusion* is that which may appear to be so, but which does not actually exist in any given moment. *Fear* is the avoidance, desire to escape from, or resistance to what is actually so.

If you look directly at something with your whole being in the present moment, and it exists, it's true, by definition. If it disappears or is not really there, it is an illusion. If you look directly at fear with your whole being, in the moment, you are no longer avoiding and escaping from looking directly at what is happening, so, by definition, fear is not present. Therefore, fear is an illusion and does not really exist.

The only way to dispel the illusion of fear is to stop avoiding, escaping, resisting and being afraid of looking at what is actually taking place within your consciousness and in the world each and every moment. This means being in a state of conscious awareness; higher intelligence; clarity of mind.

The purpose of this section of the book is to help you see clearly the nature and movement of consciousness so you can more easily enter this state of attention.

Forms of Fear

Fear takes many forms, some of which are illustrated in the tree of fear (Figure 4.1). To fully understand the branching nature of fear, you can trace back to the roots every form you encounter by saying to yourself "What is underneath this fear?" or "What am I really afraid of?" For example, underneath the fear of public speaking might be the fear of rejection. Underneath the fear of rejection is the fear of loneliness. Underneath the fear of loneliness is the memory of loneliness which occurred the first time you ever experienced it.

Manifestations of Fear

At the top of Figure 4.1 (the leaves of the tree), you see many of life's conditions arising from fear. If you have any of these in your life at present, it is an indication that you have unresolved fear.

Fear as an Emotion

Dispelling fear is appropriate on the mental level. But fear is also an emotion, and emotions must be loved and accepted before they can integrate. When you are in touch with fear on the mental level, you need to tune in to your body and feel the fear in the cells and tissues. Sometimes it is a tightening or stiffness in the forehead, or a feeling of butterflies in the stomach. Sometimes it is more subtle; a fatigue or dreariness. Intense feelings of fear may make your body restless and unable to sleep.

The key here is to have complete acceptance of the feelings and to experience them with full attention to the energy patterns. Fear in the body is often a sensation of electrical energy pulsing throughout the affected areas. If you can stay with the feeling without labeling or judging it, your body will teach you what it needs for its security. This is how you differentiate between physical fear (self-preservation instinct) and psychological fear (separation-based thought).

Physical Fear vs. Psychological Fear

When the body is in real danger, you may get a sudden adrenalin rush and an intense desire to take action. This is not really fear, but a form of body intelligence prompting action. Psychological fear, on the other hand, has nothing to do with impending danger, but is based on imagined insecurities from past experience. Because situations and events are constantly changing, there is no reason to expect the outcome of a future situation to always be the same as the past. Fear is a self-fulfilling prophecy. What you fear you tend to attract, because your thoughts are creative. When you integrate fear, you are better able to respond to a potentially threatening situation in an intelligent manner.

You will find that most, if not all, of the things that appear to threaten your security are based on the idea that the body is vulnerable to various forms of attack. If you have healed your thoughts and expanded your consciousness sufficiently, you will not draw dangerous situations to you as a means of learning life's lessons. If you have not healed your thoughts and expanded your consciousness sufficiently to avoid danger, then you must rely on your body's built-in intelligence to protect you. Either way, you always have available everything you need for your physical safety.

If an unpleasant situation happens to you despite all this, then, on a soul level, you attracted the experience to you to learn from it and you need to be grateful for this. When you are in the middle of a difficult lesson it is not easy to have gratitude, and you may need to release a lot of emotion before you can even entertain the idea. But gratitude for life's lessons is the fastest way through them.

Judgment

Judgment is an activity of the ego which, when allowed to take over consciousness, replaces the discernment of the higher mind. Judgment is always based on past experience. The problem with judgment is that it perpetuates the separation because the one who judges splits off and keeps separate that which he judges to be bad, wrong, unworthy, or unacceptable. Judged emotions are typically denied and suppressed, creating more problems. Judging parts of the self is the primary cause of getting stuck on the path of healing and personal growth. When we judge, we have closed our minds to new ways of looking at things. To break out of the circle of fear and other ego traps, we need a fresh approach. It is impossible to open to the new when our minds are clouded in judgment. Judgment is closely related to guilt. Guilt arises when we feel we have been judged as unworthy, or when we have judged our actions as bad or wrong. You will find many references throughout this book to the damaging effects of judgment and guilt.

Denial

Another primary aspect of the separation is denial. Denial is the mechanism that keeps the separation in place. When we have judged something or someone (ourselves) as being unworthy, and feel guilty about it, the resulting discomfort is usually then denied. We push the uncomfortable feelings down into the subconscious mind to fester and boil, while we happily go our merry way thinking everything is fine.

Figure 4.3 shows the tree of denial. As with the tree of fear, the way out of denial is to go to the deepest level and look directly at the whole nature and structure of it, seeing how the deeper layers create the more superficial ones. This need not involve years of psychotherapeutic analysis of each branch; only a complete willingness to face each aspect with honesty and humility. And love.

Figure 4.3 - Tree of Denial

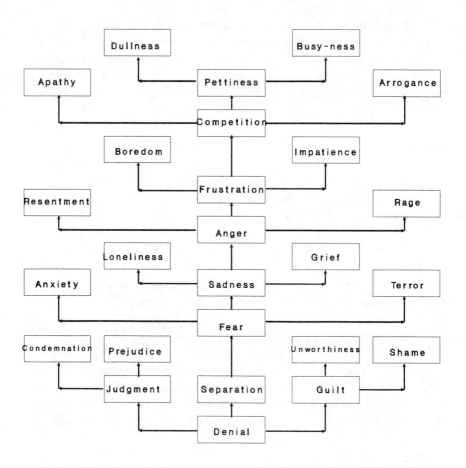

Refusing to look at an inner or outer reality separates us from that reality and takes away our ability to constructively solve problems. In Chapter 19, I've included a story, "The Gods of Denial" that describes the destructive effects of one kind of denial.

Ego Alignment

A healthy ego is one that humbly serves the higher Self, or soul. It receives its instructions from the soul and carries them out in the physical world. In its normal state, the ego does not get stuck in judgment and condemnation. Judgment and condemnation only occur when the ego is in control and not the soul. Those who seek to destroy the ego are, in fact, caught in it. The ego does not inherently fight against parts of itself and make them wrong. It only does so when it is out of touch with the soul. By allowing the ego to reign, you are giving it power that rightfully belongs to the soul.

By expanding your awareness to include the higher dimensions of yourself, you see the ego in its true perspective. It is simply the mechanism for relating in the third-dimensional world. Because the ego is the sense of an individual self, left to its own devices, it will see everything as separate. So if you identify with the ego; i.e., believe you are the ego, you will also believe you are separate from the rest of Creation. By identifying with your true essence (your soul), you will no longer see yourself as separate from others and from life - and the ego will then serve you well in your journey through life.

The ego helps you set boundaries and develop personal space from others. Those who do not set boundaries often take on (assume responsibility for) anything and everything from other people and the environment around them. Their auras become "dirty" and muddled and they find it very difficult to think for themselves. They tend to take on the thought forms of the race mind, (the composite mind of humanity, or collective subconscious). The majority of thoughts in the race mind are geared toward physical survival, the seeking of security, competition, greed, fear and defensiveness.

A healthy ego will separate you from these undesirable qualities. You cannot do very much to help others if you are caught in the same stuff they are. By claiming your own personal space, you call forth your higher self, or soul, to protect you from the discordant energies of the race mind. The wisdom of the soul can then help you discern which information in the race mind is useful to you and which is not.

The ego, or rational mind, when it is out of balance, is the cause of many of the problems in the world today. It is often the part of the self suppressing, judging and denying the emotions. It is also the part of the self that programs the subconscious mind. The ego is not synonymous with the conscious mind, because the conscious mind includes everything you are conscious of, and you may not always be conscious of the ego.

The best way to tell what your ego is doing is to become aware of your programming, conditioning and belief systems.

Programming

When you want a computer to perform a task, it is necessary to write a program. The same is true of the human biocomputer. Information is fed into the brain through the senses and stored in memory. All life experiences, events, thoughts, feelings and images are recorded in memory. If this information is thrown in at random, chaos results. However, when the information is presented in an orderly manner, it becomes a program. We are bombarded with information continuously. The first sensory input we may have received in life came at the moment of birth. If we were cared for, fed and held immediately, we may have received the initial impression that life is warm and caring.

Programs are stored in the physical body. For example, when we were born, we may have had an uncomfortable feeling in the stomach called hunger. When mother gave us milk, the feeling changed to something pleasant, thus we have a program that the way to turn physical pain into pleasure is through food.

A program is a crystallized set of beliefs that direct the self to make certain responses to life situations. For example, if someone introduces himself, you may have a program that says you must extend your right hand and shake his. Obviously, some programs are more beneficial than others. If you are a single man and you have a program that says "beautiful women do not like me," then every time you meet an attractive woman you may avoid her. This is probably not a beneficial program.

How do you recognize a program? We know many of them tend to be subtle and complex. Often we may be running several programs at once on different levels of our consciousness. The more superficial programs may be directed by the deeper ones. If we find a program that is not serving us, we may desire to change it. If this undesirable program is buried under many layers of superficial programs, we may need a great deal of self-exploration to uncover it. By changing the more fundamental programs, the other ones are easy to change.

The best way to recognize a program is to look at the mirror called "your life." Your life experience is the sum total of your programs. If your life is working 80% of the time, you probably have 80% beneficial programs in your consciousness. The areas of your life that are not working are showing you where and what the negative programs are.

There are some specific techniques that can help you identify negative programs. If there is an area of your life you wish to improve, you may use the following process. First, mentally create a picture of the situation. Next, ask yourself these questions:

1) What am I feeling right now? What happened to make me feel this way?

2) Am I rationalizing, suppressing or escaping my feelings?

3) What do I want from this situation?

4) If others are involved, what demands and expectations do I have of them?

5) If this is a recurring situation, what is the usual outcome of this experience and how do I feel about the usual outcome?

Then make a list of all the programs you can come up with pertaining to this situation. Some will be simple thoughts; others complex ideas. Ask yourself "What originated this program and why is it no longer beneficial to my life?

Conditioning

Conditioning is the environment and life experience that you created your programs from. As we grow from an infant into a small child, we acquire many programs for many reasons. If father spanked us when we behaved against his principles, the feeling is uncomfortable. We formed a definite idea about our behavior, and hence, a program.

Throughout our early years, those who are closest to us, primarily parents and family, are the main sources of our conditioning. Their values, ideas, conscious experience and the conditioning they received throughout their lives determined what information we were given as children.

Often it is not necessary to regress back to childhood friends, or a particular third grade teacher, etc. It may only be important that you see the ingrained nature of the conditioning, understand the programs formed from it, and the dynamics of it, and get in touch with how it is making you feel. Remember that you are creating your life experience through your programs and beliefs. They color your perception of the events in your life. Your programs essentially take neutral events and create emotional reactions to them.

For example, I attended a seminar once where we were each asked to share the best and worst experiences in our lives. The catch was, we could describe the event, but the others had to guess whether it was the best or the worst thing that had happened to us. People got up and shared things like "my first marriage, my first divorce, my second marriage", etc. For one person, the first divorce was the happiest time; for another, divorce was the most unhappy. Same event; completely different reaction. Some people are devastated by separation from loved ones; others feel liberated and excited about being on their own. The difference is in the programming and conditioning.

You can change your programming, but you cannot change your conditioning. However, you can understand it and refuse to be a slave to it. All of us had unpleasant experiences during our childhood. Rather than feel victimized by an unhappy upbringing, we can learn to understand how this conditioning has shaped our present responses and reactions. We have all heard stories of horrendous abuse in the lives of people who have gone on to become happy and successful in their chosen fields. John Bradshaw is one example. Although each of us is unique and special, our conditioning is very much the same throughout the world. Our problems are universal. And so are the solutions. If one human being can overcome the grief and fear of abuse, all of us can.

Obviously it is not easy. It requires patience and commitment. I'm not going to offer you a pie-in-the-sky quick fix for your issues. Many of the solutions offered by our society fail miserably to address the problem. Therapists are often expensive and inadequately trained. The pressures of modern life can make it hard to devote enough time and attention to our conditioning. We have been taught to suppress and deny our feelings for so long that many of our programs are buried under hundreds of layers of conditioning. It takes time to uncover each layer.

I have been working on my issues pretty much continuously for the last 15 years. I have made incredible progress. I feel better about myself now than I ever have before. I am involved in at least half a dozen creative projects designed to benefit humanity. I have become aware of states of being and dimensions of the universe that bring awe and reverence. For the most part, I do what excites me in life. Some of my experiences might seem like science fiction to the average human being. I feel alive and vibrant much of the time, and boredom seldom afflicts me. I have seen and been a part of miraculous healings of myself and others. And yet, I still have the same human issues as the rest of us. I still feel pain, grief, anger, fear and loneliness, although I am not controlled by these feelings. I am dealing with my own issues regarding separation, rejection, guilt, judgment and loss. I have a great deal more understanding now than when I began, and a great deal more acceptance for who and what I am. But I am not "above" the human condition, and I doubt there is anyone alive today who is.

Change

Although we must accept the fact that we are all a part of the human condition, we also need to realize that our world has gone just about as far as it can go on its present course. If we do not change, we will not survive as a species. This is a fact. And although a part of us desires to change, we still resist it. It is not based on the comfortable, the familiar, or the known. The rational mind resists change because it threatens our image of self. We have derived a sense of security from having a "stable" personality. Yet is there really security in keeping things the way they are?

True security comes from within the self. The self has the ability to grow and change in harmony with its environment; to respond appropriately to any given situation. Seeking security outside the self means we have given our power away to others, and therefore have lost our security.

No amount of money, power or fame is ever going to give us true security. Until we realize this, we will continue destroying the environment and ourselves. We must change the programming that tells us security and happiness comes from out there somewhere. We must be willing to question the belief that the right job, the right relationship or the right house is the answer to our problems. We must change our perception of the world. Our relationships must change. If we cannot get along with those closest to us, how can we expect to heal the planet?

As a species, we need to face the fact that our present behavior patterns, ideas and concepts are based largely on negative programs and beliefs. Not only must we change, but the change must be a radical and fundamental transformation.

To experience freedom, we must have a fundamental revolution in our thinking. True freedom is a state of being where we are no longer bound by our mental patterns. When we are free of robot-like programming that is no longer useful, then real learning begins. We become the masters of ourselves. We are no longer controlled by the mind; we use it as a finely-tuned instrument for perception.

We learn how thoughts arise from memory, how fear is brought about, and how to live in the moment with a fresh response to each situation. We are then free to explore the unknown, thereby transcending the old self. We discover our real Self--constantly changing, yet eternal. To change and grow we cannot cling to the security of our old self. We must move on. Change is a universal reality in the lower dimensions. We cannot fear change and be free. Our fear of change is based on our past programming.

How do we change our programming? What programs are beneficial to our growth? To answer these questions, we must learn to use our intelligence to look directly, in each moment, to exactly what is going on inside and outside us. We must learn to be actively aware in each moment, not merely acting from conditioned responses in memory. Memory is available to us as a tool when we need it. It is always there in its entirety. But it cannot dominate our consciousness if we are to perceive accurately.

Belief Systems

If a program is repeated enough times with the same outcome, it becomes a belief system. A belief system is a collection of beliefs based on commonly repeated programs. Beliefs systems are like computer applications where each application contains one or more basic programs. What we know about ourselves depends largely on the belief systems we have acquired. Our consciousness is filled with various belief systems. Some of them are superficial and have minimal impact on our lives. Others go very deep and form the basis for our outlook on life. As I said before, beliefs create our reality; i.e., the way we perceive life.

There are thousands of beliefs and belief systems. I would like to zero in on the deepest and most basic ones that affect almost every human being on Earth.

Core Beliefs

"I am unworthy." This belief comes straight from the heart of guilt and produces the emotion of shame. The belief in unworthiness probably goes back to the beginning of Creation. The story goes something like this: When God created man, He gave him free will. Man misunderstood his free will and his actions fell out of alignment with universal principles. He thereby felt guilty and ashamed of his behavior and considered himself unworthy of receiving God's love.

"I'm not good enough." This belief is closely related to "I am unworthy." When parents or others had expectations of us based on their belief systems, and we failed to live up to those expectations, we

often adopted this belief. The church has been a major perpetrator here by instilling the idea of sin and telling us that we don't measure up. This core issue is based on the belief that God demands perfection.

"Life is a disappointment." This is actually part of a vicious cycle called "expectation/disappointment/cynicism." We have an expectation about something in life; it doesn't work out the way we had hoped; we then become cynical and expect failure in the future.

"Life is a struggle." For many of our ancestors, survival seemed difficult. Due to ignorance of natural laws, oppression from others, and fear, many of us gave up our power and began believing we were helpless pawns in the chess game of life, struggling against insurmountable odds. With modern technology, it is now possible to ensure physical survival for all. Paradoxically, holding the belief that life is a struggle is imperiling our survival. This is because having such a belief leads to workaholism and extreme stress, eventually causing disease and death.

"There's not enough." The belief in poverty and scarcity goes back to the beginning of Creation when we "fell from grace." By misunderstanding free will, we forgot that the universe was abundant and unlimited, and we started perceiving ourselves as victims in a hostile universe. The belief in scarcity arises from the basic belief that we are separate from God, the source of abundance, and that the inner and outer realities are separate from one another. Some of the common manifestations of this belief include hoarding, greed and unbalanced distribution of goods and services--activities that actually create scarcity.

Some Sacred Cows

The following belief systems are believed by so many people that they are considered truths. It is very dangerous to blindly accept something as the absolute truth. Very often, a belief may be true on one level or dimension but be completely meaningless on another level or dimension. An example of this is the law of gravity. This law is very real on the third-dimensional Earth, but out in space has little relevance. The law of gravity is also superseded by different, more powerful principles in the higher dimensions. Levitation, for instance, does not violate the law of gravity; it merely utilizes higher laws that counteract the law of gravity. Unless something is true at all times and on all levels and dimensions, it is not an absolute truth.

Some belief systems thought to be absolute truth and held sacred by society include:

"The body must grow old and die." This would be true if the law of entropy were the supreme law of the universe, as some physicists claim. However, there is another law, the principle of regeneration, or centropy, which counteracts entropy. Individuals who balance regeneration with degeneration can maintain a healthy, youthful body indefinitely. For more information on physical immortality, see Chapter 20.

"God is perfect, unchanging love." There may indeed be an aspect of God that is perfect and unchanging, but if God is everything, then He must be growing, evolving and changing as well. If we were created in His image, then the traits and characteristics of man must have been present in God at the time of man's creation. Therefore, God has been angry, sad, fearful, jealous and mistaken at times. Just because He created us doesn't necessarily mean His evolution is finished or His healing complete.

"You must leave the body to attain Heaven." From the beginning, the body has been judged against for its "base" nature. Limitation does not occur simply because you have a body. It occurs because the unlimited aspect of your being has been denied. By forgetting your higher self, you forgot your unlimited aspect. This aspect can transform the body into a vehicle of light that is no longer bound by third-dimensional principles.

"I am God." Yes and no. You are a part of God. You can merge your consciousness with God. But you are also an individual soul, a god in your own right, capable of evolving to the point where you can create entire universes. A more accurate statement might be "I am a child of God." According to my perception of the Creation story, the Heavenly Father and Divine Mother gave birth to your soul much in the same way that your earthly parents gave birth to your body. You certainly don't go around saying "I am my earthly father."

"Pain is inevitable." Pain is resistance to the life force. It is also a wonderful teaching device. If it is completely accepted, there is no longer any resistance, and pain is transformed. Being a martyr is not accepting pain. Martyrdom is a belief in sacrifice; that if you suffer enough pain, somehow God will reward you. God does not require pain

or sacrifice. If you love and accept all parts of yourself, there will be no pain.

"I can't be happy all the time." It is not healthy to demand constant happiness. You need to accept how you're feeling no matter what it feels like. But this does not mean that it's impossible to be happy all the time. The belief that life has to have ups and downs is derived from guilt. Guilt says you don't deserve to be happy and that you will have to pay for your pleasure. If you begin to pay attention to what brings you down after being high, you will see that guilt and fear are the reasons. If you see guilt coming before it takes hold, you can move it back out of your being. If you love the fearful part of yourself, you can include it in your happiness. Happiness is a natural state when all parts of yourself are in alignment.

"Everything is love and light." If you believe this one, I have a bridge to sell you real cheap. For most people this is the form of denial that has created more problems on Earth than anything else. Enlightenment does not come from accepting the pleasing aspects of life and denying the rest. Real love accepts the darkness as well. You don't have to embrace darkness and take it in to your being, but you do need to have loving acceptance for the darkness. There is a difference. I can love the drunk on the street and see him as an equal to me, but I don't have to drink with him. If I have no judgment or denial within me, darkness simply becomes a contrast; a dance of duality, rather than something evil to be gotten rid of. The real evil is the denial itself.

Let me impart to you a story based on an actual experience I had in 1991. I was exploring my rage, which had been buried under many layers of denial and was now surfacing. I went deeper and deeper into the rage until I was able to picture it as a reddish-black mass of seething, pulsing energy. Then I looked still deeper and saw a two-headed serpent. One head was black; the other white.

I asked the serpent who he was, and the black head answered, "I am Pan, the God of Paradise." Then the white head answered "And I am Satan." I was shocked. I fully expected the black-headed serpent to be Satan - after all, everyone knows that evil is black and good is white. But when I listened further, the story began to make sense. Pan, the black serpent, was full of rage. He had been pushed down, suppressed, repressed and denied for aeons and aeons, and he was desperate to express his frustration at being shut down. He had become so compressed from lack of expression that he was devoid of light.

Satan, the white serpent, was the cause of Pan's suppression. Satan was cool, calm and detached and went around saying "everything is light and love." It is denial that causes separation and Satan represents denial.

One further note: The backdrop to this scenario of the two-headed serpent was an opaque, neutral color. I was told this backdrop was the body of God, and that God is completely neutral. He does not fight darkness with light, or light with darkness; He simply *is*.

Conflict

What is conflict? How does it arise? What are its effects? To fully understand these questions, we must look very deeply into the self. Conflict occurs when two or more parts of the self are not in alignment. In other words, the self has become fragmented and separated into various parts which oppose or are inharmonious with one another. This fragmentation occurs when we deny a part of ourselves or adopt beliefs, ideas and concepts which are not representative of our true nature.

The most common form of conflict involves judgment of feelings and emotions. There are three steps to this process. First, a situation arises which triggers a negative emotion. Next, we judge the emotion as being undesirable. Finally, we judge ourselves for feeling the negative emotion.

If we take full responsibility for the negative emotion and use it as an opportunity to learn about our programming and conditioning, we are less likely to fall victim to steps two and three. For example, the following statements involve negative emotions where the person is not taking responsibility for the feelings:

"She makes me angry."
"Being alone makes me depressed."
"I'm sick and tired of him."

Taking responsibility for these feelings starts with rewording the thoughts, perhaps in this way:

"I feel angry when she's around."
"I feel depressed when I am alone."
"I feel sick and tired when I'm around him."

Remembering that we create our own experience is always the first step in healing.

The Root of Conflict

Conflict occurs if we judge our emotions and judge ourselves for feeling them. For example, if we feel angry when she's around, we might then decide:

"Anger is bad."
"It's wrong to feel angry."
"I shouldn't be feeling this way."

We are then likely to further fragment ourselves with the secondary judgment:

"I'm not a good person because I keep getting angry at her."
"I must be really screwed up to feel this way."
"I'm supposed to be happy."

Now the part of us that feels angry is in conflict with the part that is judging ourselves for feeling angry.

This is so important that I'd like to use another example. Let's use depression this time. Suppose you have an experience of being depressed when you are alone. The program goes something like this:

"It is not a healthy state of being to be without companionship. It means I have nobody to depend on for comfort and I'm not being cared for. Therefore I am unhappy because I desire things to be different from the way they are."

This program is being triggered by external situations and involves conditioning by society and parents, as well as past experience - we remember being happier with friends around. So we are relating our present experience to a past reference point.

At this point, rather than understand and work with this program to create healing, another program may get triggered which drives us deeper into depression:

"I shouldn't feel depressed. It is not right to feel this way. Something is wrong with me. I desire to feel happy and yet I'm not, so I don't like myself."

Do you see what's happening here? The statement "I don't like myself" implies that "I" and "myself" are two separate entities. In reality they are not, but this judgment creates division and separation within the self. Anytime you judge a feeling or thought you split it off from the rest of you. Instead of simply feeling sad, you think of your sadness as something separate from you. "Me and my feelings", "you and your thoughts", etc.

Figure 4.4 on the next page clearly shows this division between "what is" and "what should be."

Ending Conflict

What is this self that I call "me?" Is that who I really am, or is it a collection of past experiences, ideas, concepts and information? How can this self really be me?

To end conflict, let's look at the division of self once again. How does this division come about? We know that judging parts of the self creates separation and fragmentation. So why do we judge?

Throughout evolution, our rational mind has developed into an enormous, complex entity. Its purpose is to classify, disseminate and order reality in ways that support our growth as human beings. As we grow into higher dimensions, however, we cannot remain stuck in the intellectual, logical process. We must develop new ways of dealing with life. Our rational mind categorizes and compares, putting order to irrationality and chaos. This is obviously necessary, but it is not how the deeper self works. Within us is another kind of intelligence that instantaneously comprehends information without having to sort out all the details. This is the wisdom of the soul that can see both sides of a conflict and work out a real solution.

When we look from higher intelligence at the conflict process, we see five steps:

1)   A situation arises which triggers a program.

2)   Thought is generated by the rational mind.

3)   The program and resulting thoughts are not in harmony with the situation. In other words, the situation is judged as being undesirable.

4)   Conflict results. There is a "should be" instead of "what is."

5)   There is a resulting negative emotion, which is then judged, and the process repeats itself.

Do you see that this five-step process keeps us stuck in memory? We are continually comparing our present experience with one in memory or one imagined in the future. Being stuck in memory creates fear of the unknown. Therefore, the ego sets up mechanisms to protect itself. Fear arises because our world is threatened by ideas, concepts and beliefs that are not in harmony with our view of the way things "should be." When life does not fit our concept of what should be, we become fearful and alienated from others. We then give off inharmonious energy and negative vibrations.

Yet we know we "should" be harmonious. We begin the cycle all over again. This is one of the great paradoxes. We see that we must end conflict, and yet there is conflict. So we develop a fear of conflict. We decide it is evil; something to be gotten rid of. We should ot have conflict because it results in negativity. Thus, we have judged conflict and its resulting negativity.

The process is perpetuated again and again. Fear keeps triggering more programs, which trigger more thoughts, which trigger more conflict. On and on until we see the absurdity of it all. When we try to break out of the cycle, we become frustrated and anxious and this continues the process, so, clearly, a different approach is needed. We cannot end conflict by trying to escape it, break free or suppress it. And we cannot use our rational mind to try to end conflict. Instead, we must focus our entire attention on it--not drown in it, but flow with it, experience it, and accept it for what it is. This doesn't mean you say "Here's fear. I'll be stuck with it all my life, so I might as well enjoy it." No. Simply examine it--look at it without being an observer apart from the fear. Become the fear. You created the fear, the program and the conflict. Be one with it. And in oneness there is no division and no separation.

In summary, when you see the entire process as it occurs, there is choiceless awareness and instant comprehension. This awareness stops the cycle and we are left simply with an experience. It is not good or bad, it just *is*.

Figure 4.4 - Conflict and Division Within the Self

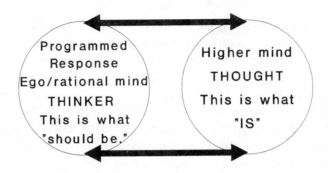

This person believes life should be
according to his models and ideals.
He continually denies his feelings
and thoughts when they do not
agree with his model of reality.

Figure 4.5 - Unity Within the Self

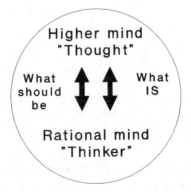

The language of love. This person
sees conflict as it arises, flows
with it, and it is therefore
dissolved. The "thinker" becomes the
"thought." This is accomplished by
accepting "what is."

The cause of the world's problems is separation and division within our beings. This division manifests as a belief that things happen to us beyond our control. We have been conditioned to believe that feelings and thoughts are external events caused by external situations. We project our thoughts and feelings outward and see a reflection in the outer world; a mirror of our own consciousness. Then we forget we created the reflection and blame the world. The belief in separation manifests as a belief that the world is separate from us. In truth, we are the world. If you reject a part of the world, you are rejecting a part of yourself. If you reject any part of yourself, you cannot love yourself. If you do not love yourself, you cannot love the world and be a positive force in it.

When you understand conflict within the self and end the division within and without, then you become a powerful force for healing.

CHAPTER 5
THE MIND

The mind is the instrument of the spirit and the bridge to the soul. It is also the perceiver and projector of reality. Its interface with the body is the brain, a vast biocomputer that relays mental messages to and from the body. The mind is the primary agent of Creation. The activity of the mind is thought, which it generates either through memory (subconscious storage) or through the superconscious (creative aspect) of the mind. The higher mind controls the psychic, intuitive and imaginative faculties while the lower mind (ego) controls the rational, intellectual and logical functions. The combined higher and lower minds of all human beings are known as the collective mind, or the race mind.

Aspects of the Mind

The Collective Subconscious

Within the race mind is the collective subconscious. (I prefer the word "subconscious" instead of "unconscious" because "sub" means beneath the surface, which is more accurate.) While every human being has an individual subconscious that stores all life experiences, the whole of humanity has a subconscious that stores all of the life experiences of humanity. Imagine, for a moment, that you have a personal computer with a disk storage system. The information on the disk is analogous to your personal subconscious. The data you bring to the screen from the disk represents the information brought into the conscious mind from the subconscious.

Now suppose your PC is linked to thousands of PCs across the country (via modem or network). These PCs are then hooked to a mainframe storage device (or network server) which contains a vastly larger memory than your own disk. Because your disk and the server disk are electronically linked, all information is available at the touch of a button. The trick is, you have to know which button to push. Without the proper knowledge, you will not be able to bring information from the server disk to your personal computer.

The Akashic Records

We can take this idea one step further and suggest that the collective subconscious, as a part of the race mind, is connected to a larger information system that encompasses the entire universe and all life forms in it. This master storage system is called the akashic records. In the akashic are records of every thought, feeling and experience of the soul since the beginning of Creation.

The Universal Mind

The akashic records are part of the Infinite Intelligence, or Universal Mind, which contains all knowledge on all levels and dimensions. This is the Mind of God, which has both a personal and impersonal aspect. The impersonal aspect is much like a giant computer that orders all of Creation into its patterns and blueprints. It contains the RNA/DNA codes, the atomic structures and the subatomic structures that determine what type of life will evolve on a given planet. More information on the akashic records and Universal Mind can be found in Chapter 10, "Dimensions."

The Universal Mind Computer

The Universal Mind Computer (UMC) contains all knowledge (data), programs (beliefs) and energy (intelligence) needed to create anything and everything. Within each individual soul is a holographic representation of the UMC. This individual miniature of the UMC is divided into three "subsystems": superconscious, conscious and subconscious. From now on, the term "mind" will refer to the totality of these three subsystems within an individual. As you can see in the following figures, I have included several models of the mind and its various ways of filtering information.

Mind Models

The most useful mind model I've found is the hourglass (Figures 5.1a through 5.1d). I've used four different diagrams to illustrate this because I feel it's helpful to be able to view abstract ideas from many angles. In these models, information from the UMC enters the superconscious mind and is filtered into the neck of the hourglass (the conscious mind). The portion of the information accepted by the conscious mind is stored in the akashic records as soul experience, and the part rejected or denied by the conscious mind goes into the subconscious as suppressed or repressed experience. If the information is beneficial to soul growth, but is ignored or suppressed, it goes into the subconscious programming and mixes with the programs (beliefs) already resident there.

Figure 5.1a - Map of Consciousness (hourglass model)

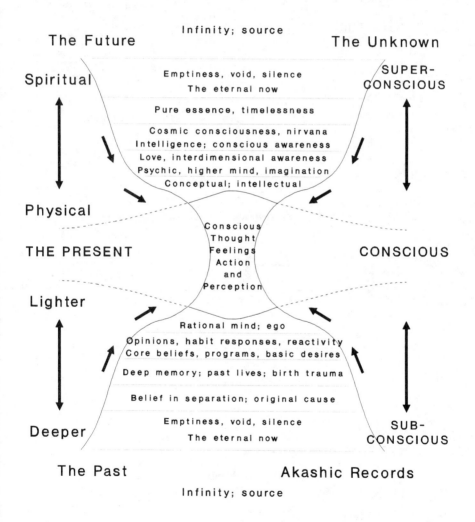

Figure 5.1b - Egg Model   **Figure 5.1c - Small Hourglass**

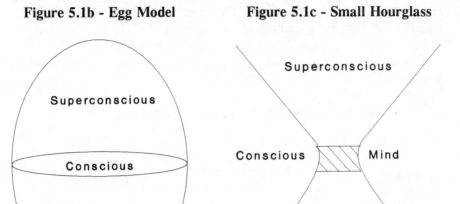

Figure 5.1d - Frequency Bandwidth Analogies

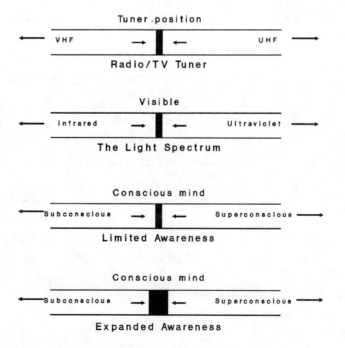

All outer stimuli (earthly experience) enters the three mind regions simultaneously and is filtered according to: (a) the soul's desire for experience; (b) the soul's protection; and (c) the programs resident in the subconscious. Option (a) implies that the soul draws to itself the experiences it wishes to have based on its model of reality. Option (b) safeguards the soul's mind from information overload. For example, certain autonomic body functions such as one's heartbeat may bypass the conscious mind so it can focus on something more relevant to the soul's growth. The mind's protection mechanism also filters out experiences which can harm the physical or emotional body. Option (c) is where reactivity takes place. Outer stimuli trigger a programmed response based on conditioning in the subconscious.

Tools for Expanding the Mind

Before we can explore the higher mind, we must be able to expand our consciousness. Therefore, I suggest you try the following techniques for mind expansion. In addition to the techniques described below, there are several more detailed exercises in the Appendix.

Relaxation and Concentration

I'm sure you have a pretty good idea of what relaxation is. At least physically. But what about mentally? What happens when the body is relaxed but the mind is not? Most likely you will drift around with random thoughts, then zero in on something and start going off in that direction. Pretty soon you are engrossed in a particular train of thought.

True relaxation occurs when the mind is allowed to drift aimlessly without being forced to focus in any one direction. Both relaxation and concentration are important, depending on the goal of your awareness process.

Meditation

What passes for meditation is usually a form of concentration and mental discipline. True meditation occurs when the mind becomes quiet and still. The meditative mind is silent, but watchful. It sees thought as it arises without being controlled by it. How does one quiet the mind? Forcing, controlling or resisting the activities of the mind only makes it more active. You cannot be silent if you are thinking "I must quiet my thoughts." Have you ever tried not to think of a pink elephant? To achieve true meditation, we must use a roundabout method of quieting the mind. We must trick the mind into going beyond itself. One way to do this is to ask "impossible" questions; i.e., questions that cannot be adequately answered by the intellect, such as "Who am I?", or "Who is asking the question?" One of the exercises in the Appendix contains several impossible questions. Closely related is the impossible parable, or "koan." Koans and impossible questions are often used in the practice of zen to trick the mind into silence.

The ultimate method of meditation is simply pure awareness. This requires an extraordinary amount of relaxation, concentration and choiceless awareness and is usually achieved only after many years of self-exploration. It involves the ability to completely follow every nuance of thought and feeling as it arises and to comprehend it in its totality. The great Eastern philosopher, J. Krishnamurti, taught this process, although only a few of his students ever achieved it. However, pure awareness is not attained by following any method or philosophy. It only comes about by resolving all the distractions of the mind caused by incomplete processing of psychological issues.

If you follow your train of consciousness, you will find that after brief periods of quietness, the most common thoughts that come up have to do with unresolved emotional or physical issues. Maybe you remember the criticism of a boss the day before and wish you had responded differently. Or, if you are unemployed, maybe you begin contemplating your search for employment. Pretty soon, instead of meditation, you find yourself fantasizing all the possible scenarios that could result from the job interview tomorrow.

To achieve pure awareness, you must be able to balance choiceless awareness with selective awareness. In this world (even if you live on the mountain top), there will always be practical activities that require selective awareness. The real key is the ability to turn the selective mind on and off at will. If you set aside one hour per day for meditation, you want to spend that entire hour in choiceless awareness. But if you have unresolved issues, you will most likely spend the hour dealing with those issues. This is a necessary and valuable prerequisite to pure awareness.

Pure awareness is attained when you freely express thoughts and emotions as they arise while at the same time being able to understand them from a space of choiceless awareness. This means if you feel hurt, you express it fully in the moment instead of suppressing it. This is not always easy to do, especially in today's society. In the past, a monastic life was often advised for serious students of meditation. Reduce or eliminate as many worldly responsibilities as you can and you increase the chances of being able to live in choiceless awareness.

Today, for the most part, a monastic life is not necessary or even advisable for most people. We need to experience life fully in all its aspects. Even if we only achieve five minutes per day of choiceless awareness, we are well on the way to enlightenment.

Discipline

The root meaning of discipline is "to learn." This does not mean beating the mind into submission every time it thinks about sex when you are trying to meditate. Rather, it means learning about your mental and emotional patterns, noticing your distractions, and creating an environment that helps you explore the self. This environment may involve sitting in a lotus posture 30 minutes twice a day, or it may not. Often when you first begin meditating, it is useful to create a structure; i.e., the same time every day, the same posture, etc.

Eventually you want to become more flexible, however. For me, meditation is an internal discipline that has very little to do with outer structure. Certainly it is easier to quiet the mind if you are not running a dozen business errands every hour. But it is not impossible. It is even possible to be in meditation while having a conversation with someone. In fact, total attention is the primary key to good listening. If you listen with your whole being to another, you notice all the details of the conversation; the way he moves his hands, the tone of his skin, the words behind the words, etc. When you see the whole picture behind what the other person is saying, you are better able to respond. Response from a state of inner silence is a complete response. If you are too busy thinking about what you are going to say next, you are not in choiceless awareness.

Even if you are discussing something practical and highly technical, you may be able to go in and out of meditation, depending on the response needed. A well-trained intellect can fetch facts and figures very quickly and then go back into silence until the next time activity is required.

A good friend of mine calls this process "balancing linear time with momentary time." Linear time is the dimension of the intellect and selective awareness; momentary time is the domain of the higher mind and choiceless awareness.

Psychic Awareness

While the psychic is a level of awareness, for convenience we will define the various psychic functions as part of the higher mind. The shared mind concept (collective subconscious and collective superconscious) explains how psychic functioning works. In Figure 5.2a, we see the "Wheel of Life", a way of depicting the Oneness of all beings.

Figure 5.2a - Wheel of Life

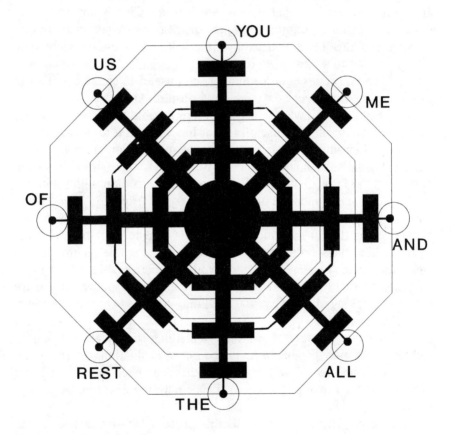

The deeper one goes into the Self, the more information is shared with the collective. In the higher mental planes, souls have access to information not available to the physical senses.

(NOTE: the term "psychic" is not to be confused with "intuitive." Psychic is a mental process of perception, whereas intuition is a feeling-oriented process.)

When we look at the psychic realms in detail later in this chapter, you will see exactly how this information is accessed and communicated.

Figure 5.2b - Energy Web

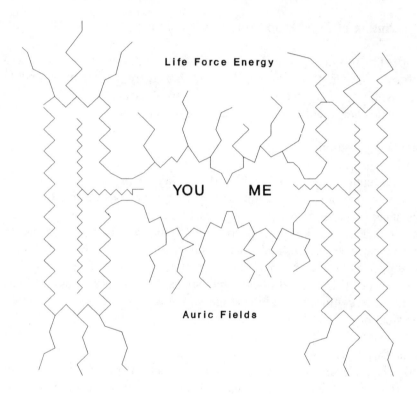

Life Force Energy

YOU   ME

Auric Fields

Intuition

Psychic awareness is a quality of the spirit, or masculine pole of Creation. Intuition is a quality of the will, or feminine pole. Psychic awareness is perceived, intuition is felt. The three lower chakras are used to intuit; the three upper chakras are used to perceive psychically. The 4th chakra (the heart) is used for both. See Chapter 10 for more information on chakras.

Intuitive people have great knowledge, but it is not mental knowledge; it is a deeper knowing. When asked how they know, they will respond with "it's just a gut feeling." This is a reference to the solar plexus, or third chakra, where intuition resides. By contrast, the psychic functions tend to correspond to a point between the eyebrows commonly called the "third eye." While intuition is considered a feminine quality, obviously men are just as capable of developing intuition. And certainly women can be, and often are, very good psychics.

Description of Psychic and Intuitive Functions

The following describes in detail some of the more common ways information is received psychically and intuitively. Some of this could be review to many readers, but I hope to shed a new light on these properties and functions of the higher mind and will.

Mental Projection

Mental projection involves the ability to project a holographic image of oneself through time and space to perceive information at a distance. There are varying degrees of mental projection. You can project only the imaging portion of your mental body so as to clairvoyantly see events and situations happening elsewhere in the world or universe. Or you can project a complete replica of your physical body through the mental planes and "appear" at another location. This is not to be confused with bilocation, which is actual creation of another physical body in a different time or space.

Mental projection is usually used in conjunction with other techniques, such as psychic healing. In the Silva Mind Control Method, there is an exercise where participants mentally project to a distant location and clairvoyantly perceive health problems in an individual whom they have never met. They then have the option to perform "healing at a distance," which we will cover next.

When you first begin mentally projecting, you may feel you are making up the images that come to mind. In some cases, you may be. After a bit of practice, however, you will be able to discern the difference between internal images and external perceptions. If you are not highly clairvoyant, you may simply sense that the information is accurate or not by the feeling in your body. In the Silva Method, a "control" person (or third party) is used to verify accuracy; i.e., someone who knows the person being perceived. Most people are able to function with at least 80% accuracy after a short training period.

The key to effective projection is to relax the Beta activity of the brain through meditation and relaxation and to simply focus your attention on the target to be perceived. There are certain triggers and associations that make it easier, such as visualizing a movie projector screen in your mind's eye and placing the person or object upon it. It is easier to perceive accurately if you know nothing consciously about the person or object being perceived. Having preconceived knowledge about something tends to distract from the ability to project, because most people tend to doubt the validity of the information if it does not agree with their outer memories and knowledge.

Usually, acquired knowledge is less accurate than information perceived psychically. Often psychic information is true on a deeper level than acquired knowledge. For example, you may know John Pubiic as a basic, all-around nice guy. When you look at him psychically, however, you may perceive an angry, fearful person. Chances are, the nice guy is a superficial layer of the personality and the deeper self is embroiled in emotional issues.

Psychic Healing

There are really two kinds of healing: psychic healing and spiritual healing. Psychic healing involves the ability to detect and correct abnormalities in the body by utilizing the life force energy of the cosmos, commonly known as "prana." This may involve laying on of hands, aura clearing, chakra balancing, psychokinesis, visualization or invocation of other-dimensional entities. Psychic healing is a specialized form of spiritual healing, which focuses more on bringing the soul into complete alignment with the various parts of itself. Psychic healing is more concerned with the mechanics of healing, while spiritual healing deals with the root causes of illness and seeks correction on all levels. Spiritual healing can include not only the psychic techniques mentioned herein, but also counseling, hypnotherapy, prayer, meditation, rebirthing, reiki, and many other disciplines.

Spiritual healing starts with the premise that a soul is already perfect in the spiritual dimensions and that the physical, emotional and mental selves are simply out of alignment with that spiritual perfection. It also takes into account the soul's free will and seeks permission before attempting any psychic or mechanical healing processes. If a soul is not evolved enough spiritually, psychic healing is a waste of time. Even if the healing is temporarily effective, sooner or later the soul will recreate the problem in another form until the root causes are healed. For more information on specific forms of healing, I recommend browsing the healing section of any metaphysical bookstore.

Healing at a Distance

It is possible to direct healing energy over any distance and even through time. I have been involved in "miracle" healings in this manner where I had never even met the person involved. I would simply project to the person, perceive the health problem and begin correction. IT IS EXTREMELY IMPORTANT THAT YOU HAVE PERMISSION FROM A SOUL BEFORE ATTEMPTING HEALING IN ANY FORM. Some souls do not wish to be healed, even though they may express an outer desire for it. When healing at a distance, it is especially difficult to tell if the person is willing, on a soul level, to be healed. You need to be in touch with your own inner essence to really know if you are violating the free will of other souls by trying to heal them.

Healing is a multidimensional event. People become sick when one or more levels of their being is out of alignment with their soul. When you perceive a problem, it is usually multi-layered in nature. You may begin with a physical sign or symptom. If you are healing at a distance and you mentally project to the person, you may immediately see a growth or tumor in his/her abdomen, for instance. After receiving permission to proceed, you may direct energy to the afflicted area (there are several techniques for doing this) and see the tumor dissolve.

However, you may then get in touch with an emotional issue behind the physical problem. Perhaps the person has been very angry for a long time and has suppressed the anger in the stomach. The healing then progresses to the will, and you help the person come to peace with the anger and find the cause.

Next, you may receive an image of the person's childhood where he/she was abused or neglected. This may be the origin of the anger. You could then be directed to comfort the person while helping him/her heal the childhood trauma.

At this point, you may be wondering how all this can be accomplished at a distance. Certainly, face-to-face contact is easier when dealing with therapeutic situations. However, all that is really necessary for complete healing is to obtain a soul agreement that healing will take place. On a soul level, you and the patient can connect, regardless of time and space. You may be able to telepathically suggest actions for the patient that will resolve the trauma; it may be that the energy received during the healing is sufficient to trigger any emotional release necessary. The soul connection may precipitate understanding of the cause of the problem, so that true and permanent resolution can take place.

Almost everyone has at some time been involved with the practice of healing at a distance, at least subconsciously. Holding someone in your prayers during a church service is a form of healing at a distance. Even sending a "get well" card can transmit healing energy. Healing at a distance is an extensive topic and there is other literature available, so I will not go any further into it now.

Clairvoyance

Clairvoyance is often used when healing at a distance. Clairvoyance involves seeing with the mind's eye (third eye) events or situations occurring in another location. With highly developed clairvoyance, one can see in colorful detail what is actually taking place, although beginning clairvoyance often comes in symbols. Sometimes symbolic perception is preferable, especially if the clairvoyant is working with someone who may not be able to grasp the direct implications of a particular event or situation. Often the symbols and colors seen by clairvoyants do not make sense intellectually, but have deep meaning on another level.

One of the primary challenges of psychic communication is to take impressions which are often non-verbal and find words that portray the essence of what the psychic is experiencing. In my Tarot and clairvoyant readings, I always get a complete, exact energy reading for the client, but the real skill is in how to verbally communicate what I receive in a way that the client can not only understand but use to further his/her growth.

Clairvoyance can be readily developed by visualization exercises. Some people seem to be naturally clairvoyant; others require much practice. Occasionally, I meet someone who never sees energy but only feels it. A person's degree of clairvoyance does not necessarily correspond to his/her level of spiritual evolution. If you are one of those that does not seem to be able to visualize in living color, do not judge yourself unfairly. Your skills may be emphasized in other areas.

Clairvoyance can be used to see subtle energies that vibrate too quickly for the physical eyes to see. This includes the auric field, electromagnetic anomalies, discarnate entities, etc. If an energy field is especially strong, it may be marginally visible as dancing or sparkling light or "grid lines" which resemble interference on a TV screen.

Clairaudience

Clairaudience is the ability to hear (with the inner ear) sounds that are beyond the range of normal hearing. The clairaudient may hear the voices of discarnate entities or beings from other dimensions. Music is often heard coming from the etheric planes, and has been called "music of the spheres." Some of the sounds heard clairaudiently may include a low-pitched humming noise, a high-pitched squeal or a sound like a choir of angels. The low-pitched humming may be the atomic structure of the universe vibrating. It has been said that the universal vibration is the sound "OM." High-pitched sounds may be actual sound frequencies just beyond the range of normal hearing caused by physical machinery, electromagnetic fluctuations in the earth's field, emanations from the auric fields of entities or objects, or the close proximity of entities from other dimensions occupying the same space as the listener.

Clairsentience

Clairsentience is the ability to feel subtle energies. These may include a sense of being touched by discarnate entities or it may be an actual physical sensation in the body caused by something in another realm or dimension. Clairsentience is different from intuition. Intuition is an inner feeling or inner knowingness while clairsentience is a sensory experience. Whether or not a physical sensation is imagined or real, the clairsentient will feel connected to a vast realm of other-worldly sensations. The most dramatic and physical demonstration of clairsentience is the experience of kundalini. Some energies perceived by the clairsentient may be strong enough to cross over from the etheric to the physical, creating actual physiological changes in the body. More subtle forms of clairsentience may include a feeling of being brushed by spirits, or a feeling of hot or cold in a room of normal temperature.

Precognition

Precognition is the ability to foresee future events. It can involve any combination of clairvoyance, clairaudience and/or clairsentience. An example of precognition that utilizes all three would be the prophecy of doom where the subject is suddenly seeing volcanoes, feeling earthquakes and hearing screams for help.

There appear to be two types of precognition. The first type, which is the most common, involves fourth-dimensional seeing of probable realities currently being created by the person being perceived, or by a third party. This is the category most prophecy falls into. Precognition can happen during the dream or waking states. When the precognitive event happens unconsciously, memory of it may be triggered if the event actually happens. This is called "deja vu." For example, you may have a dream of being introduced to a certain red-haired man by a good friend. Upon waking, you forget the dream. A couple of weeks later, your friend introduces you to the red-haired person you saw in your dream. If you don't remember the dream, the person may look familiar but you don't know where to place him. If the sequence of events happens the way you saw it in the dream, you may be convinced you have experienced this before, hence, deja vu.

There is another kind of precognition that seems to involve seeing a soul's time track completely, before the soul experiences it. This fifth-dimensional precognition occurs when all the soul's possible futures have been seen simultaneously along with the ultimate outcome. This implies that one can move forward in time and experience the future self directly. It also appears to imply that free will gives way to predestiny. However, I believe it is simply a way of viewing all of a soul's free will decisions at once.

Is it possible that one can see through all the veils of perception to the absolute truth beyond all relative realities? Truth, if it exists, would have to encompass all of space and time completely, and therefore, recognition of it would mean being able to simultaneously comprehend past, present and future. From this vantage point, all of Creation is happening at once; a million years becomes the blink of an eye; entire universes are created and destroyed in a fraction of a second.

A soul in a state of God consciousness experiences being everywhere at once; everything in Creation is a part of him/her. Is it possible that you are simply God experiencing itself one soul at a time? In other words, right now you are experiencing one version of the cosmic drama behind the eyes of one body, mind and soul. Perhaps each soul in the universe is simply another part of you that you haven't yet chosen to experience personally in linear time.

Don't try to comprehend this with the rational mind. Simply let it digest for awhile. And now, back to our discussion of the psychic realms.

Telepathy

Refer to the following diagrams. Telepathy is the natural form of communication between souls who have awakened to their higher dimensional selves. Everyone is telepathic, but very few are aware of it. Telepathy between two souls requires that both parties be open and receptive, and also be able to transmit successfully. Telepathy is commonly known as thought transference and can occur between souls in any time, space or dimension. One common form of telepathic communication is between discarnate entities and physical humans. When the interaction occurs energetically as well as mentally, it is known as channeling.

Figure 5.3a - Mental Projection

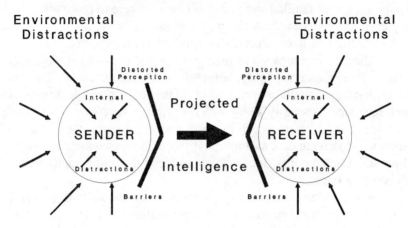

Sender perceives Receiver.
Sender sends thoughts or energy
to Receiver. Receiver may
be unaware of Sender.

Figure 5.3b - Telepathy

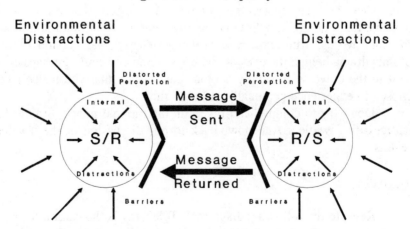

S/R transmits to R/S. R/S acknowledges message
and sends reply. S/R acknowledges reply.
There are four times as many possible distortions
during telepathy as opposed to mental projection.

Figure 5.3c - Precognition

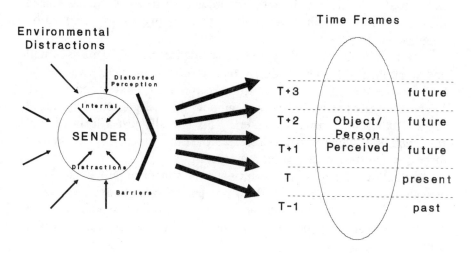

Sender perceives object/person in several
simultaneous time frames--past, present and
future. Sender then tunes into future time segment
for precognition or past time segment for retrocognition.

Channeling

There are several levels of channeling. The most basic is simply
telepathic communication where the receiver reports what the sender is
saying. When the energy of the sender is merged with the receiver, the
sender "comes through" the receiver, adding an extra dynamic to the
transmission.   Souls can merge in varying degrees; if the sender
completely merges his energy field with the receiver, he "takes over" the
body of the receiver. If this is a true merger, there are effectively two
souls occupying one body. More common, however, is the "transfer",
where the receiver's soul either enters the sender's energy field or goes
elsewhere in the universe while the sender communicates through the
receiver's body.

In trance channeling, the receiver's soul usually goes elsewhere in
the universe, often to another realm to be tutored by guides and teachers.
Full trance channelers have little or no memory of what took place
through their bodies while their souls were out and about. Most soul
transfers or displacements are temporary and only last for the duration
of the channeling session. In the rare case where the receiver's soul
chooses not to come back and the sender's soul chooses to remain in the
receiver's body, the phenomenon is known as "walking in." At last

count, there were approximately 26,000 walk-ins residing on earth. Many souls who claim to be walk-ins are not. A true walk-in has placed his or her entire non-physical being into a body previously occupied by another being.

The fact that most of us are fragmented into various aspects of will and spirit makes it highly unlikely that we could completely vacate the body on the spur of the moment to make room for another soul. More likely, it is only the spirit aspect of our soul that has chosen to leave and allow another spirit aspect to enter. This is really just a form of soul fragmentation, which usually decreases overall awareness. Chapter 20 discusses soul fragmentation in more depth.

Soul transfers can also occur when the spirit and will are so much at odds that they no longer wish to occupy the same body at the same time. Without another soul entering, the physical body would die. If a soul feels he cannot go on but is terrified of dying, he may choose a soul transfer.

The most common form of channeling is higher self channeling. This really means that the rational mind of the channel is taking a rest and allowing the soul essence to speak directly from the superconscious mind. Often, the channel will claim to be channeling some entity with a certain name when in fact, it is only his/her own soul that is speaking. The most important thing to remember about channels is not who is speaking but what is being said. Is the message useful? Does it help you grow and evolve?

Some channels are bringing forth what is known as "group souls." These entities are sometimes oversouls or soul groups from higher dimensions that have a broad overview of what is happening on Earth. They may have discrete names, but usually refer to themselves as "we."

When an entity or entities speak through another soul's body, the entity or entities usually access the subconscious mind and akashic records of that soul in order to answer questions from the channel's perspective. Many entities have not been in embodiment for a long time and may not even understand the language spoken by the channel. Without accessing the channel's subconscious and akashic, the message will not make sense. Entities often describe themselves in terms that will be easy to understand by humanity, but do not be deceived and believe this is how they think about themselves. For example, entities and group souls with names like "Galactic Confederation" and "Brotherhood of Light" will, in all probability, have no use for such names apart from getting their message across. Many levels of intelligence are so far beyond the concept of names that such labels would seem absurd if we really grasped where they are coming from.

Even the concept of spiritual hierarchy needs clarification. If an entity is truly evolved into higher realms, he does not see himself as part of a "pecking order." The idea that one soul is higher than another becomes meaningless in the higher dimensions. It is present-day humanity that relates to a hierarchy.

Obviously, not all channels are working for the good of humanity. Be especially discerning when studying so-called channeled material. If the words sound right, but the energy feels strange, question it. Many entities speak of love and light, but some of these beings have judged heavily against the shadow side of themselves and thus, their messages seem hollow and phony. Others are using such platitudes merely for their own personal gains or the personal gains of the channel.

There are very few clear channels on Earth at this time. Most channels, even in deep trance, tend to mix their own energy and information with the energy and information of the entity coming through. Usually, in order for a channel to bring through a being who is truly highly evolved, the channel needs to also be highly evolved. There are many well-known channels who seem unable to sustain the high vibrations of the beings they are bringing forth. Often their messages are contradictory. One day they are on, the next, they are off. One day the channel may bring through a very enlightened perspective; the next day the message may be manipulative and confusing.

Information that originates from a truly loving entity will not advocate actions that create judgment and separation. It is one thing to point out the issues and problems going on in a listener, and quite another to sound condescending and overly critical. Beware of pat answers to complex questions. Beware of platitudes. Convenient or vague responses are often a way for a channel or entity to avoid admitting they do not have the real answer to a question. On the other hand, beware of entities that are overly specific. You may not want some spirit who has never been on Earth telling you exactly how many shares of a particular company's stock you should be buying. You probably know more about the company than the entity does.

Personally, I am not that excited about channeling. Most channeling comes from the higher self (or soul essence) and I would rather simply operate from my soul essence consciously and come from my center in day-to-day communication. Because channeling is a phenomenon, it is easier to charge money for a channeling event than to simply sit in front of a group of people and come from your higher self. As a rule, people do not like to take responsibility for themselves and want some outside authority to do it for them, and channeling provides a convenient way to do that and line the pockets of the channel at the same time.

I am not judging channeling; I am only pointing out some of the pitfalls of believing everything you hear just because "Jesus" said it. No matter who the source claims to be, check it out carefully and feel it in your gut.

PK and TK

Psychokinesis and telekinesis are advanced psychic abilities that involve moving or influencing people or physical objects directly through the use of subtle energies or thought. True PK and TK involve the knowledge of how to manipulate the electromagnetic field (EMF) around an object by tuning into its consciousness. All objects have some degree of consciousness. All forms of laying on of hands involve PK to some extent. However, if the person is unreceptive to the intent of the healer, the results will be minimal.

There are very few people on earth who are successful at PK and TK. To be able to influence objects directly with the mind, you must build a rapport with the object. In a sense, you must merge your EMF with the object and imprint the desire into it. To bend a spoon, you must become the spoon and desire to bend. There are rare exceptions where particular energies and thought forms are already so highly imbedded in an object that it moves rather effortlessly. Although technically, PK and TK are different names for the same phenomenon, I will differentiate and say that PK involves moving an object in your immediate physical vicinity and TK involves moving or influencing an object at a distance. The absent healing described earlier makes use of TK in addition to clairvoyance and mental projection.

Psychometry

Psychometry involves the ability to obtain information about an object simply by holding it in your hands or contemplating it. For example, if you hold an ancient artifact, you may clairvoyantly see images of how the artifact was used, who used it, and even the thoughts present in the people who used it. What you are actually doing is tuning into the akashic field surrounding the object and reading the information stored there. Psychometry can also be used to find missing objects or people. By tuning into a piece of clothing, a hair sample or a personal object, it is possible to attune to the akashic field of a missing person and perceive his/her location and state of being. Sometimes, the name of the person is enough to attune to his or her akashic imprint. More often, a photograph is used. I have looked at a photograph and given a detailed reading of a person I've never met.

Actually, it is possible to read someone with no psychometric anchors. Because we are all connected on a spiritual level, information about every soul in the universe is available at any time, provided you have the permission of that soul. Names, personal objects and photographs are only triggers that make it easier to home in on the person you desire to read.

Teleportation

Teleportation is an extremely advanced method of relocating the physical body. It is technically not a psychic ability because it involves far more than just the psychic faculties. True teleportation involves disassembling the atomic structure of the physical body in one place and reassembling it in another. This requires tremendous mastery of the physical body, as well as spiritual mastery. 99% of what has been reported as teleportation is really a sophisticated form of mental projection where the image of a being is projected holographically to another location while the physical body remains in one place. For psychic communication to take place, holographic projection is preferred, primarily because it is far easier to perform than teleportation. Over the last 10 million years, there have been perhaps a dozen advanced teachers who have teleported on Earth. The rest are either holographic projections or inaccurate stories.

Bilocation

Closely related to teleportation is bilocation, which is the ability to manufacture more than one body and project consciousness into it. This is also related to cloning and replicating. To clone or replicate an image of the body requires thorough knowledge of RNA/DNA constructs and an ability to redirect the atomic structure of the universe to mold itself to that construct. Needless to say, this requires a level of evolution beyond that of humanity at present. Bilocation has been performed on earth by three or four master teachers who came here from higher dimensions with full knowledge of how to replicate themselves while in a physical body. These beings are from the 9th to 12th dimensions, and only appear on Earth during extraordinary times. Today, they are here as part of a special dispensation for humanity. (I will have more on this in later chapters.)

The Imagination

The imagination is the imaging faculty of the mind. It has two primary functions: (1) to perceive realities already in existence ("receptive" imagination); and (2) to create new realities ("creative" imagination). Clairvoyance is one of the qualities of the first function; artistic achievement is an example of the second function.

The mind is always creating. If you have an active imagination, you are an active creator. The key is how to channel that active imagination in ways that are fulfilling and productive.

How do you know when you are creating and when you are simply perceiving realities that have already been created? Unless you are a practicing psychic with many years' experience, you probably can't tell the difference. Like all faculties of the mind, the imagination can be driven by higher intelligence, love and clarity; or it can be driven by fear, worry, anxiety and doubt. When you imagine disaster, you are creating that reality on some level. If you give imagined disaster sufficient power and belief, it will precipitate into your life. Consequently, the same is true of more desirable things.

To perceive clairvoyantly that which is already created, you must quiet your mind enough to temporarily suspend your creative imagination so that your receptive imagination can go to work. If you have preconceived ideas about something, it is much harder to differentiate between creative and receptive imagination. Therefore, the accurate psychic must often "forget" the past and become like a blank screen. The clairvoyance techniques in the Appendix are designed to help you harness the power of your receptive imagination.

Uses of Imagination

The chart on the following page shows that each part of the mind has its own type of imagination.

Third level imagination (also called "synthetic imagination")

This is the process of recalling images. It involves using photographic memory and vividly visualizing a person, place or event that happened in the past. This is one way we use memory to supply information to our present reality.

Figure 5.4 - Three Types of Imagination

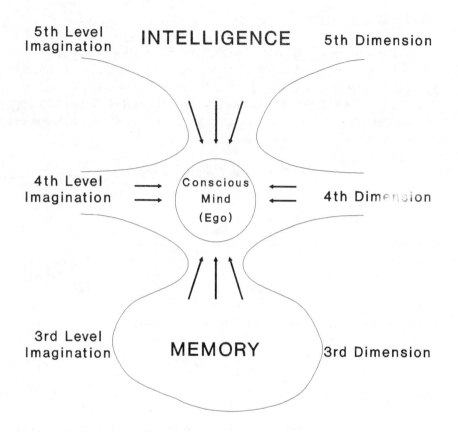

Fourth level imagination (or "spontaneous creativity")

    This is creating an image or picture with no basis in established reality, or drawing upon the subtle levels of the creative dimension (perceiving the astral, mental or subtle planes and drawing information from them to create).

Fifth level imagination (or "psychic/clairvoyant")

    Using information from the collective subconscious, superconscious or Universal Mind to perceive what is actually taking place in another time, space or dimension.

Developing Creativity

<u>The Creative Process</u>

  The only way to develop the creative imagination is to use it. So I've included, in the Appendix, some creativity exercises, including spontaneous writing, the 10-step creative thought process, and creative visualization. Once the creative imagination is kindled, it can be used to manifest your dreams and visions in your outer reality.   Below is a flowchart of the creative process.

Figure 5.5 - The Creative Process

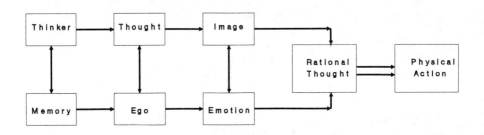

  Creating reality happens in several steps. The process begins with an idea or thought, often triggered by an outer experience. This thought must then become activated by triggering the emotional and physical body.

  <u>Example</u>: You have an experience which triggers the memory of ice cream. You have the thought "I want ice cream." A mental image of you eating the ice cream occurs. A sensation occurs in the body along with an emotional desire. The rational mind then debates whether or not you should obtain the ice cream. If you decide to proceed, it plans how to get the ice cream by directing the body to perform certain actions. We can look at the process from both an inner and outer perspective:

Figure 5.6a - Inner Model

Figure 5.6b - Outer Model

These two models are both valid. I suggest you use the one that is easiest to grasp.

Limits to Creative Potential

We are all creative, but many of us have blocks to our creative potential. Here is a list of the blocks to creativity most commonly experienced by humanity. You will recognize some of these from our earlier discussions:

Table 5.1 - Barriers to Creative Potential

1. Ignorance of oneself and one's mind, emotions, and body.

2. Blindly following ignorant authorities. Conforming to the societal patterns of parents, teachers, leaders, etc.

3. Clinging to old beliefs, traditions and programming.

4. Guilt. The belief one is bad and deserving of punishment.

5. Self-condemnation. Being unwilling to forgive one's past mistakes.

6. Attachment to the body; to physical form.

7. Identification with the ego; the self-image; the personality.

8. Belief in separation, in general.

9. Fear of self. Avoidance and escape from looking at oneself.

10. Fear of being out of control.

11. Not living in the here and now moment (fear of the present).

12. Projection. Blaming others or the environment for one's lack of creativity.

13. Wallowing in self-pity. Looking for someone to come to the rescue.

14. Being overly dramatic. Making mountains out of molehills. Getting caught up in the drama of life.

15. Belief in lack, scarcity and limitation.

Table 5.1 (continued)

16. Belief that one can never get enough (love, money, etc.).

17. Belief that one is unworthy of love, money, etc. A form of guilt.

18. Fear of death. Fear of endings or goodbyes.

19. Insecurity. Fear of losing the familiar. Fear of loss.

20. Fear of pain and suffering.

21. Fear of life.

22. Fear of the unknown.

23. Fear of death.

24. Fear of rejection.

25. Fear of disapproval.

26. Fear of loneliness.

27. Fear of becoming attached. Fear of commitment. Fear of getting caught up in the material world.

28. Fear of not achieving.

29. Fear of parental disapproval. The need to earn parents' love.

30. Birth trauma. Early childhood trauma. Infancy patterns.

31. Fear of God.

32. Fear of the devil (a form of guilt).

33. Belief in having to overcome lifetimes of karma (guilt).

34. Desire to escape from Earth into Heaven (fear of attachment).

35. Attachment to sexual pleasure (ego/body identification).

Table 5.1 (continued)

36. Jealousy, anger, envy, and greed - i.e., demands for security.

37. Seeking power, control, and recognition (underlying belief in weakness and undeservingness)

38. Over-achiever's syndrome (fear of disapproval).

39. Self-indulgence (bad habits, junk food, alcohol, smoking, drugs, etc. - a form of avoidance and denial).

40. Bad habits in general. Addictive behaviors.

41. Laziness and apathy.

42. Boredom.

43. Fear of expressing oneself (a form of fear of rejection).

44. Fear of negative emotions (a form of fear of losing control).

I'm sure you can add to this list.

The Purification Process

Now that I've depressed you with all the blocks to creativity, I would like to describe what I call the purification process, or simply, *the process*. Because most of us have accumulated hundreds of limiting beliefs and have suppressed many layers of emotional trauma, this "stuff" is usually the first thing we encounter when we begin expanding awareness, or desire to break free of limitation.

Many of us have gotten all excited about being the masters of our lives, creating our heart's desire, and being happy, unlimited and free. We then set out on a path full of expectation. "All I have to do is think positive, do affirmations, and look and feel the part." Wrong. If we were already clear inside, this would probably work. But inevitably, doing affirmations, thinking positive and asking for freedom and abundance will bring up everything in the way, first.

Many years ago when I began affirming for happiness and love, I began experiencing just the opposite ever more intensely every time I affirmed. Although I didn't realize it at the time, the techniques were working, because all my "stuff" was coming up to be healed. The danger here is that we sometimes become discouraged at this point and think the process is not working. We may find the stuff so unpleasant that we decide not to look at it and shut down instead. If our dreams do not come true immediately (and they rarely do when we have so much stuff in the way), we may become cynical and start believing we will be forever stuck in negativity. Once we lose faith in the techniques, they stop working due to the power of belief.

Obviously, we must find a balance between cynicism and pollyanna; between getting discouraged and being unrealistically optimistic; between believing it will take centuries to heal and blindly expecting everything to fall into our laps without having to raise a finger. The former pole is where the martyr hangs out; the latter is the realm of the space cadet who lives in a fantasy world.

A healthy purification process happens in cyclic stages. I call the cycles "loops on an upward spiral." Each loop of the spiral consists of the following:

(1)   Assimilation
(2)   Expansion
(3)   Consolidation
(4)   Integration

1.   Assimilation.   During the assimilation phase, new information and experiences are entering awareness; these can take the form of revelations, visions, and surges of new energy. This spurt of new growth results in expansion of consciousness.

2.   Expansion. This is where the new experiences become real for us. We have new knowledge, greater understanding and more power over our lives. Step 2 is the peak of the cycle. Here, we may feel on top of the world, ecstatic in our new state of being.

3.   Consolidation. This is where our "stuff" comes up. Stage 3 is a retraction; a stage where our energy seems to drop, all our old beliefs and habits seem to return, stronger than ever, and we begin to doubt the validity of our new experience. If we get stuck in consolidation, we may become disillusioned and believe it was "too good to be true." What keeps people stuck in Step 3 is self-judgment and criticism -- in other words, failing to see that this step is part of a cycle.

4.   Integration. In order to reach integration, we must allow the new energies of assimilation (Step 1) and the resulting expansion and

growth (Step 2) to fully sink in to the depths of our being. Anything not in alignment with these new realities is pushed to the surface for healing during Step 3. Integration occurs when we embrace our stuff, allow it expression, and come to an understanding about it. We then see the whole picture of why we feel the way we do and have insights to help us take the next step.

An example of the 4-step cycle is as follows: Suppose we desire a greater income doing what we enjoy. Step 1 would include the belief that we really can make a living doing what we enjoy. We then get all excited about it and new ideas begin pouring in on how to proceed. We feel a sense of elation and expansion (Step 2). However, when we start to follow through with the new ideas, a lot of unworthiness issues start popping up. We begin to doubt if we are really ready to proceed (Step 3). We then process the issues and see how these issues have kept us stuck in the past. We begin to feel a sense of certainty and solidity as we clear the old issues and take action (Step 4).

Between cycles, a state of limbo may exist. It may seem as though nothing is happening or things are in a void. Or we may seem confused. If this happens, it is time to become quiet and receptive, allowing the new energies of Step 1 to enter once again.

Purification cycles may vary tremendously in duration. During a period of rapid personal and planetary acceleration, one might experience several major and minor cycles in a year. During a "retrograde" or stagnant phase, one cycle can take years to get a handle on. Patience is certainly a virtue here.

How do you know when a cycle is complete? How do you know when there's no more "stuff" in a given area of your life? As you approach each deeper layer of stuff, the cause goes back further and further. If you have issues of abandonment, for instance, the first time you explore these issues, you may remember being left alone as a small child. The next time, you may remember a past life when your husband or wife left you. Eventually, you may go back to the beginning of time and see the whole issue from Original Cause, realizing how it has played itself out lifetime after lifetime up to the present. If you have truly integrated abandonment, you may feel a powerful certainty deep within. Future situations where you are alone will not bother you, and you will no longer create scenarios of abandonment.

Consciously creating what you want in life becomes easy, natural and straightforward if there are no more issues in the way. You may find the emotional charge gone regarding whether or not you are successful at creating what you want. You may prefer things to be a certain way, but you don't demand it. If things don't turn out as planned, it doesn't bother you - you simply realize that everything happens in its right time. And, paradoxically, this attitude allows things to happen more quickly. It's like squeezing grains of sand - they fall through your fingers. You must allow them to rest gently in your open hand if you wish to keep them.

Conscious Soul Growth

Once a soul reaches a certain level of awareness, he or she may begin consciously drawing experiences that maximize growth. Up until that point, the soul would often attract a lesson and the ego would fight, resist or complain instead of accepting the lesson as a gift. This is especially true if "no pain, no gain" is one of the soul's core beliefs. Consciously accepting and appreciating life's lessons is the key to rapid growth. Someone once said "if you cannot be grateful for what you have, how can you expect to get more?" Making a real commitment to growth will bring lessons fast and furiously. If you are grateful, you might find the lessons enjoyable and consciously seek them out.

Life lessons do not have to take the form of unpleasant outer reflections. Difficult circumstances and cataclysmic events only occur if you refuse to learn the lesson when it presents itself in a gentler way. The purification process can be an inner experience with no serious consequences in the outer world. If you pay attention to the messages your spirit and will give you, if you integrate the stuff as it comes up, and if you express your true feelings without suppressing or denying them, then there is no reason to suffer "bad karma." Negative outer conditions are a result of denying or suppressing negative beliefs until there is no other way to learn the lesson. This is especially true of physical health. If you are sensitive to the body and emotions, you will be instructed in what to do to prevent illness. It is only when you repeatedly ignore your soul's messages that the body will manifest illness.

By gladly seeking out those experiences that "push your buttons" you can avoid ever having to see negative reflections. This doesn't mean you become a masochist and spend all your time processing. Processing, like anything else, can become an addiction. If you force yourself to grow faster than your soul is ready for, you will be unable to enjoy life or even catch your breath. You will then end up spending most of your time in the consolidation phase of the cycle, while waiting for the rest of you to catch up.

Intelligence

Intelligence (also known as "conscious awareness") sees the whole, rather than the parts, of a situation, especially when looking at conflict within the self. When inharmony is created by demanding that things "should be" a certain way instead of accepting "what is", intelligence acts by seeing the conflict instantly and ending it instantly. Then there is only "what is." The responses, reactions, events and conclusions are all a part of what is. We may not be able to change the external event, but we can change our experience of it. And once we create a armonious response to the event, it becomes much easier to change it, if that is what the soul desires.

Intelligence uses all the faculties of the mind, but it is not controlled by them. It instantaneously evaluates all the criteria in a given situation, draws on Universal Mind for the proper information and generates its own response. Intelligence is impersonal. It is a dimension of energy; a field of conscious awareness. It is part of the fifth dimension, which transcends time and space. Your higher self, or soul, naturally resides in this field of intelligence, but your rational mind and emotional body often do not. That is why it is so important to align all the parts of yourself so that information can flow unimpeded from higher intelligence.

What is intelligence? It is the energy of mankind in a highly refined form. It is an infinite stream of consciousness originating from the Godhead. It is pure awareness, in the moment, but it includes linear time. To evolve into a state of intelligence, you need three things:

1)   Awareness of the moment
2)   Acceptance of being
3)   Transcendence of "self"

Awareness of the moment means choiceless awareness - noticing all the subtleties and movements taking place. Acceptance of being includes all levels and dimensions of yourself, but it also means accepting "what is" in all areas of your life. Transcendence of self means you expand your awareness beyond the individual ego and include the larger you that is omnipresent. Transcendence of self is transcendence of time and space. You have heard the expression "be here now." *Now* is where intelligence resides. *Now* includes past, present and future. *Now* is where you will find true wisdom.

Intelligence is outside of time and space. This is why it is possible to see into the past or future, and other dimensions. Time and space are constructed in layers, or frames. From the perspective of the higher self (intelligence), multidimensional awareness becomes your conscious reality.

The following diagrams show several ways to explain the idea of multidimensionality:

Figure 5.7a - Historical Consciousness

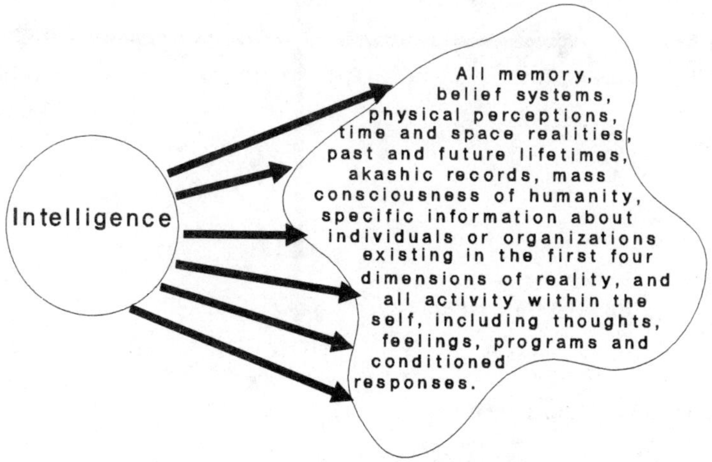

Intelligence

All memory, belief systems, physical perceptions, time and space realities, past and future lifetimes, akashic records, mass consciousness of humanity, specific information about individuals or organizations existing in the first four dimensions of reality, and all activity within the self, including thoughts, feelings, programs and conditioned responses.

Figure 5.7b - Reincarnation

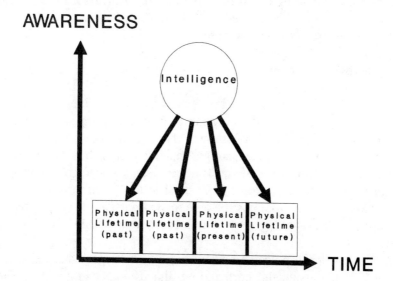

AWARENESS

Intelligence

| Physical Lifetime (past) | Physical Lifetime (past) | Physical Lifetime (present) | Physical Lifetime (future) |

TIME

Figure 5.7c - Time Frames

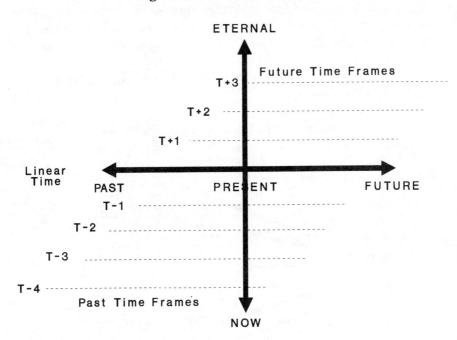

Collective Consciousness

From the perspective of the higher self (intelligence), it is possible to access virtually any information from anywhere within the collective subconscious, including the akashic records and Universal Mind. This is because you are able to step out of your personal knowledge and access the universal knowledge (See Figure 5.7a).

Reincarnation Revisited

This is also how you can become aware of past lives. Actually, from this perspective, the lives are not past, but simultaneous, because you can see any or all of them at once. How is this so?

If you recall the movie analogy, imagine that each lifetime is like one frame on a filmstrip. If the film represents linear consciousness moving through the projector one frame at a time, then in order to see what's past or future, you must be able to step outside the continuity of the film, thereby viewing several frames simultaneously (See Figure 5.7b).

If you wish to perceive beyond the limits of space and distance, you must step outside the normal four-dimensional continuum. The reason most of us are not able to perceive from a higher perspective is that we are identified with one time frame or dimension and are so heavily focused on it (selective awareness) that we are unaware of the other time frames and dimensions. In our model of precognition (Figure 5.3c) we saw how our true being exists simultaneously in many levels and dimensions, but our "normal" awareness occupies only a fraction of that area.

In Figure 5.7c we see another concept; that of vertical time vs. horizontal time. Imagine that time is composed like a stack of pancakes. If you look horizontally, you will only see one layer at a time, but if you look vertically, you can see the whole stack. The key here is to be completely in the present and to detach from all thoughts of past and future. After all, every time frame and dimension exists right now, and the only way you can know this is to *be here now*.

Figure 5.8 - Multidimensional Man

Perception of Actuality

In order to perceive from intelligence, it is necessary to have clear, undistorted perception of what is actually taking place, within and without. In order to have clear perception it is necessary to examine the factors that limit the accuracy of the perception. As we said before, noticing what blocks you is always the first step. There are many good questions you can ask yourself to determine whether or not you are perceiving a situation accurately. Some examples are:

- "What conclusions am I drawing from this situation?"

- "What qualities of my perception am I taking for granted?"

- "When I want to perceive information about something I have never experienced before, how do I usually go about it?"

- "Am I really aware of what another person is saying, or am I attaching my own meaning based on my past experience?"

- "When another person is relating an experience to me, do I really understand what he or she is saying?"

Let's suppose you are involved in a conversation with another person and you desire to perceive what is actually so in the situation. To perceive truly, you cannot rely on memory because the person is constantly changing, and you cannot experience the other intellectually, for this is still in the past. You must be attentive moment to moment, not engaged in past thoughts. You cannot be thinking about what you are going to say next. You must have a passionate desire to understand the other person. You need to ask yourself "what is he really experiencing?" In addition to noticing your own inattentiveness, notice his. How is he reacting to the conversation? What is he feeling? Ask yourself if his experience is triggering memories of similar experiences in you.

To further illustrate this, I've included, in Figure 5.9, a list of the most common distractions and barriers to effective communication.

Figure 5.9 - Barriers to Perception

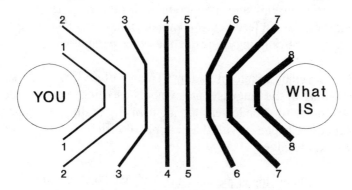

1 ▪ Environmental Distractions
2 ▪ Personal Physical Distractions
3 ▪ Unrelated Emotional Distractions
4 ▪ Personal Programs/Emotions
5 ▪ Race Mind Conditioning
6 ▪ Symbolic Interpretation
7 ▪ Undeveloped Mental Faculties
8 ▪ Personal Reference Point

    1.   <u>Environmental distractions</u>. These are the external distractions, such as random noise, nearby talking, machinery, distortion of the physical senses (i.e., the room is too dark to see the person's facial expression, etc.).

    2.   <u>Personal physical distractions</u>. These include whether or not you got enough sleep last night, the pain in your left leg, overeating, clogged sinuses, etc.

    3.   <u>Unrelated emotional distractions</u>. This is how you feel while the situation is happening. Maybe you are upset over something that happened last night and your mind keeps wandering back to it. Maybe you desire a particular outcome before you even begin the conversation.

    4.   <u>Personal programs and immediate emotional distractions</u>. These are your personal issues and feelings that are triggered by the situation. They include judgments you may have about the person, beliefs you have about the things he or she saying, emotional reactions in you that are triggered during the conversation, etc.

5.   Race mind conditioning. These are all the ideas, concepts, beliefs, models and thoughts that you have taken into your subconscious regarding relationships and interaction with others. They include past knowledge of the subject being communicated, pre-conceived notions about what is really going on inside the other person, etc.

6.   Symbolic interpretation. This involves your understanding of the meaning of the language and symbols used in the communication, and your ability to decode sensory input in the brain. We touched on this concept in Chapter 1 with the example of different interpretations of the word "knowledge."

7.   Undeveloped mental faculties. This involves the ways your senses receive the experiences of another person. Maybe you can hear him/her accurately, but are unable to feel the energy he/she is radiating out toward you.

8.   Personal reference point. This is your awareness of being a separate entity from the other person. It includes your position in time and space relative to the other person. It is the perception "I am here listening and you are there talking." There is still a receiver separate from the communicator, so there is still a barrier to perception.

9.   Physical limitations. These are the actual physical limitations on the situation. You may be totally merged telepathically, intuitively and spiritually with the other person, but because you have a separate body, your experience of the other person will never be exactly the same as his/her experience.

Our intention here is to perceive with total awareness; to know completely what is taking place. Therefore, we are seeking to overcome the first eight barriers and experience a true oneness with our fellow human beings. This soul-to-soul connection can only take place when all the issues between the persons are resolved.

I could write a whole book just on interpersonal communication, but I will leave you to explore the subject more fully on your own.

Universal Intelligence

In summary, this chapter has examined not only the mental level of awareness, but also psychic functioning, creativity, intelligence and conscious awareness. Although higher intelligence is a very lofty level of perception, there is still a sense of individuality; a perceiver separate from that which is perceived. The ultimate level of awareness is that of universal intelligence, also known as "cosmic consciousness" or "Oneness with God". But before we look at Oneness, there is another, extremely important level in between personal intelligence and universal intelligence.

It is impossible to go beyond the mental level of awareness as long as you maintain the sense of a separate self. For a key ingredient is missing: Love.

CHAPTER 6
LOVE

Before I talk about love, let me relate another subject dear to all of us: freedom. What is freedom? Is it the ability to make your own decisions? To travel? To do anything you want? Or is it something that you feel deep inside when you discover your true essence? The poem below sums it up:

Freedom

Freedom is being unlimited.
Freedom is releasing your attachment to the past.
Freedom is moving effortlessly through the realities of life without getting caught and tangled in traps along the way.
Freedom is being open and receptive to the immeasurable presence of the Divine.
Freedom is being a silent observer of the good and bad, realizing that perfection is there.
Freedom is being without fear, without restraint.
Freedom is boundless love and compassion for all.
Freedom is flowing with the river of bliss.
Freedom is when our minds are free of old content.
Freedom is being here and now without thought of attainment.
Freedom is knowing the meaning of life.
Freedom is loving and serving unconditionally.
Freedom is just being who and what we truly are.

What is Love?

Love is beyond time. Love is beyond thought. Love is beyond illusion. Love is beyond description. Most of all, love is beyond separation. Love is the beginning of eternity. It is the beginning of enlightenment. Love is a state of being beyond polarity.

Love ends karma. Love ends duality. It is the meeting place of the spirit and the will; it is the heart. It brings together the masculine and feminine. In the lower worlds, this occurs in sexual union; in the higher worlds, the Mother-Father principle unites in Christ consciousness.

Love is more than a level of awareness; it is also a dimension, a world of its own. Although love is beyond time, it can reach into time and affect all the levels and dimensions of time.

Love can be given and received directly without the need for vast amounts of mental knowledge. A simple glance, a touch or a kind word can catapult a soul into its fragrance in an instant, shortcutting years of karma and inner struggle.

Love is a miracle; the greatest miracle. As "A Course In Miracles" so aptly states, "Love is a law without an opposite." When you are in love, whether with another person or with God, all you see is love. Darkness, guilt and judgment have disappeared and have no memory; beauty is all there is, forever and ever.

Love is the greatest healing power. Its presence can dispel the deepest, most chronic forms of disease. You can try a million healing techniques, but if love is not present, the effects will be temporary at best.

Love can appear in many forms. Anything that gets you out of your head and into your heart is a miracle of love, although for many, pain and suffering seems to be the path. Often it takes a firm kick in the rear to get one to realize that the mind cannot solve all of life's problems. Sometimes it takes utter despair; when every trick has been tried and every idea used to no avail. This is what spiritual teachers really mean when they say surrender is the only way. It is not surrender of the will, or even of the mind; it is the attachment to the mind; the letting go of the preconceived ideas and concepts and the opening to something new.

The key to opening the heart lies in balancing the spirit and the will. The spirit is the God force present in all Creation; and the will is the feeling nature of life; the experiencer. By opening to spirit and becoming aware of your feelings, you make room for love to descend upon you.

For most of us, the emotions are what block us from opening the heart. We have been battered and bruised so much emotionally, whether from childhood, past lives or Original Cause, that we have all but given up on love. Hurt so many times, by so many unfulfilling relationships, we often become cynical and give up our dreams. The childhood tales of fairy prince and princess give away to bitter disappointment as we wend our way through alcoholic nightmares, spousal control and manipulation, divorces and legal proceedings, child abuse, sexual abuse, and all manner of dysfunction.

Even with good therapists, many of us seem forever stuck in childhood patterns and broken dreams, with layer after layer of rage and grief waiting to consume us if we dare look deep enough. Without spirit; without God to lift us out of our mire, there seems little hope. And so we turn to religion only to find the same dysfunctions masquerading behind the cloth and the pulpit. "If only I give enough money to church, somehow I will be saved." "If only I say enough 'Hail Marys.'"

It is only now, in what Christians have called "the end times", that we have finally gained enough wisdom to step beyond the seemingly endless cycle of pain and suffering. And we have many souls who have gone before us, assisting from the higher dimensions. We also have Divine intervention. With our backs against the wall, there is no place to go but up. And so we are thrown a rope, just as the enemy (our own guilt) closes in on us. The friend on the other end of the rope is love, brought to us from On High, and although we must climb the rope ourselves, we are given much encouragement and support from those above who are cheering us on.

The Earth would not have survived some of the past wars if it had not been for the love of those in the higher realms. Several times they have intervened to keep us from destroying ourselves. But they did not intervene without our permission. Collectively we, the ones who have yearned for freedom, asked for their assistance. Not long ago, perhaps 30 years back, we reached a critical mass. The number of souls desiring freedom grew so large that the request could not be denied. And so now we are being shown the way out.

It is my hope that this book is providing one of the steps out of bondage. Without assistance and love from On High, it could not have been written. The ideas have been flowing continuously since I made the commitment to write, and many more ideas will come before I am finished. So together, let us lovingly explore new worlds and dimensions.

Enlightened Relationships

There are very few healthy relationships on Earth at this time. All of us have issues from childhood and past lives that influence our ability to be fully present with another human being. If we allow these issues to control us and prevent communication with another, we will be forever stuck in dysfunctional relationship patterns and behaviors.

Based on my own experience, it seems almost essential that one must learn how to be alone before one can be intimate with another in a healthy, fulfilling way. The length of this individual "soul-searching" will vary from person to person. Most of us go to one of two extremes, however. Either we jump from relationship to relationship with no breather in between, or we spend most of our lives alone, being afraid to jump in the water.

A person cannot wait until he or she has attained a state of "perfection" before entering into relationship. A soul may need to learn lessons about being alone for several years, but eventually, that soul will need to have experiences that can only be found in relationship with another.

To have a truly enlightening relationship, it is necessary for us to stop projecting our own issues onto the other person. We must take responsibility for our own feelings, and express those feelings openly and honestly. If the person (or persons) in our lives is unable or unwilling to accept us the way we are, complete with our human feelings, then it usually means we are unable or unwilling to accept ourselves the way we are.

Once we gain enough self-worth and self-esteem to accept ourselves completely, we can then attract a partner who accepts him or herself completely. However, we may not attract the perfect partner immediately. This is because we often attract someone who mirrors the issues we have just recently cleared. This other soul will draw us into his/her life because we are just far enough ahead of the game to give a helping hand over the rough spots, but not so advanced as to be completely incompatible.

If we listen to our higher selves, we will intentionally create relationships that maximize our growth, until we are sufficiently healed to create a relationship that is primarily for co-creating and playfulness.

The key to a successful relationship is communication. The natural state of human beings is to communicate telepathically. However, until we return to our natural state, we need to stop assuming the other person knows our needs and wants. We must be willing to be vulnerable and imperfect in order to heal. We must also be willing to say "no" to someone who is unwilling to accept our vulnerability and imperfection. We need to have a clear sense of our own boundaries and the boundaries of our partner. There must be both individuality and union between couples. Being alone and being together are simultaneous realities; i.e., they are both happening all the time, depending on which dimensions of reality we are focused on. (We will look at these dimensions in depth in Chapter 10.)

There are many good books on relationships, and I encourage you to read as much on the subject as you can. It would also be a good idea to learn about time management, since the pressures of modern life can leave little quality time for couples to be with each other. However, if you are truly committed to creating a healthy relationship, you will make time for it, and you will do whatever is necessary to heal the hurts of the past that keep you isolated and separate, even if you share the same house and bed with another. If we heal our relationships, we heal our world. For in reality, we are in relationship with over five-and-a-half billion people. And yes, love *is* the key.

CHAPTER 7
THE SOUL AND OVERSOUL

The Soul

The soul represents the pure essence of the Self. My perception of the soul is that it is similar to a vast star or cosmic light, forever travelling the corridors and mansions of the infinite universe, while continuously creating in the lower realms of existence (body, emotions, mind, etc.).

When all the layers of conditioning and programming have been peeled away and only the essence remains, we live from the wisdom of the soul. We become aware of countless "mansions" in the Father's house. Great beings, invisible to our lower bodies, reach out and touch us with their wings of light. And we are welcomed back to a place we never really left.

The soul is not the same as the spirit. Spirit is the glue, the cohesiveness, that holds all of Creation together. It is the energy and intelligence, the order behind all Creation. Soul, on the other hand, is the individual spark, the basic unit of being of which we are all made. Each soul is like a tentacle flowing out from the body of God - forever connected to the whole, yet unique and individual.

The Oversoul

Individual souls spend many incarnations reawakening to who they are and purifying themselves of all the false images they have taken on throughout their Earthly journeys. Once the soul is purified, the love and wisdom of Self begins to extend beyond itself to reach out and bond with its long lost counterparts - its vast cosmic family of kindred souls. Each soul family comes together in a great star cluster, or oversoul. One by one they come at first, then two by two as each soul finds his or her twin flame counterpart. Then four by four and eight by eight until the soul family is completely reunited.

Figure 7.1 - Souls and Oversouls

Thus, all ascends back into Oneness and the process begins again. Yet, this is not the end. For the oversouls are but one of the many creations of spirit - the God essence that gives life, that bonds us to everything in the Universe.

Time and time again, we will return to this holy place, for the soul is eternal, being the basic unit of God; a complete hologram of the Infinite.

This chapter is very brief, for it is designed to be a glimpse of things to come. In later chapters, we will explore the soul and oversoul in more depth.

CHAPTER 8
MEDITATION, TIMELESSNESS AND COSMIC CONSCIOUSNESS

The Meditative Mind

NOTE: There are two definitions of meditation: (1) the practice, and (2) the state of mind. In this chapter, we will use the term "true meditation" to describe the still, meditative mind.

In true meditation, the mind becomes silent and reality as we know it comes to an end. Time no longer has any meaning. There is no longer a "me" and a "you." There is no longer an experience of life; there is simply life itself. In this state of silence, all the aspects of life still exist, but there is no separation between the self and the experience. There is no comparison, no image-making, no word-forming or idea conception taking place. There is no "me" looking at a tree and thinking "this is a tree and I am seeing it." There is simply the experience of the tree, with no label, no model, and no thought.

In a state of true meditation, "models of reality" becomes a meaningless concept. There are no levels, no dimensions, no states of being. Things simply are as they are. Life becomes merely a drama; a dream. All the striving, seeking, acting and even growing become insignificant; a silly, absurd activity in a world of sleepwalkers. At the same time, something vast and nameless comes into existence. Suddenly everything has supreme meaning and sacredness, although it is not anything the mind can grasp. A sense of boundless freedom takes over and consumes the self. Every moment becomes brand new and stretches forever in all directions. Without thought, there is no past or future and so there is no time. There is nowhere to go and nothing to do. Desire becomes irrelevant.

And yet, all the aspects of self become very real. The body still eats, the emotions still feel, the mind still functions, though somewhat on automatic. The natural world becomes a thing of wonder; each blade of grass is a thing of perfection; the wind becomes the breath of God. All of life continues as before, but the separate self, the ego, is no more.

It is this state the masters were in when they said "all is illusion" and "the world is not real." And from this lofty perspective, it truly *is* all a dream.

Every time I have entered this state, I have always returned to "linear" consciousness. I do not know if it is possible to stay in this timeless place and still function in the world. Most people I've met who spend a lot of time "beyond time" are what we commonly refer to as "space cadets." None of the "normal" values of society mean anything any more. Without desire, there is no motivation to do anything in the world, except perhaps to attempt to teach others how to reach this state.

The last time I entered this state, I looked at whether or not one could integrate it with the more worldly states. Can one function in timelessness and still play the worldly game impeccably? Can one come from inner stillness and still have desires, feelings, goals, plans and a so-called "grounded" experience?

Certainly, some functions of consciousness can be put on automatic. Driving a car does not require a lot of focusing if it has become a habit. I have been able to meditate while walking, and occasionally, even when carrying on a conversation. And to write this section requires some sort of balance between time and timelessness. To be honest, the first part of this book was difficult to write, not for lack of knowledge or writing skill, but because I kept going in and out of time while trying to write about levels and dimensions. For those who are stuck in time, the concepts are meaningful and help answer a lot of questions that are necessary on the soul's path. But from a timeless perspective, levels and dimensions are ridiculous. So every time I wrote about the "higher" levels, I would run into resistance and lump them all together.

This is one of the reasons I've included so many versions and models of reality, and why I sometimes prefer the seven-level model over the 12-level one (see Chapter 11). However, I encourage you to use whatever works for you and don't get hung up on the difference between the 9th level and the 10th. From a state of meditation it is all a silly game.

Cosmic Consciousness

Once a soul enters a state of true silence, a number of things can happen. Perhaps he or she returns, reluctantly, to a world that no longer seems to have meaning. Or maybe a new joy descends on what was once a humdrum life. The state of meditation cannot be sought and attained. It must be allowed to come of its own. This is what Krishnamurti meant when he said "truth is a pathless land."

Another state of awareness that cannot be consciously attained is the state of cosmic, or universal consciousness. For most, it comes rarely and unexpectedly. This is the state of true oneness -- not a sense of feeling at one with Creation (the heart), but a sense of actually being all of Creation (the spirit).

Imagine, for a moment, that everything in life is really the opposite of the way you think it is. Look at all that you think is you - your sense of self, your body, emotions and mind, etc. Now imagine that none of that exists at all. Instead, all that you think of as being outside of you has become the real "you." That distant star, the flowers in the meadow, the person over there, the car, the tree, is all you. And the person thinking all this, is no longer you at all. You have become all that you thought you were not. And all that you thought you were before is gone. How can this be so?

There is a something, somewhere, that is aware of that distant star, that field, that meadow, that sky. It exists, it has a reality. So there must be someone who is experiencing it. Who is the experiencer? Who is the being that knows that star, that tree and that sky? Not the body, emotions or mind. They no longer exist. But something is experiencing them. And if you have gone deeply enough into this exercise, you <u>know</u> they are there. And you are experiencing them as they are, not according to a belief or perception.

Cosmic consciousness is the realm of the spirit. The spirit is everywhere at once, beyond time and space. It is not your spirit and my spirit, it simply IS. And we are that spirit, and that spirit is us.

Although the realms beyond the intellect are truly awesome, I'm going to introduce some concepts designed to bring us back down to Earth long enough to create alignment between the intellect and the higher consciousness. The next three chapters explore various aspects of the Universe in detail, beginning with densities.

CHAPTER 9
DENSITIES

(NOTE: In this book, "higher" densities are less dense than "lower" densities, because "higher" and "lower" refer to actual frequencies of vibration, not to the degree of density.)

Densities are discrete vibratory levels within the frequency spectrum of Creation. Generally, densities are divided into harmonics, or octaves. We can arbitrarily assign density levels to various vibratory frequencies in the Universe in order to communicate about how the Universe is constructed.

To further illustrate the idea of harmonics, I've given the following examples:

On a piano, there are eight whole pitches which make up each octave. Depending on the type of piano, there could be anywhere from five to eight octaves on the keyboard. Each octave is a specific harmonic, with the vibratory, or density level increasing as you go up the keyboard to higher notes.

Another way to view the idea of densities is by using the light spectrum. If each color on the light spectrum were to represent a density, then we could arbitrarily assign a number to a color; for example, if yellow equals third density, then orange would be second density, and green, fourth density, etc.

Of course, we could define densities using actual frequency measurements. For example, 100 to 1000 Hz (cycles per second) could be first density; 1,000 to 10,000 Hz could be second density, etc. As you can see, densities do not have to be linear; they can be logarithmic.

The main attribute of a density is its harmonic relationship to other densities. In the TV series "Star\Trek" they talk about warp factors when describing the speed of spacecraft. Each warp factor could be a density; the higher the warp factor, the higher the density.

Densities can be harmonics of a basic unit of measure, such as the speed of light. In the new physics, there is a concept of parallel time frames. It is theorized that each time frame is accessed by achieving speeds that are harmonics of the speed of light. While it may not be possible to exceed the speed of light linearly, it appears to be possible to "dial" harmonics of the speed of light, as represented in Einstein's famous equation $E = mc^2$, where c^2 is a harmonic of the speed of light. In this example, c^2 could be second density, c^3, third density, etc.

In this book, densities will correspond to various life forms along the evolutionary scale. The higher the vibration of a given life form, the higher its density. As you will see later, each density roughly corresponds to the dimension with the same number, but dimensions are more like worlds within worlds that overlap each other, while densities do not overlap.

In Chapter 1, we listed the 12 densities. Figure 9.1 below shows each density along the light spectrum.

Figure 9.1 - Densities as a Function of the Light Spectrum

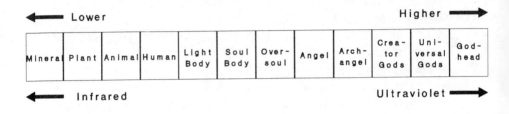

First Density: The Mineral Kingdom

First density refers to the mineral kingdom. The vibratory level of this kingdom is very dense, but it has its own level of life and consciousness. I'm sure you have known someone who claims to talk to rocks or crystals, or has imagined being one. You can communicate in a rudimentary sort of way with this kingdom. In this model, we are assuming the mineral kingdom is the first stage of evolution in the manifest universe.

Second Density: The Plant Kingdom

Second Density refers to the plant kingdom. This kingdom is more organized than the mineral kingdom and has limited ability to move about. It has reproductive and photosynthetic awareness and an instinct to survive, but its perception is still rather limited.

Third Density: The Animal Kingdom

Third density is the level of the animal kingdom. The "lower" level human being also resides here. Third density humans are souls experiencing the animal kingdom in humanoid bodies. Contrary to popular belief, animals have basically the same abilities as third density humans: the instinct to survive, reproduce and care for their young, as well as a rudimentary intellectual awareness.

It is important here to differentiate between third density and third dimension. Obviously, the third dimension includes the plant and mineral kingdoms, whereas the third density refers specifically to animals and "lower" humans. I also want to mention that the term "lower" here refers only to the frequency involved and is not a judgment against anyone. I am not implying that third density humans are any less Divine than "higher" fourth density humans. This would be as absurd as arguing that I am better than a rock because the rock is in fir density.

Those who judge others for their level of vibration are displaying their ignorance of the perfection of the evolutionary process. Some of the most aware souls in the universe have chosen to re-experience third density to gain valuable experience not available in the higher realms. You cannot remember who you are if you insist on judging and comparing yourself to others. Although you may prefer to be in higher densities, if your motive for being there is to escape the lower densities because you disdain them, then the unwillingness to accept your lower nature will keep you stuck there. The fastest way to evolve is to love all parts of yourself.

At the time of this writing, it is my perception that approximately 80% of all humans are experiencing the third density. What are the characteristics of third density humans? Besides the survival and sexual urges, third density humans have the belief that they are victims of outside circumstances and have very little power to change their lot in life. This is the epitome of separation. Most third density beings try to alleviate the inherent pain of separation by conforming to various movements, ideologies, religions, etc. Because they have not yet developed their fourth density awareness, they find it very difficult to think for themselves, and so they are ruled by the cultural beliefs of their society.

Currently, many people are "sitting on the fence" between third and fourth density. This means a part of them has stretched into fourth density while the remainder is still in third. If you strongly desire to be in fourth density and you honor and accept the parts that are still in third density, you will soon find your entire being in fourth density or higher.

To be completely free of third density requires being willing to no longer buy into the belief systems of third density. Living on a planet where 80% of the people are in third density creates a very strong force field in the aura of the planet. As we have said before, beliefs are very powerful. If you do not consciously choose your beliefs, you take on the prevailing beliefs of your environment. That is why it is important, if you are vibrating at fourth density, to surround yourself with people who are in alignment with your fourth density beliefs until you are able to break free of the influence of your environment. When you reach a high enough vibration and enough of you is aligned, then it is possible to immerse yourself in a group of third density humans without being affected, but this takes a great deal of awareness and discipline.

Fourth Density: The Higher Human

Fourth Density is the vibration of the "higher" human. Fourth density humans are not necessarily lighter or more loving, but they are definitely more powerful and creative than third density humans, because people in fourth density are aware that they create their own experience through their thoughts and belief systems. Fourth density humans have awakened the psychic and intuitive centers, have keen imaginations and frequently tap into the astral realms. Outwardly, they look very similar to third density humans, but they tend to be more mentally and intellectually refined. Although they may not be conscious of it, they use their psychic and intuitive powers to draw to them the experiences they need for their soul growth.

The ego is still very much a part of fourth density. Many fourth density humans are rugged individualists and free thinkers. They tend to be rebels and radicals, shaking up the status quo. Although their ideas are often very creative and at the leading edge of humanity, they are still polarized against those with opposing viewpoints. Many protest marches, demonstrations and counterculture activities have met with increased opposition from those who do not want to disturb the sense of security that comes from the heavy denial inherent in the more conservative lifestyles. For the protesters to truly make a difference, they must move beyond polarization into fifth density, a step a few leading edge humans are about to embark on.

Polarization notwithstanding, positive fourth density beings use their abilities for the good of humanity. They focus on changing their thoughts and beliefs through affirmations, reprogramming and other techniques. Negative fourth density beings use their abilities to control and manipulate others. There are many beings in the universe who are technologically advanced but use their psychic powers to control entire planets for their own ego pursuits. These powerful beings have mesmerized others with psychic phenomena while taking power from their followers and giving little in return. A lot of fourth density entities get stuck in the astral levels of the fourth dimension. To a fourth density being, the astral planes are often mistaken for the more heavenly realms because, through the power of thought and belief, the astral can be made to look any way you want it to.

About 20% of humanity has evolved into fourth density.

Fifth Density: The Light Body

Fifth density is the level of the light body. This is the beginning of the state known as ascension. A special dispensation has been granted to the more evolved humans allowing them access to fifth density before they have attained complete self-mastery. Therefore, fifth density humans are ascended beings, not necessarily ascended masters.

Chapter 20, "Building Your Crystal Light Body," explains the mechanics of mutating from a carbon-based life form to a silicon-based one. This is a precursor to actual ascension and follows the "quantum shift" principle spoken of in Chapter 2.

To reach fifth density requires opening the heart and learning to love yourself and others unconditionally. Love will lift your vibration above the Earthly levels of third and fourth density and turn your mortal, carbon-based body into a radiant, immortal, crystalline one.

The vibration of fifth density is etheric. The fifth density body is visible to fourth density humans as a luminescent outline of the physical form. It is generally not transparent, however. As humankind continues to evolve into fourth density, more and more people will begin to see luminescent beings in their midst. At first, such visions will be psychic. Early on in fourth density evolution, the third eye opens and all sorts of entities are discovered existing within the fabric of the ethers.

In the Renaissance period, artists often depicted holy men (and women) with gold halos around their heads (and bodies). The saints were highly developed into fourth density and so were many of the artists, having constantly used their creative faculties to the point of becoming visionaries.

To third density humans, fifth density is completely invisible. Fourth density humans are still visible, but those nearing fifth density may tend to fade in and out. To the trained eye, the body takes on a radiance or glow as a soul gets close to ascension. However, most third density people do not really notice fourth density all that much because their minds are pre-occupied with trying to survive. Even so, there are accounts in the Bible (and elsewhere) of people disappearing in a pillar of fire and smoke. To some observers, ascension involves the sudden disappearance of the body in a flash of light, hence "one is taken and one remains." However, many of the "pillar of light" scenarios involved people being taken aboard spacecraft, so it is often up to the reader to correctly interpret these accounts.

The fifth density body is capable of flying through the air (ethers), walking through walls, and existing peacefully in normally hostile environments.

Sixth Density: The Soul Body

Sixth density is the level of the soul, also known as the higher self or pure essence. In addition to being able to fly about the Earth, the sixth density soul body is capable of travelling the stars. This ascended form is no longer bound by Earthly space at all, and can traverse "the corridors of time" and the "highways of light." In other words, the soul body can travel forward and backward in time, and often does so in order to learn more about the nature of the Universe.

Sixth density is the gateway to the angelic realms, which are a part of the celestial heavens. The sixth density body is celestial in appearance to the fifth density eye -- translucent, brilliant and constantly vibrating in ever-changing hues and colors. Everything is crystalline in character. The causal and crystal worlds, the crystal temples, castles in the air, pegasus and all manner of mythological creatures are visible in these densities. Nature spirits, devas and other fairy folk from the inner Earth also occupy the etheric realms of the fifth and sixth densities.

Beings who occupy a particular density can see visions from the next-higher density. To sixth density, the angels of the seventh density appear as great winged creatures that dazzle the skies with their brilliance.

Sixth density, being ethereal, is completely non-physical and is not subject to any of the physical laws of Earth. There is a great civilization on the planet Venus that lives in sixth density, even though the third density atmosphere of Venus is composed of poisonous gases and temperatures in excess of 600 degrees.

Etheric cities can seem suspended in air, and often correspond to the upper aura of a planet (the stratosphere). The Holy City spoken of in Revelations exists in the ethereal sixth density and will only be seen by "those with eyes to see and ears to hear" - i.e., fifth and sixth density ascended beings.

Sixth density, being the level of the soul, is the highest and purest form of individuality. Having stripped away all the layers of incarnation and life experience, the soul emerges as a spark of God, the basic unit of Creation. Each soul is completely unique and has its own "signature." The ego self of third density is only an image of the real self which actually exists three levels higher in the evolutionary spiral.

In a sense, evolution ends when a being reaches sixth density, because time is no longer linear. The soul essence is eternal; it has always existed and always will. So one does not actually evolve into a soul, one simply returns to soul awareness. Later, I will explain how souls emerge from the Godhead to journey into material form.

An evolved soul is one in which all five lower bodies (physical, emotional, intellectual, psychic and etheric) have aligned themselves with the free soul in the sixth density. Until this happens, the soul body remains "cut off" from the rest of the being, not in truth, but in awareness.

In a little while, I am going to tie together all the models I am presenting by exploring the idea that "where you put your attention is where you vibrate." Returning to the soul simply means you put your attention (awareness) on your true essence (soul) until it is reunited with the lower bodies.

Seventh Density: The Oversoul

Seventh density is the oversoul. This density is the beginning of an entirely different spiral of Creation. While evolution ascends up through the first six densities becoming more and more refined and individual, the higher densities (seven through twelve) become more and more joined and indivisible.

Seventh density is where true union between souls occurs. Up until this point, souls that attempted to join would take on essence from other souls, thereby creating layers of psychic material that clouded their auras and confused their purposes. This is because true joining can only occur after a soul is purified and made complete. A complete soul is one whose lower bodies have been cleansed and "made new again." All foreign energies (essence from other souls) must be returned to their rightful places. When all the layers are stripped away, only the eternal, unchanging Self remains. This Self can then return to its family of souls where true bonding is possible.

The oversoul is a group of souls, or soul family, comprised of a number of individual souls who have merged into a larger whole. See Chapter 20 for a more detailed explanation of group souls.

Souls first begin to bond as couples, or "twin flames." These twin souls then seek out other twins from the same ray, or family tree. As each twin unites, the souls form a cluster, which fuses together into one master soul - the oversoul.

Each oversoul "fragments" by sending individual souls out into incarnation or other levels of experience. The souls later re-merge back into the oversoul and the cycle repeats for as long as each soul feels the need for more life experience. Sometimes, souls from the same soul group (oversoul) meet on the Earth plane and recognize each other. Some form lifelong relationships as lovers, parents or friends. Often, one soul family member will remain in the higher planes and assist another who is stationed on Earth.

In this accelerated time, twin souls usually use this arrangement because the Earth-bound soul tends to evolve more easily if his or her twin flame is in the ascended state helping. Only on rare occasions do twin flames incarnate at the same time and meet in the Earth. If a soul is not sufficiently evolved, such a meeting can be a distraction, rather than a help. It is not unusual for twin flame relationships on Earth to be just as co-dependent and addictive as any other relationship.

Eighth Density: The Angels

Eighth density is the angelic realm, also known as the lower celestial heavens. Many visionary artists have captured a glimpse of the colors and vibrations of the angelic worlds. Although the angels have a fine, glorious vibration, they are considerably more dense than the archangels of ninth density.

As a being increases in vibration, he or she encompasses more and more of the energies of the realm corresponding to that vibration. Angels, therefore, have access to many levels and dimensions simultaneously and are capable of communicating with many humans at once because they have the ability to create multiple holographic images of themselves and appear in different places simultaneously. The angels create an aura of light wherever they go and their presence has been felt by most of humanity at one time or another.

Fallen angels are those who have lowered their vibration from eighth density. There are many reasons for this. Some angels have never been in physical embodiment and want to gain experience this way. Others become trapped in lower densities and forget their origin. There are many stories around the subject of fallen angels. We will touch briefly on the subject again later.

Ninth Density: The Archangels

Ninth density is the vibration of the great archangels. In a sense, the archangels are to the angels what the oversoul is to the soul. Archangels are vast beings of light that encompass large areas of the universe, much like galaxies on the physical level. Many of the archangels have been given names and labels, and they appear throughout religious literature.

Tenth Density: The Creator Gods

Tenth density is the vibration of the Creator Gods. The Creator Gods are vast beings who create entire universes and whose light emulates the light of the Heavenly Father and Divine Mother. In religious literature they are often referred to as the Ancient Ones or the Paradise Sons. They are the supreme rulers of the spiritual hierarchy, second only to the Heavenly Father and Divine Mother.

Eleventh Density: The Universal Gods

Eleventh Density is the vibration of the Universal Gods. These are the gods of the different universes, or parallel dimensions, that exist beyond the spiritual hierarchy of this universe.

Twelfth Density: The Godhead

Twelfth Density is the vibration of the Godhead, the Great Central Sun, and the unmanifested aspect of the Heavenly Father and Divine Mother. It is the gateway to the void, the Tao, the Great Mystery, the unknown.

CHAPTER 10
DIMENSIONS

Dimensions are very different from densities. While densities shift harmonically from one vibratory frequency to another, dimensions involve a total shift in reality construct. While densities are discrete and do not overlap, dimensions tend to encompass entire realities and overlap each other. In fact, the greater the dimension, the more all-encompassing the reality it represents.

"Lower" dimensions are contained within "higher" ones. For example, the third dimension contains the lower two dimensions in their entirety in addition to being a unique reality construct of its own. If the first dimension represents a line (or distance), and the second dimension is a plane (or area) and the third dimension includes height and depth (volume), then certainly the third dimension includes an infinite number of planes and lines within its construct.

Another way to look at the concept of dimensions involves the idea of subsets. In basic mathematics, different types of numbers form different subsets of the real number system. Perfect squares (1,4,9,16...) are a subset of integers (1,2,3,4...) which are in turn a subset of the real numbers. The real numbers are like the third dimension; the integers, second dimension; and perfect squares, first dimension.

If mathematics is not your cup of tea, we can use geography. Let's pretend the first dimension represents your house or apartment. The second dimension is your street; the third dimension your town, the fourth dimension your state, etc. Using the concept of subsets, all of your house is along your street, your street is a part of your town, etc. Obviously, there are parts of the fourth dimension (your state) that are unique and not in the third dimension (your town); however, all of the third dimension (your town) is in the fourth dimension (your state).

If you wish to perceive the truth about a given situation in life, the best way to do this is to enter a high dimension where you can see the whole picture. Imagine you are lost in the woods, and suppose the ground were the first dimension, the forest the second dimension and the sky the third dimension. To find out where you are and how to get where you're going, the best way is to go into the third dimension (the sky) where you can view the entire forest and see what's ahead in all directions. In a nutshell, this is how psychics acquire information not available through the basic physical senses. They simply shift their perception to a higher dimension where the entire picture becomes clear.

This is also what happens when someone detaches, or steps away from an issue they have been embroiled in. When you are immersed in a problem, it is hard to see the solution, but when you lift yourself above and view the problem from a greater vantage point, you see the solution inherent within the dimension of the problem.

Figure 10.1 - Dimensions

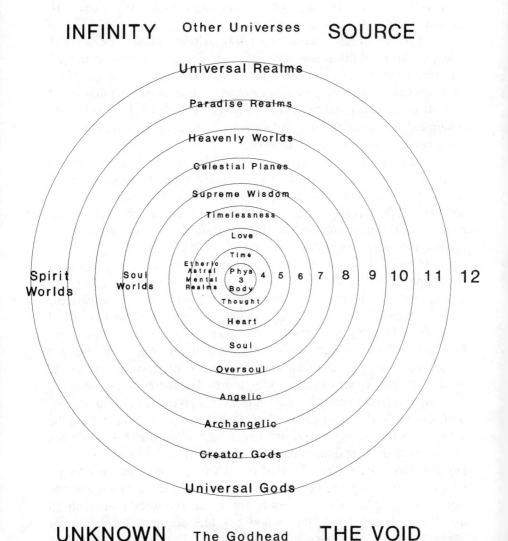

What really constitutes a dimension? Basically, a reality construct is valid if it is comprised of a certain set of universal laws and principles that are consistent within the construct. In Figure 10.1, we have defined 12 dimensions. Each dimension is a world unto itself, complete with its own set of laws and principles. Within each dimension are subdimensions, or discrete worlds and levels of existence. For example, the astral worlds and the mental plane are both part of the fourth dimension.

The First Dimension: Existence

The first dimension is that of existence itself. To have existence, an object must have a location or point in time and space. The sum total of all the locations (loci) in the universe constitutes the first dimension. This can be visualized as a line or path through infinity.

The Second Dimension: Magnitude

The second dimension is defined as magnitude, or distance. There is a path (straight or curved) between every first dimensional location in the Universe. The sum total of all the paths between any given two or more locations in time and space constitutes the second dimension. This can be visualized as a plane through infinity.

The Third Dimension: Depth

The third dimension is the one we are most familiar with. This is the dimension seen with the physical senses. It is the sum total of all the magnitudes, or planes of existence in the physical universe. It has its own set of laws and principles including gravity, attraction, polarity, etc.

The Fourth Dimension: Time

The fourth dimension will be discussed in more depth. Physicists often define the fourth dimension as time. Time is an aspect of the fourth dimension because it exists any place there is movement in the universe. Movement can occur at a location, along a path, or within a plane. It can also occur in an intangible realm called "thought." Thought and time are the two main characteristics of the fourth dimension.

Time

There are two kinds of time. Physical time is simply a measurement of relative motion between two heavenly bodies in the physical universe. We use clocks to measure this relative motion. If there is no movement, there is no physical time. On Earth, physical time exists because the Earth and sun have relative motion. We decided arbitrarily to use one revolution of the Earth around the sun as our basic unit of time. Physical time is a variable, as Einstein demonstrated with his theory of relativity. When objects approach the speed of light relative to each other, time begins to slow down. It has been theorized that objects travelling faster than light would travel backwards in time.

There is another kind of time which Krishnamurti called "psychological time." This is our sense of time; our feeling of time. This is controlled by thought and memory. Psychological time is a variable also. I'm sure you can remember a time when you were so engrossed in something that time seemed to fly, or a time when you were bored and time seemed to crawl. Psychological time is a function of thought, so if you have no thought, you have no psychological time. This sense of timelessness is one of the keys to higher awareness because by stepping outside of the dimension of time and thought, you can enter the fifth dimension.

Thought

The fourth dimension is far more than just physical and psychological time. It could be said that the fourth dimension is the realm of creativity. It is the universe created by the mind and having substance in the outer world. If thought is the ruler of the fourth dimension, this dimension must be vast indeed. After all, we are constantly thinking, so we must be constantly creating. There are no such things as idle thoughts. Certainly some thoughts are more powerful than others and have more ability to manifest in the outer world. But every thought and every mental image exists in some part of the fourth dimension.

The Mental Plane

The domain of the mind is the mental plane. The mental plane is a subdimension of the fourth dimension. This is where all mental activity takes place. The mental plane consists of the collective reality of each individual's mental world. Contained within the mental plane is the collective subconscious, a Jungian term denoting the collective reality made up of all individual subconscious minds.

The collective creations of the mind make up several realities, all of which are part of the fourth dimension. If you look again at the hourglass model of the mind in Figure 5.1, you will see it is open at both ends. There is no actual separation between individual minds. The open space at the top of the superconscious and bottom of the subconscious is where minds join - in the vast realms of the mental plane.

The mental realms are where all ideas, concepts, images, symbols and thought forms reside. This is not merely a repository, however. It is an active, changing laboratory of creation where the elements fuse and merge in a sea of consciousness. This is the creative source of the four lower worlds, the planes of "maya", as they are called in Eastern philosophy.

The key to accessing the worlds of the fourth dimension is belief. "What you believe in, you will experience. As you sow, so shall you reap. You create your own reality." These are all expressions for what Ernest Holmes called "The Law of Mind."

The fourth dimension is the realm of metaphysics, of mind over matter. It is where inner and outer reality begin to meet. It is the bridge between the worlds of matter and the worlds of spirit. It is also the bridge between linear time and momentary time.

Within the fourth dimension are what we call the parallel worlds. These realms do not have a higher vibration than ordinary fourth dimensional time and space, but exist simultaneously with ordinary reality in a sort of "parallel dimension." The most widely known of these is the astral plane, described below.

How do you tell the difference between a parallel world of the fourth dimension and something from the fifth dimension or beyond? This question has confounded many a seeker on the path to truth. Some have confused the more beautiful aspects of the fourth dimension with Heaven, nirvana or the Godhead. But there are some litmus tests that reveal the larger picture.

First of all, the fourth dimension is relative. This means each person perceives it differently according to his or her beliefs. If I believe in poverty, that is what I will create. If you believe in wealth, you will create it. Many religious people see images of their Lord. Because their belief is so strong, it creates that reality. In most cases, they are not actually seeing the true essence of an entity. They are seeing a mental or astral image -- an entity or thought form created by the mind. Their Lord is very real to them, but to a non-believer, it does not exist.

Secondly, the fourth dimension is the realm of phenomena. It is the realm of the psychic, the intuitive and the dreamer. It is the playshop of the creative imagination, the workbench of the magician. It is also the gateway to the astral, and to a vast realm of twilight characters - the "lovely and the grotesque", the creations of "gods in training."

The Astral Plane

The astral plane, also known as the astral world, is a subdimension of the fourth dimension. It can be thought of as a repository for the creations of lesser gods. An appropriate analogy would be the artist's scrapbook. Every "miscreation" or "mistake" gets discarded into the astral realms. The astral plane is divided into subplanes, each filled with creations corresponding to the vibration present within each creator. The lower astral plane has been called by some the "sewer" of Creation because it tends to be the home of all the unwanted creations. All denied thought forms end up here eventually if they are not reclaimed and brought to consciousness. Like all fourth dimensional entities, the lower astral creations are real in the mind of their creators and within their confines, but have no power beyond the fourth dimension.

Like the dream state, which represents the higher astral realms, the lower astral is unique to each soul; i.e., no two souls share the same astral space in exactly the same way. One person's monsters may not exist in another person's astral space. While each astral world is unique to its creator, souls can share astral space by "dialing" the same frequency. This is analogous to a computer workstation with a password. If more than one user has the password, the same programs and files can be accessed.

Unless you have monsters in your own thoughts, you may not be able to "dial" the same frequency as the soul with monsters in the astral plane. Thus, his/her monsters will not be real for you. However, if you believe strongly enough, you can create your own monsters, but most conscious creators prefer something more palatable.

The higher astral realms are where will fragments and astral "dream" bodies tend to hang out. These are also the realms of the imagination, the "practice pad" for creator gods. Each soul has an individual astral body and an individual astral "sacred space." (See the Glossary for more complete definitions of these terms.)

Dream States

During the dream state, you may have several types of dreams. Below I've listed the four basic types of dreams in order of commonality and level of awareness. The most common is the "subconscious recycling" dream where the dreamer's subconscious is working out daily issues during sleep. These dreams are usually mundane and actually occur more on the mental and subtle levels than on the astral. Characters in the dream are subconscious images and not actual astral beings.

The next type of dream is the symbolic. These can occur on the mental or astral level, but still tend to involve only the sacred space of the dreamer and not the shared astral plane at large. The events and actions in symbolic dreams represent life lessons and soul information. Like recycling dreams, the characters are projections of the subconscious and not actual astral beings.

The third type of dream is the lucid dream. Here we begin to see crossover from the personal astral to the collective astral. In essence, the lucid dreamer awakens from the realm of subconscious projection and enters the true astral realm. He may be fully conscious while in this state and may seek out astral experiences. The images here are clear and vivid, and it is possible to share dreams with other astral entities or dreamers, although this requires a very aware state of mind. A lucid dreamer becomes aware of his astral body and often uses it to fly around. I've studied my astral body during a lucid dream and have found it to be waxy and somewhat rubbery. When looking in a mirror, the astral eyes tend to be almost devoid of pupils and tend to shimmer and wax in the ethereal light of the astral plane.

The fourth type of dream is the transcendental, or interdimensional dream where the dreamer actually takes his astral body into other dimensions via the "silver cord." This is the true out-of-body experience and is quite rare for most people. Unlike the first three dream types, interdimensional dreams can occur during trance and meditation as well as regular sleep.

Discarnate Entities

When a soul experiences physical death, a number of things can happen, depending on the level of consciousness at the time of death. If the soul has not aligned the will and spirit (and most souls whose bodies die have not), the will is unable to ascend into the higher realms and instead goes into the astral plane. This will is now a discarnate entity;

a soul fragment. The rest of the soul (the spirit) may ascend into a higher level, thereby creating a split. The will then awaits reincarnation of the spirit so that it can reunite; but often, the will may fragment or attach itself to another soul in physical embodiment. This process is described more fully in Chapter 20.

Will Fragments

Will fragments are aspects of the emotional body that get separated from the soul and physical body during death, or that get cast out or projected from the body during "cording", a type of psychic attachment between two or more souls. When two or more souls interact, their wills (emotional bodies) mingle and merge. Pieces of will essence from one soul can attach themselves to the other soul. When the two souls separate, it is possible that not all the will fragments will return to their original state. For example, I may have some of your will fragments and you may have some of mine. Will fragments can be cast away from the body through denial. If they do not attach themselves to another body, they may drift around in the astral plane. Will fragments are one of the explanations for ghosts and apparitions. Although physical death is the most common way for wills to fragment, ghosts of people still living are known to exist.

Thought Forms

Thought forms are energy impulses that radiate from souls into the ethers (the etheric realms) and the mass consciousness (the collective subconscious). They are the building blocks of fourth-dimensional creation, and the process of bringing things into manifestation. Without emotion, will, desire and power, thought forms have very little ability to precipitate into outer reality. Instead, they drift aimlessly through the mental realms and, if not reinforced, eventually dissipate into static energy fields (after being imprinted in the akashic records).

Thoughts that are repeated over and over tend to crystallize into more powerful thought forms, much like a tiny snowflake (one water droplet) crystallizes into a larger cluster containing many frozen water droplets. Eventually the thought form becomes substantial enough to precipitate into outer reality, just as the snowflake becomes heavy enough to precipitate down through the atmosphere.

The actual mechanics of precipitation involve subatomic particles, neutrinos and quarks, which is too complex to go into here. Suffice it to say that physicists are already discovering the basic units of consciousness in subatomic research; these quanta (particle-energy packets) behave exactly the way the scientists expect them to, because they are really looking at their own consciousness precipitated into a laboratory environment.

Thought forms can be projected consciously or unconsciously from one person to another and may appear in the mind's eye of the receiver as an image, symbol or entity. Holographic mental projection is a technique employed by some extraterrestrials (ETs) and advanced humans, whereby an image of the being is projected to someone else in another time or place. If the receiver is clairvoyant, the thought form may look just like the body of the sender, "materializing" in the room, at least to the inner vision. In some cases, mental projection can be seen with the physical eye.

The Laws of the Fourth Dimension

The law of karma, or cause and effect, is the supreme law of the fourth dimension. Beyond this dimension, the concept of karma is meaningless. Karma is not punishment; something to be atoned for. It is really a synthesis of two other laws of the fourth dimension, the law of mind and the law of reflection. The main difference between karma and reflection is that with karma, there is often a lag time between intent to create and actual creation. The law of reflection states that what you believe in, you will see in the outer world. The law of mind states that thought is creative. The law of reflection is really "instant" karma; that is, you create an image in your mind of the way things are and that is what you see when you look out into the world.

When you think creatively, it may take time for the effects of your thoughts to manifest in your life. There are many reasons for the lag time; these reasons are too complex to go into here. However, the biblical phrase "as you sow, so shall you reap" is a good metaphor for the law of karma, because it likens it to sowing a field. You plant the seeds (thoughts), which then grow into food (manifestation). This process certainly takes time. If you wish to change the crop, you must change the seeds. If you wish to change the results in your life, you must change your thoughts.

One of my favorite analogies is the movie scenario (you can tell, because I keep using it throughout this book). You are in a theatre watching a movie called "Your Life." Suppose you don't like the film. Imagine how ridiculous it would be to go running up the aisle of the theatre to the screen and try to move the characters around on the screen with your arms because you don't like the way they are acting. Yet this is exactly the way most people behave regarding their thoughts.

If your mind is the projector, then the film is your thoughts and beliefs, and the screen is your life. To change the screen (your life), you must change the film (your thoughts and beliefs). Of course, you could always walk out of the theatre (detachment), and sometimes this is the best move, especially if you are hopelessly caught in the drama and unable to see how you created it. But sooner or later you must learn to master your mind and become an excellent movie maker and film director.

To summarize, the topics we have covered here are vast, and I encourage you to seek out metaphysical books and classes that go into time, thought and the mind in more depth. But now, let's continue our tour of the dimensions.

The Fifth Dimension: Love

The fourth dimension is the bridge between the worlds of matter and the worlds of spirit. When we cross the bridge to the fifth dimension, we leave the worlds of duality and enter into an entirely different world of love and unity.

The fifth dimension begins with the etheric plane, an invisible realm beyond the astral and mental levels, and a doorway to the heart.

The Etheric Plane

The etheric plane refers to the electromagnetic ether that surrounds and penetrates the physical universe. The etheric body is a general term to describe the electromagnetic field (EMF), or aura, around the physical body. The etheric body is similar to the emotional body, but the etheric body includes more than just emotional energy. The emotional body occupies space in the etheric body, and individual emotions are stored in different parts of the auric field. The etheric plane is less dense than the physical plane but can be measured by physical instruments and can be felt physically. All physical objects have an auric field that protrudes out from the center of the object into the far reaches of the Universe.

The etheric plane is a vast sea of energy containing all the auric fields of every object and entity. Within each field, the akashic records are imprinted. These imprints contain the blueprints, or schematics, of the physical objects, much like a mechanical drawing contains all the data necessary to build a house.

The Aura

The aura is the electromagnetic field surrounding objects or persons. It is easily seen by clairvoyants and felt by clairsentients. It consists of gross and subtle fluctuations in the EMF extending out infinitely far from the object or person. As the distance increases, the EMF decreases. The EMF around a typical human usually becomes undetectable by scientific instruments a few feet out from the body. However, your auric field extends throughout the Universe in all directions, so there is really no place in all of Creation where you are not. By the time you get a mile away from the body, however, the auric field is so subtle that even most psychics cannot detect it.

You can measure the intensity and polarity of the auric field using dowsing rods, pendulums and other devices. Simply stand in front of a person, beginning several feet away and walk slowly toward the body while holding the rods straight in front of you. When they cross, you have reached the edge of the gross auric field. For all practical purposes, we will concern ourselves with the gross field, or the area commonly detected by psychics and dowsing devices.

The auric field increases and decreases in size depending on the consciousness of the person. If one is "spaced out" and engaging in non-directive thought, the aura tends to be larger than when one is focused on a discrete thought or feeling. You can shrink the size of your auric field by using grounding techniques (explained in the Appendix). People who are highly charismatic tend to have large auras that envelop a lot of people. People who are introverted and withdrawn tend to have auras that stay close to the body.

The colors of the aura tell a great deal about the state of consciousness of the person. Generally, bright vivid colors portray good health while dull vague colors portray illness. There are many shades and subtleties to the aura and many layers. Most people have several layers, or "shells" to their auric field. The inner layers correspond to the more physical levels of being while the outer layers are more subtle. Most people have external energies imbedded in the outer layers of their auras, often from family and friends. Those closest to the person (lovers, children, etc.) may have energy imbedded in the inner layers of the aura.

The following depicts the usual meaning for different colors in the auric field, as seen clairvoyantly:

Table 10.1 - Auric Colors

Color	Meaning
Bright Red	Passionate, sexual, energetic
Dark Red	Angry, volatile mood
Orange	Social, party mood
Yellow	Intellectual, conceptual
Bright Green	Loving, heart energy
Dark Green	Life force, healing, nature
Turquoise	Healing from spiritual guides
Light Blue	Healing specific areas of body
Dark Blue	Expansive, high awareness
Indigo	Deeply centered, intuitive
Purple	Transmutational, intense purification
Pink	Love, compassion
Blue-white	Purification, transcendence
White	Christ, purity
Silver	Divine Mother energies
Gold	Heavenly Father energies
Brown	Confused, muddled
Black	Shut down, in denial
Gray	Lack of life force, low energy
Colorful with black splotches or streaks	Psychic ties or hooks to others; demands placed by others
Colorful with black or brown layers	Taking on burdens of others; guilt, self-judgment
Color followed by white or gold	Divine protection invoked
Scrambled color	Confusion, lack of identity
Blue colors with red splotches or streaks	Anger being processed out; intense healing of emotions

The Chakras

Chakras are vortexes (concentrated areas) of electromagnetic energy in the etheric body. There are many books on the chakras, so I will be brief here. I like the rainbow analogy, so I will go with it. There are 12 basic chakras along the vertical axis of the body and several smaller ones on the hands and feet. The 12 major ones correspond to the 12 densities and are as follows:

First Chakra   (Red - base of the spine) - The first chakra grounds the physical body on the Earth. It deals with survival and procreative issues.

Second Chakra   (Orange - sexual organs) - The second chakra is primarily concerned with sexuality and social interaction, and includes emotions related to sexuality and need for approval from others.

Third Chakra   (Yellow - solar plexus) - The third chakra is the seat of the will, intuition and desire, and deals with issues of personal power and competition.

Fourth Chakra   (Green - heart) - The fourth chakra is in the etheric heart and represents balance and life force. The spiritual heart emanates a pink color and is sometimes considered a chakra of its own.

Fifth Chakra   (Blue - throat) - The fifth chakra is centered in the mental and conceptual area and deals with expression and communication.

Sixth Chakra   (Indigo - third eye - forehead) - The sixth chakra is the psychic and inner visual center and represents higher mind.

Seventh Chakra   (Violet - crown) - The seventh chakra is the gateway between the physical and higher dimensions and represents inspiration from spirit.

8th-12th Chakras   (White - above crown) - The eighth through twelfth chakras represent the subtle bodies and their connection with spirit.

Healthy chakras radiate their native colors and tend to spin like a flywheel in a clockwise direction. Unhealthy chakras tend to be faded and do not spin, or spin in a counterclockwise direction. The chakras are etheric body energy focal points that correspond roughly to certain physical organs. For example, a problem in the third chakra is usually related to stomach and abdominal distress. If there are unresolved emotional issues, the solar plexus chakra is often unhealthy and the corresponding abdominal organs may tend toward disease. To heal discord in the etheric body, one needs to enter the finer vibrations of the fifth dimension and cross the bridge to love.

The Bridge to Love

If the fourth dimension is time and thought, the fifth dimension is love. Love begins in the fifth dimension but it is not limited by it. Here, time takes on a completely different meaning. In the fifth dimension there is still individuality, but it is unfettered by the creations of the mind. It is the realm of the heart, where "I am my brother's keeper" becomes meaningful. Here, we see clearly that all of life is a reflection, that I am in you and you are in me. Our issues, our dreams, our visions become shared - and yet we remain unique, multi-faceted beings. We are still experiencing life; we are not yet completely one with the experience.

The fifth dimension is what "A Course In Miracles" calls the "real world." Here is a world created by love that reflects the higher, heavenly realms. Like the gods in training, the gods of love have their playground also, but theirs is a happy, joyful place, full of abundance and shared experience.

Opening the Heart

The pinnacle of Earthly knowledge is at the top of the fourth dimension of mind. Here are all the personal growth methods mastered, all life's experiences explained, all paths of time and space seen with mental understanding. Here are those with mastery of time and space; the great scientists and mathematicians. Here is the cunning and clever intellect, highly refined and brought into alignment with the psychic, intuitive and imaginative faculties.

There comes a point in every soul's evolution when he or she travels to density magnitude 4.99 - the highest step in the mental realm. But to jump to 5.00 - the fifth density (corresponding to 5th dimension) - requires the opening of the heart.

This jump is so tiny in the overall picture, but can seem so large when one is stuck in the mind; stuck in time. For no amount of Earthly wisdom or exalted thought can touch love. The ego and the rational mind must fade away and become totally receptive before love's presence can lift the soul gently above karma, cause and effect, and all the phenomena of the fourth dimension.

True Unity

The unity of the heart is the inner unity of personal alignment and integration. You are still an individual soul, evolving into godhood. It is not until you reach the fifth dimension that true unity is possible. Until that point, the process of evolution seems to be more of a stripping and peeling away of the layers of the Self until only the true essence remains.

There is no formula, no magic wand, no method to love. As the soul is purified and understanding is gained, the way is cleared for the quantum leap into the heart.

The heart is the center. When you are centered and all parts are brought into alignment, the awareness of your soul - that eternal, individual spark of God, is finally realized. And from beyond the love, light and bliss of the fifth dimension, a new song is heard, one from beyond the beyond, from a timeless realm where words can never go.

The step from the 5th to the 6th dimension is gentle and swift. Suddenly, time takes on a whole different meaning and the memory of eternity returns, with the realization that it never left - only your awareness of it.

The Sixth Dimension: The Soul Plane

The sixth dimension is often called the soul plane because it is the true dwelling place of the soul. It is here that eternity begins. Without beginning and without end, the sea of love extends throughout the universe, calling on all to join in unity and oneness. In the sixth dimension there is no longer an ego or personality. There is a single Self, a single soul, immersed in a world of dancing, vibrating light and pure consciousness. There is still a "you" and "me" but there is no sense of separation. Everything is connected to everything else.

The soul plane is the highest level of individuality. In this realm, the pure essence, higher self or soul (whichever term you choose) evolves into a greater and greater universe of its own, eventually learning how to create entire new universes.

While the soul can merge with other souls, and often does, it remains a complete, unique reality unto itself, a holographic image of God. The fully evolved soul can create infinite varieties of life forms, each a holographic representation of itself.

The Causal Plane

The causal plane is the collective creation of individual souls and contains the akashic records and the building blocks of the etheric plane. Seen by visionary artists as a crystalline world of exquisite beauty, the causal realms are like the master control center of the worlds of time and space. A tiny adjustment in the crystalline structure of the causal plane can create radical shifts in the entire time-space continuum. This plane contains the very fabric, the very essence of evolution.

The causal plane is where highly evolved souls go between incarnations to review their evolutionary progress. From this vantage point, the entire timeline of evolution can be seen spread out below them. They can decide where on the timeline to incarnate next, depending on what lessons have yet to be learned in time and space.

Soul guidance comes from the celestial heavens immediately above them. These are the realms of vast intelligence and wisdom, home of the oversoul. But before we explore the oversoul, let me touch on another subject dear to my heart.

Music

For me, music is the doorway of the soul; the doorway to the sixth dimension. Certain pieces of music can instantly lift me beyond time and space and even beyond the heart to the timeless essence of life itself; the soul plane.

Before I began this incarnation, I existed in the aura of the planet Venus, attending the mystery schools and temples of initiation residing there. This is one of the places where individual souls go between incarnations for instruction from the higher dimensions. I can still remember the music of Venus and the sixth-dimensional worlds of incredible beauty that inspired this music.

There are a few recordings available today that emanate from the soul plane. Every time I listen to one, the love and ecstasy of Venus comes back to me and fills my heart. I've included some of this music in the Appendix.

The Seventh Dimension: The Lower Celestial Heavens

The seventh dimension is where we begin to understand the meaning of twin flames and oversouls (group souls). It is the bridge between the individual souls and the realms of spirit and the Godhead. It is a realm of timeless beauty and love where magic and enchantment reign.

The Oversoul

In Chapter 7, we introduced the concept of the oversoul. Now I'd like to go into more depth. The oversoul is the collective soul consciousness of individual souls. It dwells in the seventh dimension. This is where individual souls receive their plans for incarnation. It is here that souls evaluate their progress in evolution.

Although the soul family is one in spirit, individual souls come and go as incarnations take place, always returning again and again, like Earth families at Christmas time.

No longer alone, each soul begins to merge and join in harmonious rapture, with its twin counterpart and soul group. Just as it is difficult to imagine how free will and predestiny can exist simultaneously, so it is difficult to comprehend, with the mind, how a soul can remain individual in the fifth and sixth dimensions while simultaneously merging and joining in the seventh dimension.

In order to understand the higher realms, you must go beyond mind into timelessness and silence. From deep within the silence comes the song of creation, ancient, yet forever new, changeless, yet forever changing. And as the heart fills with the beauty of this realm, the soul is transported into Oneness where all else fades to insignificance. The seventh dimension is the gateway to the Celestial Heavens. In the Celestial worlds, oversouls become fused into Master oversouls, great beings of light who are so vast and magnificent that even the fifth-dimensional awareness has difficulty comprehending it.

The Lower Celestial Heavens

The seventh dimension is the beginning of the true heavenly realms, what Eckankar calls the "God Worlds." Dwelling within the lower celestial heavens are the oversouls, or group souls. These magnificent beings are clusters of individual souls who have merged into Oneness. The oversouls instruct individual souls and offer guidance on how and where to incarnate.

The celestial worlds are bright, vivid, translucent realms of pure light that exist far beyond the worlds of time and space. They are everywhere and nowhere; the concept of distance and magnitude are meaningless here, yet because they are part of the seventh dimension, all the lower dimensions are accessible here. This explains why oversouls can "look in" on Earth and see what is going on here.

The seventh dimension is also a level of supreme intelligence and wisdom; an inexhaustible storehouse of knowledge that guides every soul on its journey through eternity. The angelic realms are just above, in the eighth dimension, and so the universal wisdom of God is directly accessible here.

The Eighth Dimension: The Angelic Worlds

The eighth dimension contains the higher celestial heavens, the realm of the angels. Here, densities and levels of awareness begin to become merged with dimensions.

As we go higher and higher into the spiritual universe, words become more and more meaningless. The concept of levels and dimensions becomes rather insignificant in the heavenly realms. The concept of spiritual hierarchies may be useful on Earth, but here, everything simply IS. Within the ISness is great variety and depth, however. Colors that are inconceivable with the mind are nevertheless pulsing, coalescing and shimmering in an ocean of Divine Love, Power and Wisdom. Angels soar through the celestial oceans, creating rainbows and dazzling pillars of light.

The old image of Heaven where angels play harps and sit on clouds is only a tiny fragment of the total picture, perhaps one person's rather boring dream. The reality of Heaven quickly dispels any sense of boredom. Everything sparkles and shines with newness and there are an infinite number of things to do. Abundance is limitless and available instantly in any form imaginable.

Beyond the 8th dimension are the mansion worlds, dwelling places of the Eternal Ones, beings of light that are merged with the Godhead.

The Ninth Dimension: The God Worlds

The ninth dimension is where the enlightened masters dwell. The energy of this realm is directly connected to the Christ. Here is where the mighty archangels are; vast beings of light who oversee the lower worlds with their wisdom and intelligence.

The Tenth Dimension: The Paradise Worlds

The 10th dimension is the realm of the creator gods and paradise worlds spoken of in "The Keys of Enoch" and other writings. The energy of this realm is connected to the Heavenly Father and Divine Mother. This is the realm of universal birth and creation; the womb of the Godhead where everything springs forth in eternal newness.

The Eleventh Dimension: The Godhead

The 11th dimension embodies the Godhead. This is the realm of the Great Central Sun of the Universe and exists in a state of timelessness. This dimension can only be accessed by the still mind in the state of no thought and no time. When all has become One, there is no one there to experience it. For we have become that which we once experienced. We have become the universe. The universe is us. We are God.

The Twelfth Dimension: The Great Mystery

Beyond the 11th dimension lies the Great Mystery. The 12th dimension is the Tao, the unknown, the great void, the unknowable, the Source Itself. It is everything and nothing. It is the beginning and the end; the Alpha and Omega. In the 12th dimension, everything is new every moment. Without the limitation of time and thought, there is a peace that passes understanding, a freedom that can never be bought, a love that can never be captured or understood. The 12th dimension, being completely outside of time and space, must remain forever in the unknown.

The 12th dimension is the doorway to other universes; universes that will never be known by this universe; universes that have entirely different laws and principles; entirely different gods. Words cannot go beyond this point; thus ends our exploration of the infinite universe.

CHAPTER 11
MODELS OF REALITY -
BRINGING IT ALL TOGETHER

Comparison of Models

We have looked at several models of reality, each with its specific drawbacks and limitations. Probably some of them have evoked the response "Yes! That's how I see it, but I couldn't quite put it all together." Perhaps others brought more confusion and doubt: "I'm confused. I don't know what he's saying. I got lost back in the fourth dimension."

To put the pieces of the puzzle together, we need to compare models and find common ground.

Relationship Between the Models

In order to understand life, we must be able to bring divergent points of view into a cohesive whole. So far, I've given pieces of the puzzle that conveniently explain how the universe operates. But how do they tie together? And how can all this be practical in everyday life?

In my many years of personal growth, I've observed the difficulties people have reconciling the various levels and dimensions with each other. And I've found a very simple key to understanding.

You will notice several references throughout this book to "selective" and "choiceless" awareness. I'm now going to extend this concept to include "limited" and "expanded" awareness. Limited awareness means focusing on one dimension at a time. Expanded awareness, or simultaneous awareness, is the ability to be aware multidimensionally.

Limited Awareness

Most people's concept of enlightenment involves shifting the focus of awareness from the lower densities to the higher ones. This shift in focus creates a vibrational shift within the soul. In other words, what you focus on, you become. For example, if you focus your awareness on third density, you become a third density being. If you shift awareness to the archangelic realm (ninth density), you eventually become an archangel (or equivalent). However, you must begin where you are. The problem is that many beings try to take a shortcut by focusing on a high density while denying the others. The soul is multidimensional by nature. We all exist simultaneously on many levels at once. By focusing on one or two levels only, we deny (exclude) the other levels. This creates a split, or fragmentation, in the Self.

You can see the split caused by limited awareness in the world. Basically, most of humanity is divided into two camps. Those who focus on the material (lower densities) while excluding the spiritual (higher densities), and those who focus on the spiritual (higher) while denying the physical (lower).

Religions have taught us to limit our awareness to the higher densities. Maxims such as "the world is an illusion" perpetuate this schism. Many "New Agers" have rebelled against mainstream society by judging it as wrong, bad, or undesirable. True rebellion should be directed against limited awareness. The problem with materialistic thinking is not the materiality itself. It is the denial of the spiritual by focusing narrowly on material comforts.

So what we have with limited awareness is the practice of taking a narrow focus and moving it up and down the density scale, much like the moving part of a slide rule.

Eventually, a soul becomes evolved enough to go up and down the density scale at will, like riding an elevator, simply by focusing awareness. Such a being can assume the body of virtually any life form in any level or dimension. But this is not until the soul has cleared all the judgments and denials present in each density level. At present, there are very few human beings who have completely cleared the third and fourth density levels. Until we clear them, we need to embrace our "lower" nature and become aware of dynamics of these "base" levels.

Expanded Awareness

Expanded awareness is the ability to include more and more levels of reality in overall perception. Instead of shifting to the right or left on the spectrum, you expand the width of perception in both directions. If you are spiritually oriented, you stop denying the material and become more aware of it. If you are materially focused, you open to your spiritual nature. Expanded awareness is the process of true awakening. By ending denial of parts of yourself, you awaken to your multidimensionality. Then you can effortlessly move into any reality you choose at any time. One day you are wearing a business suit and attending a stockholders' meeting; the next day you are on the mountaintop meditating. True mastery is not about living in 12th density out in the "south forty" of the galaxy somewhere. It is your ability to encompass all the levels and dimensions of life.

Before we continue, I want to back up and take another approach regarding limited and expanded awareness. If you have already grasped the concept, please bear with me. Understanding this is so important that I feel I cannot spend enough time on it.

The Evolutionary Process

Soul Experience

Your soul experience consists of your total experience in each of the densities, dimensions and levels of awareness at a given point in time. The evolution of a soul often involves entering (immersing consciousness in) a dimension (usually the third dimension) and gradually expanding awareness to include several dimensions.

Evolving Through Densities and Dimensions

To review, "density" refers to the actual vibratory state of your conscious awareness, while "dimension" is the realm in which you are vibrating. We exist in all 12 dimensions simultaneously, but our level of awareness determines which density we will be and which dimension we will vibrate in. For example, if we are primarily focused on the physical body, we will vibrate at third density. We still exist in the fifth dimension and have a fifth density light body blueprint, but because we are not focusing our awareness on it, it is not manifesting for us.

We cannot make densities and dimensions synonymous because focusing on the third dimension does not make us suddenly shrink from 12 dimensions down to three. But we will have the third-dimensional form, so we can say we are a 12-dimensional being vibrating at third density. Figure 11.1 shows yet another way to look at our multidimensionality.

Figure 11.1 - Our Being in Time

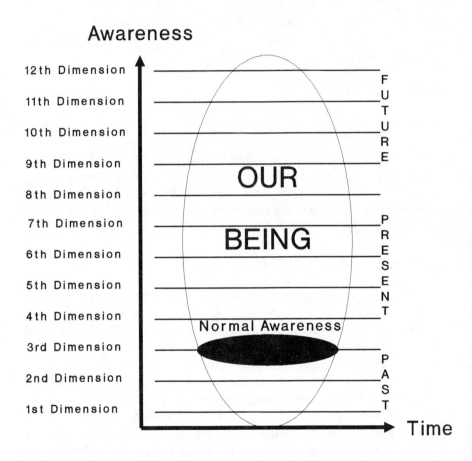

Figure 11.1 shows that ultimately we all exist in every dimension simultaneously, but that our level of awareness determines what form (density) we will experience. Our density (vibration) at any given time is the composite of our total awareness. What you focus on, you become. Many souls on Earth today have chosen to focus on third and fourth-dimensional aspects and have therefore incarnated into third and fourth density bodies.

For example, if our awareness is 20% in the third dimension, 60% in the fourth dimension and 20% in the fifth dimension, we will be primarily a fourth density being.

In the past, souls have moved from left to right on the light spectrum, gradually entering finer (higher) densities, and usually experiencing one density at a time. Evolving from left to right on the density spectrum is considered "normal" evolution. Most souls on Earth are currently evolving from animal/lower human (3rd) into higher human (4th) density.

However, once a soul evolves to a high enough density, he or she gains the ability to move from right to left along the spectrum. Thus, a soul may elect to re-experience a lower density to expand its soul experience. A soul with full God consciousness can move up and down through the density scale at will.

(NOTE: The way I am defining densities, I am not including the experiences souls have between physical embodiments in the astral realms.)

As we have said repeatedly, souls can exist in any density simply by choosing to focus their awareness into a particular level. For example, a person can project his/her consciousness into a ɔck and experience first density.

In Chapter 2, Figure 2.7, we graphically saw how evolution proceeds from lower densities to higher densities, with each life form increasing its vibration gradually until it reaches a certain point. Then there is a mutation or quantum shift to the next density. The point where the quantum shift begins is called critical mass. The evolutionary process is conscious until critical mass is reached; at that point, the process becomes automatic and the life form suddenly finds itself at the next density.

Actually, the process is a bit more complex than this, because certain aspects of a soul tend to grow faster than the rest. The mind, for instance, may already be embracing fourth density ideas while the rest of the soul is still vibrating in third density. The best way to visualize the quantum shift is to think of a soul as a rubber band. As he or she begins to stretch into higher densities, tension develops between the parts moving ahead rapidly and the parts lagging behind. If the part in front moves too fast, the rubber band breaks and the soul "fragments" (i.e., one part goes on into the higher densities and one part stays behind in the lower densities). The most common way this happens is through physical death.

However, if a soul is conscious enough to keep all the parts of the self together, the rubber band becomes more like a yo-yo. As more and more of the soul stretches into higher densities, eventually the lower density part snaps forward suddenly to re-join the rest of the soul. This can be visualized by holding a rubber band and stretching it. Your right hand represents the higher densities and your left hand the lower ones. Keep moving your hands apart until the rubber band becomes real tight. Then let go with the left hand.

This quantum shift, or snap of the rubber band, can sometimes be traumatic, which explains the phenomenon of "instant" enlightenment. It is no accident that sudden awakening often happens during or immediately after a traumatic incident, such as a near-death experience.

The evolutionary process can also be illustrated in the microscopic world. On the atomic level, the quantum leap between densities occurs when electrons in a given element are excited enough (build up sufficient energy) to "jump" into the next shell of an atom, thereby changing the nature of the substance.

Another analogy involves Einstein's Theory of Relativity. As an object approaches the speed of light, at some point (maybe .9999 times the speed of light) it reaches critical mass and "jumps" into the light stream. Although there are some flaws in this theory, it is true that time and space cease to be linear at such speeds. In the above example, .9999 is still infinitely slower than the speed of light, although linearly, it is only .0001 times slower. However, there is no linear acceleration possible between .9999 and 1.0000. To jump into the light stream requires a quantum shift. (You might recall the illustration of the two trains, one travelling at .9999 times the speed of light and the other travelling at the speed of light. To an observer on the first train, the second train is still travelling at the speed of light, although linear thinking would argue that the second train should creep by the first train at a rate .0001 times faster.)

Level Confusion Revisited

I want to once again point out an example of level confusion. Earlier I touched on free will and predestiny. Now let's look at this another way.

Most people believe either in free will or predestiny, but see them as mutually exclusive. In my perception, they are both valid, but exist on different levels. Free will is a component of the fourth dimension and involves the ability to choose what you want to create and how and when you want to create it. Predestiny is a fifth density reality involving the ability to see the results of free will in advance, and the knowledge of what path a soul will decide on in advance, based on one's understanding of that soul's will. A true fifth-dimensional perspective involves being able to see in advance all the probable realities for a soul and to intuitively know which probable realities will be precipitated into conscious experience for that soul. One way to integrate these fourth and fifth-dimensional perspectives is to think of viewing a soul's time line and seeing all the free will decisions made along that time line.

There are potential problems for souls that do not understand this process. Predestiny has been misunderstood to mean that a person has no control over the events in his/her life. But a soul is always creating, even if he appears to be doing nothing. Most of what passes for predestiny is simply a process of extrapolating a soul's future by assuming he will not change. Therefore, the decisions that soul is making now are ones he will be stuck with down the road. However, free will allows a soul to change his mind down the road and alter the course of events, and so it is not as simple as that.

True predestiny transcends time. Although free will can determine when a soul reaches a certain stage of evolution, predestiny will show the ultimate path the soul will eventually take. Predestiny can only be seen outside of time because, from a timeless perspective, you can see all the past, present and future realities spread out before you and can perceive information from anywhere in the timeline.

Figure 11.2 - Another Model of Our Being in Time

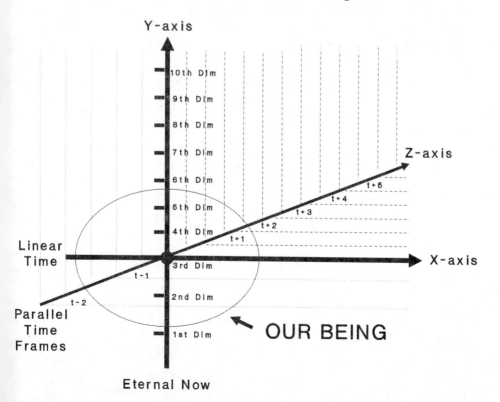

Additional Reality Models

On the following pages, I've included several tables that compare levels of reality using various constructs. Choose the one or ones that work best for you, or make up your own. The first table lumps all the dimensions from seven on up into one category. This is often useful because it is nearly impossible to differentiate between the various levels once you go beyond the seventh dimension. Nor would we be interested in categorizing levels of reality if we were already in a high state of awareness.

Part I Conclusion

The inner journey we have taken together during these first 11 chapters has been a necessary and desirable one. Although many of the ideas presented in Part II are intriguing and may border on the sensational, they are, in many ways, of lesser importance than the concepts in Part I. There is little you can do to change outer reality if you do not have a thorough understanding of the self. Reading the information in Part II is not going to suddenly solve all your problems. If you don't like what's happening in the world, re-read and practice the tools presented in Part I over and over until you reach true self-realization. Then you will be a force for change in the world.

Table 11.1 Comparison of Models in a 7-Dimensional Universe
(Levels 3 - 7 breakdown)

Dimension	Density	Aspects of Self	Levels of Awareness
Third -- Earth -- Physical Universe	1 - Mineral 2 - Plant 3 - Animal	Body Will Ego	Physical, instinctual, emotional, sexual, intellectual, rational, selective awareness

Fourth
 	
-- Astral
   Plane
- Mental
   Plane
	4 - Human	Mind	Dreaming, imaginative, psychic, intuitive, creative, karmic, conscious awareness

Fifth - Etheric Plane - Love	5 - Light Body	Heart	Love, oneness, unity, intelligence, insight, synthesis, wisdom, choiceless awareness

Sixth
 	
- Causal
   Plane
- Soul
   Plane
	6 - Soul Body
	7 - Oversoul
		Soul
		Oversoul
			Meditation, silence, freedom, eternity, pure essence, timelessness

Seventh
 	
- Celestial
   Plane
- God Worlds
- Godhead
- The Void
	8 - Angel
	9 - Archangel
	10 - Creator
	     gods
	11 - Universal
	     gods
	12 - Godhead
		Spirit
		Christ
		Universe
		The Tao
			Enlightenment, nirvana, ecstasy, bliss, newness, no self, true oneness, unknown, unknowable, great mystery

Table 11.2 Dimensional Breakdown by Levels of Awareness

Aspect/ Dimension	Physical State	Emotional State	Mental State	Universal Laws
1--Existence (BODY)	Body	Survival instinct	Conscious sensation	Gravity, entropy
2--Magnitude (WILL)	Emotions	Sexuality, security	Reactivity, subconscious mind	Procreative, centropy
3--Depth (EGO)	Ego, self	Competing, striving	Intellect, rational mind	Separate identity
4--Time (MIND)	Astral, mental	Healing, purifying	Creativity, imagination	Cause and effect, karma
5--Oneness (HEART)	Etheric, light	Love, joy, compassion	Insight, intelligence	Integration, synthesis
6--Eternity (SOUL)	Soul, oversoul	Ecstasy, nirvana	Timeless, meditation	Evolution, reincarnation
7--Universal (SPIRIT)	Angelic, Godhead	Ecstasy	Christ, cosmic	Infinity, eternity
8--Beyond the beyond (VOID)	N/A	N/A	Unknown, unknowable	N/A

Table 11.3 - A 12+1 Dimensional Model of the Universe

Dimension	Density	Aspect of Self	Level of Awareness
1. Existence	1. Mineral kingdom	Body	Physical body
2. Magnitude	2. Plant kingdom	Will	Emotional body
3. Physical Universe	3. Animal kingdom	Ego	Intellect, rational mind
4. Mental, Astral	4. Human kingdom	Mind	Psychic, ima inative, creative mind
5. Etheric Planes	5. Light body	Heart	Unity, oneness, love
6. Causal Planes	6. Soul body	Soul	Timelessness, eternity
7. Oversoul Planes	7. Oversoul body	Oversoul	Intelligence, wisdom
8. Celestial Heavens	8. Angelic body	Spirit	Enlightenment, nirvana
9. Heavenly Worlds	9. Archangelic body	Spirit	Supreme enlightenment
10. Paradise Worlds	10. Creator Gods	Christ	Eternal consciousness
11. Other Universes	11. Universal Gods	Godhead	Universal consciousness
12. Great Central Sun	12. Father-Mother God	Godhead	Tao, Great Mystery
13. The Void	13. The Source	Unknown	Unknowable

Table 11.4 - Cosmic Cycles of Twelve and Beyond

Dimension	Aspect	Color/Ray	Chakra
1--Existence	Physical Body	Red	Base of spine
2--Magnitude	Emotional Body	Orange	Sexual center
3--Depth	Intellect, ego	Yellow	Solar plexus
4--Time	Mind, psychic	Green	Lower heart
5--Etheric	Heart, love, light	Pink	Upper heart
6--Soul	Pure essence	Blue	Throat
7--Causal	Oversoul	Indigo	Third eye
8--Celestial	Spirit	Violet	Crown
9--Heaven	Christ principle	White	Above crown
10--Paradise	Mother principle	Silver	Above crown
11--Universe	Father principle	Gold	Above crown
12--Godhead	Great Central Sun	Clear	Above crown
13--Void	Other Universes	Black	N/A

****

PART II
THE CUTTING
EDGE

****

Warning

The material in this section could be shocking to those who believe everything the media tells them. Reality is much larger than any news story that reaches the mass consciousness. Staying on the cutting edge of evolution means staying aware, moment to moment, of the new energies entering the Earth, and being willing to discard old, outdated realities quickly and easily.

The information on extraterrestrials (ETs) is being updated continuously as their presence changes and more people become aware of the big picture. Shortly after I wrote this section, the media began exposing the truth behind ETs, abductions and government coverups. By 1996, much of the material in this section could be common knowledge among the mass consciousness.

I therefore invite you to jump ahead of the mass consciousness and examine several subjects with me that affect us today and will probably influence most, if not all, humanity in the immediate future. Being aware of the big picture can help us make intelligent decisions about the New World Order.

To help us understand what's really going on, let's begin with a look at the story of Creation and the <u>real</u> history of Earth.

CHAPTER 12
THE STORY OF CREATION

There are many theories of how the Universe began. I believe the real story is much more complex than simply a "big bang" or wave of the Creator's wand. If God is all that is, He/She is both personal and impersonal, simple and complex, known and unknown.

It is not possible to describe the indescribable. But I will use models to help stimulate awareness. The Creation models supply a piece of the cosmic puzzle and if we put them together correctly, we will have a working model that can help us understand and appreciate the Infinite Creation in all its mysterious splendor.

There appear to be two main levels to Creation. To put it simply, the first is the idea that All Is One, and the One is, at any given moment, either separating and fragmenting into individual parts, or joining and merging back into the Godhead.

The second level parallels the physical birth process. It states that God/Goddess gave birth to individual souls and that those souls eventually evolve into individual gods who then go on to create entire universes of their own.

At first glance, these two ideas seem contradictory; however, if we remember the concept of level confusion, it might be possible they are both true within a particular construct. It may be that individual souls are evolving into individual gods and at the same time are infused with spiritual essence that joins and connects each one to all of Creation.

Simultaneity

While one part of the universe is expanding, another is contracting. Have you ever looked through a kaleidoscope while turning it continuously? At any given moment, colors are expanding and contracting simultaneously--sometimes disappearing into the center, sometimes moving out. It is greatly oversimplifying the Creation story to say that the expansion is God breathing out and the contraction is God breathing in. If God is everywhere at once, He/She is breathing in and out simultaneously in different places. And what about the pauses between breaths?

The Trinity

In the Hindu model of Creation, the Creator embodies a trinity - Brahma, Vishnu and Shiva. Brahma is the creative, or expansive process (the outbreath), Vishnu the constant, unchanging aspect (the pause), and Shiva the contractive, or destructive process (the inbreath). In Christian theology, the trinity is depicted as Father, Son and Holy Spirit, which can be very roughly equated with Brahma, Vishnu and Shiva. If we carry the trinity idea one step further, we could say the creative, electric, expansive property of God represents the Father; the static, unchanging, eternal aspect is the Son and the destructive, contractive, magnetic aspect is the Holy Spirit.

The chart below represents the trinity as seen from many different viewpoints.

Table 12.1 - The Triune Nature of God

EXPANSIVE	STATIC	CONTRACTIVE
1. Birth	Life	Death
2. Brahma	Vishnu	Shiva
3. Heavenly Father	Child	Divine Mother
4. Father	Son	Holy Spirit
5. Creator	Maintainer	Destroyer
6. Masculine	Neuter	Feminine
7. Spirit	Heart	Will
8. Electric	Electromagnetic	Magnetic
9. Entropy	Superconductivity	Centropy
10. Devolution	Reincarnation	Evolution
11. Outbreath	Pause	Inbreath
12. Yang	Balance	Yin
13. Positive	Neutral	Negative
14. Action	Stillness	Reaction
15. Ideas	Knowledge	Experience
16. Individualization	Union	Coalescence
17. Divergence	Oneness	Convergence
18. White Holes	Quasars	Black Holes
19. Yahweh	Christ	Kali
20. Wisdom	Love	Power
21. Mind	Body	Emotions
22. God	All That Is	Goddess
23. Separation	Unity	Reparation
24. The Bible	A Course in Miracles	Right Use of Will

The Birth-Death Cycle

When we look at the cycle of birth and death, we see the trinity at work. Mother and father come together in sexual union (Static) and conceive a child. The child is born into the world and experiences separation and individualization (Expansive), then begins evolving into his/her own mature self, drawing the parts of the self together through life experience (Contractive) and eventually re-uniting and beginning the cycle anew.

Maximum Separation and Maximum Union

It is also possible to use a four-cycle model, or quadrinity, to conceptualize the universe. The cycles would be: (1) inbreath, (2) hold at peak of inhale, (3) exhale, and (4) hold at peak of exhale.

The point of maximum contraction - the end of the inbreath right before the next outbreath - is the point of maximum union, or the unmanifested state before the beginning of Creation. This is the static state depicted in the Trinity model.

At the point of maximum expansion - the end of the outbreath right before the next inbreath - is the point of maximum separation, before souls begin evolving back into Oneness. This could be called the void, darkness, or space beyond the outer reaches of Creation - the maximum distance from the center of the Godhead. It could also be considered to be the point of maximum density in the physical; i.e., the manifestation aspect of the trinity of Father-Mother-Christ and the end product of the creative process. In the quadrinity model (Figure 12.2), this is depicted as the Body of God, also called the fourth part of God. The quadrinity of God would therefore consist of four parts: Mother (inhale), Christ (top of inhale), Father (exhale), and Body (bottom of exhale).

The Paradox Explored

Now that I've created a nice, neat little model of the trinity, and gone even further to propose a quadrinity, I want to say that this is only part of the story. For a long time I was perplexed by the paradox of individuality and unity, and how they seem to contradict each other. However, if we turn to nature, perhaps we can find an explanation. For example, the analogy of physical birth and death seems to fit nicely here. A soul becomes aware and starts evolving back into a state of Oneness. At the same time, the soul grows and expands into an individual god, capable of creating entire universes "in the image and likeness of the Father." At some point, the soul reaches cosmic adolescence and "leaves home" to start a life of its own, eventually creating a family. The soul never separates from the spiritual essence which permeates all things, but it does become a unique universe of its own, unlike any other universal being.

When this soul merges with another soul, the two souls, being complete, unique universes, create another unique being from out of their midst - becoming cosmic parents, in a sense. At the same time that the parental souls are merging, new souls are diverging and beginning the cycle anew. Like the kaleidoscope, souls merge into oversouls which merge into master oversouls, until all disappear into the center of the wheel, emerging into another universe entirely. All the while, new souls are growing up and giving birth to offspring, etc.

Ultimately, this model of Creation must fail in the end, because the principle of holographics states that every soul contains the entire blueprint of Creation from the very beginning. In other words, each time a soul emerges, an entire universe is created in miniature. Have you ever contemplated that your physical body is a universe unto itself? The cells are like multidimensional galaxies, each containing atoms, which are like miniature solar systems. The protons are the suns and the electrons, planets. Whether you go inward or outward, you eventually come to the same infinite Creation.

Now let us narrow the Creation story down to the current cycle of trinity - the expansion since the Big Bang. The Big Bang began, in linear time, approximately 20 billion years ago. This is the birth of the physical universe (and many parallel dimensions of the universe). In the book Original Cause (Four Winds Publications) is a chronicle of the various souls created since the beginning of time. I do not have any direct soul memories earlier than 100 million years ago because I had not emerged as an individual soul until around that time. Therefore, I will cover the early years of Creation only briefly, before jumping ahead in history to the beginning of life on Earth. Since I will not duplicate the information in Original Cause, you may wish to add the following information to what is there, keeping in mind that I make no claims to be as knowledgeable as the source of those writings.

Since I seem to have a love affair with diagrams, here are some more gems for your contemplation. For you artistic types, please feel free to embellish these or create your own.

Figure 12.1 - The Trinity

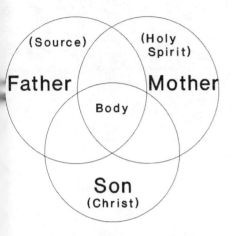

**Figure 12.2 - The Quadrinity
(or Four Parts of God)**

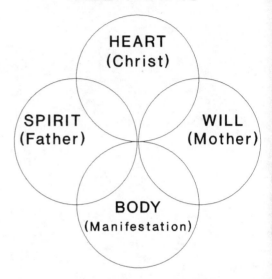

Figure 12.3 - A Symbol of God

Figure 12.4 - Alignment with Spirit

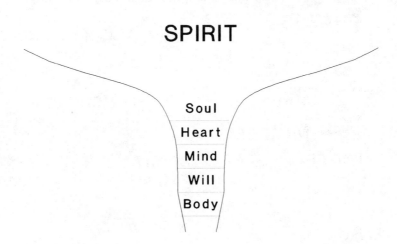

CHAPTER 13
THE REAL HISTORY OF EARTH

The Founders

Earth was created by the Divine Mother approximately five billion years ago, but it was not until around one billion years ago that the first life forms appeared on her surface. Shortly after the beginning of time, aspects of the Godhead fragmented into a group of souls called the Eternal Ones. One of the Eternal Ones established the Central Sun of this sector of the Milky Way Galaxy in a star cluster now known as the Pleiades. This great soul then fragmented into smaller souls called the Founders. The Founders are 12th-dimensional beings that have evolved back into the Godhead while at the same time, keeping their individuality and remaining unaffiliated with the spiritual hierarchy. These great beings travel throughout the universe, using pure consciousness as their vehicle. They have no limitations; they can mold themselves into any form they choose and enter any dimension they want at any time. They can go forward and backward in time at will.

The Founders created a paradise planet in the Vega star system and called it Lyra. This was a special place they could go to experience form. It was the original Garden of Eden, long before the Eden of Earth. Current cosmology calls Lyra the beginning of the human form. Contrary to the thinking of the mass consciousness, the human form did not originate on Earth; it originated on Lyra and was re-introduced on Earth through genetic engineering (a process that is partially explained on the next page) many millions of years later.

The Pleiadeans who started life on Earth were offshoots of this ancient Lyran race from the Original Creation. The Lyran star system vibrated at 12th density, which is within the realms of the Godhead. When the Godhead decided to experience duality, the Lyran world and the souls present on her emerged from the Godhead, dropping five levels in vibration to seventh density. This was the original fall from grace.

From a scientific point of view the Lyran star went supernova around one billion years ago, forcing the Lyrans to migrate. Some of the Lyrans took up residence in the Pleiades and began evolving on a seventh density world there. These Pleiadeans eventually engineered life on Earth. Many of these beings have since evolved back to 12th density, but are still involved in the Earth experiment. Other offshoots of the Lyran race include the Vegans and Sirians which will be discussed later.

The Great Experiment

Around 100 million years ago, the Pleiadeans began terraforming the Earth by introducing carbon and silicon-based life forms onto the Earth's surface. Before I continue with Earth history, I would like to digress and explain how life is created.

All physical life is created from an etheric blueprint - a coded geometric pattern formed from higher intelligence and stepped down in vibration until it can be fused into the RNA/DNA molecular format. The protein molecule is much like an organic computer; the etheric blueprint is the actual program.

The program is evolved from pure consciousness to the sub-atomic state, and finally, to the atomic. Pure consciousness can be thought of as similar to the binary digits of a computer program (i.e., the basic building blocks of the program). The subatomic level of creation could be analogous to the machine language program, and the atomic level could represent a higher level language, such as BASIC or COBOL.

All life support programs originate in the Universal Mind - the vast complex of intelligence representing the mind of God. Within this field of intelligence are the akashic records, which are much like memory storage devices except that they are really fields of energy held in place by the time continuum. As evolution progresses along the time line, it leaves an electrical charge in the etheric substance, much like a neutrino leaves a trail across a petri dish or an electron leaves a trace across an oscilloscope. While the trail, or imprint, is only a record of the actual event, the akashic medium creates a holographic image of the event. This image can then be re-experienced as a sort of "virtual reality" simply by tuning into that particular place on the time line.

This is like viewing a 3-D video of past events, not only visually, but with the physical and emotional sensations as well. In essence, this is how humans remember past life experiences. Each human's personal akashic is contained in the auric field of his/her fifth density etheric light body. The brain is simply a receiver of the EMF impulses that emanate from the aura. Memories from the soul's present life are also stored in the cells of the physical body. It is possible to bring past life memories from the etheric body into the cells of the physical body and thus experience in one's present body a traumatic event from a past life.

This rather detailed explanation of the blueprint of life is simply to illustrate that life was not a sudden accident or "one-shot" event that occurred serendipitously, but rather, a pre-conceived, pre-programmed event that can later be re-programmed and modified into any number of permutations, each of which can be experienced multidimensionally as many times as the experiencer desires.

From an extraterrestrial perspective, Earth represented such an opportunity for the Pleiadeans. Spread out before the higher dimensional mind was Earth's time line, representing infinite possibilities for evolution. If you are at all familiar with computer programming, you know that you can run a program any number of times, getting the same result each time. However, if you change one line of code, the whole program changes. The Pleiadeans, when they engineered Earth's evolution, were great experimenters. They would introduce a blueprint, and if the emerging life form did not meet their specifications, they would akashically record the results in a discrete segment of the time line and then permutate the blueprint and try again.

For almost 90 million years, Earth was a giant laboratory for evolving exotic and unpredictable life forms, most of which are no longer present on Earth today. One such form, the dinosaurs, remained on Earth for many millions of years.

Then, roughly 10 million years ago, the Pleiadeans themselves decided to come to Earth and experience the fruits of their labor. Although the Pleiadeans had carefully programmed and terraformed a humanoid to incarnate into, they were not prepared for the experience they had. Being from the seventh density, the Pleiadeans had never taken physical form. The closest approximation to form they had experienced was that of massive balls of blue-white light similar to the stars themselves.

They had tried manufacturing bodies and landing directly on the Earth many times, but the intensity of the magnetic field made it difficult to stay on the surface for more than a few days without undesirable changes to their manufactured bodies. So they prepared biologically evolved humanoid forms on Earth and infused these forms with fragments of their essence using the process of incarnation, while the remainder of their essence (99%) stayed behind in the higher realms.

Despite the massive drop in vibration, the Pleiadeans incarnating on Earth 10 million years ago created a garden paradise. At least it was paradise by today's standards. Earth's density was four octaves below the level of their Pleiadean world. When the descent into form was complete, they began to lose the conscious awareness they had projected into the tiny fragments of soul essence residing in the humanoid bodies, and as a result, a great amnesia overtook them. They forgot about their vast oversouls in the heavens. They lost many of their intuitive and psychic abilities. They become enmeshed in the energy field of Earth and felt trapped in their humanoid forms.

They mated and their offspring became the port of entry for

additional souls from the higher realms. Some of these incarnations were done consciously with agreement between parents and incoming souls, and some were not conscious, due to the denseness of Earth's magnetic field. The unconscious incarnations brought souls to Earth who did not have the understanding and balance needed to grow and evolve peacefully. As a result, the soul consciousness on Earth continued to drop in vibration.

The Pleiadeans on Earth were a gentle, feminine race that became bonded to the feminine nature of Mother Earth. As they dropped in vibration, they began to attract energies that were not in harmony with their origins. In addition to unconscious incarnations, warrior races from other star systems began to notice Earth. Some of these races were already vibrating at a low enough rate to land directly on the Earth and intermingle with the Pleiadeans. Pretty soon, the Earth became a melting pot for souls from all levels of Creation, some highly evolved and some not. Well, as you probably know, strife and conflict eventually broke out and the young civilization was shattered and scattered about on the face of the Earth. Thus began the rise and fall of 16 different civilizations over the next 10 million years.

Planet Earth's civilization today consists of many races of beings interwoven through interbreeding and experimentation. The native race of Earth (those who descended from the original Pleiadeans) are called the Adamic race. These are the souls who have chosen this planet as their primary sphere of evolution and whose genetic roots go back to the first soul embodiments here. In other words, Earth is their "home" planet.

The story of Adam and Eve in Genesis is largely symbolic, although the dynamics of it were played out on Lyra one billion years ago; in the Pleiades 100 million years ago; and on Earth 10 million years ago. Adam actually represented the Heavenly Father and Eve, the Divine Mother. The garden represented their pre-separation state of consciousness, and the tree of knowledge of good and evil represented the worlds of duality into which they incarnated. Once the masculine and feminine aspects of God descended into duality, they forgot their true origin and became fascinated, mesmerized and attached to the lower densities.

Walk-ins and Star Seeds

As time went by on Earth, beings from the higher realms tried to devise various ways to enter Earth's magnetic field without losing consciousness and forgetting who they were. They would attempt to incarnate with full memory through the birth process and mingle with the Adamic people. Such beings were called "star seeds" because they had no prior Earthly programming and no prior Earthly incarnations. The star seeds were different from the majority of Earthlings and some of them became great scientists, while others became outcasts and misfits. However, they all had one thing in common: at some point during their incarnation, they would forget almost totally who they were and where they came from. Some would forget immediately upon densification and entry into the womb. Others would be born with complete awareness, but gradually lose it as they interacted with the Adamic race.

It was determined that the most likely stage of development for amnesia was the period between two and eight years of age; so another technique was devised, called "walking in." A soul would volunteer to enter for the first several years of biological life and then "trade places" with another incoming soul. The new soul would take over the biological form and continue from there. This was a little tricky, because the new soul would have to "download" the life information of the previous soul into its memory banks and immediately begin functioning in third density. Some walk-ins were more adept at this than others.

Over the last 10 million years, many races of beings from many star systems and galaxies have come to the Earth from many levels and dimensions, some through incarnation, some through implantation (walk-ins) and some directly from ships. It is estimated that no fewer than 55 star systems have been involved in Earth at one time or another. In the following chapter, I will describe more than a dozen of the most visible and influential of the races coming to Earth. I will detail the name of the race, its appearance and mode of travel, a brief history of its involvement with the Earth and reason for coming, and the current percentage of each race residing on or around the Earth. The races are given in order of proliferation.

ETs on the Earth

NOTE: The following information has been greatly oversimplified, because, to accurately track the genetics of Earth's current population, after taking into account reincarnation and other factors, would require a highly sophisticated computer program not currently available on Earth. However, this model portrays, in consciousness at least, how Earth is truly a melting pot of ETs and humans. The figures that follow are based on a 50% bloodline model; i.e., if a soul is more than 50% Adamic, he/she is considered a member of the Adamic race. In this case, "50% Adamic" can mean either: (1) a soul's physical genetics are more than 50% intact from the original bloodline, or (2) a soul has had a majority of his embodiments on Earth, having begun this cycle of incarnations at a time when the Adamic race was still relatively intact.

Here are the approximate percentages of races in the Earth's present civilization (circa 1993):

Table 13.1 - Cosmic Makeup of Earth

Race/Star System	Percent of Whole	Population
Orion	76.5%	4.3 billion
Adamic (Pleiadean)	20.5%	1.2 billion
Sirian	1.0%	50 million
Venusian	1.0%	50 million
Vegan	0.5%	25 million
Zeta Reticulin	0.4%	22 million
Other races	0.1%	5 million

Here is the percentage of humans currently residing on Earth, listed by type of embodiment:

Table 13.2 - Type of Embodiment of Earthlings

Mode	Percentage	Population
Incarnation (humans)	99.5%	5.6 billion
Implanted (walk-ins)	0.5%	26 million
ETs direct from ships	.01%	16,000

Here are the current density levels of humans on Earth, and a projection of how they will have evolved by the year 2012:

Table 13.3 - Density Levels of Earthlings

Density	Current Percentage & Population (1993)	by 2012 A.D.
3rd	80% 4.45 billion	50% 1.0 billion
4th	20% 1.15 billion	50% 1.1 billion
5th	-	0.4% 20 million
Total population:	5.60 billion	2.12 billion

NOTE: In addition to the approximately 16,000 ETs in physical bodies currently residing on the surface of the planet, there are nearly 20 million ETs encircling the globe in various spacecraft or interdimensional cities.

The following chapter describes in more detail the prevalent ETs currently on or near the Earth.

CHAPTER 14
TYPES OF ETs
ASSOCIATED WITH EARTH

The Orions

The Orions are the dominant race on Earth today, but this was not always so. Although many groups had visited Earth and in some cases, interbred, it was not until about 500,000 years ago that the Adamic race was sufficiently diluted so as to become a minority. Around that time, beings from the star systems Rigel and Betelguese in the constellation of Orion came to Earth. The Adamic race was, at that time, very peaceful and feminine in nature. The Orions were masculine warrior-types who came "bearing gifts." Being experts in mind control and manipulation, they soon took over the Adamic people and proliferated. The Rigel faction were somewhat reptilian in appearance and the Betelguese faction were tall, red-skinned people similar in appearance to the Vikings. The Rigel faction became known as the "Dark Lords" and the Betelguese faction as "Lords of Light." These labels are for convenience only to demonstrate the extreme polarity between these factions.

The Orion factions were not only aggressive toward Earth, but toward each other as well. Between 500,000 B.C. and 200,000 B.C. there was planetary and galactic warfare between the Orions from Rigel and the Orions from Betelguese. These two civilizations fought for control of Earth, and thus, Earth became dominated by warrior energies. Many wars were fought on her surface. Several civilizations came and went during this time. Most were destroyed by chemical and nuclear weapons, with Mother Earth herself getting in the act as well.

Although both Orion races were aggressive and warrior-like, the souls from Betelguese were more peaceful than those from Rigel. The "Council of Light" from Betelguese wanted to establish their presence as the rulers of Earth, but the people of Rigel kept wrestling control of the planet from them. This is where the name "Urantia" originated in some writings.

Lucifer

The angelic being Lucifer influenced both Orion factions. Lucifer is the god of duality, whether it be light vs. dark, or dark vs. light. Lucifer is actually a great being of light who became polarized against the darkness to the point of actually giving power to the darkness. There were many loving beings in the Heavens who were appalled at the plight of Earth and wanted to assist in restoring the light there. Lucifer approached these light beings and convinced them to take sides with Betelguese and fight against Rigel. When these beings of light took sides, they took on the veil of duality and became caught in the lower vibrations of the Orions. This is referred to as the "Lucifer Rebellion" in ancient writings.

The light and dark Orions were, in a sense, reflections of each other's lack of acceptance for the self. Both Orion civilizations were masculine in nature and, along with the Sirians (discussed later in this chapter), have continued to dominate the more feminine races of the Earth to the present day. The Orions brought the patriarchal system to the Earth to replace what had once been a somewhat matriarchal world.

The Illuminati

Over the last 200,000 years, control of the Earth has seesawed between the Rigel and Betelguese factions. The most recent vehicle of Orion control is through an organization commonly called the "Illuminati" which means "the illumined ones." This began as a secret society of "occult" practitioners and mystics thousands of years ago and has since evolved into several forms, including fraternities, brotherhoods, mystery schools and financial institutions. The true history of the Illuminati is too involved to go into here with any real depth. Suffice it to say that in the beginning, the Illuminati was designed to be a way for the Adamic people to take back their power from the Orions through advanced spiritual teachings and scientific methodology.

The Illuminati flourished during the time of Atlantis and inspired many of the great technical and spiritual achievements of that time. Originally brought to Earth by the Pleiadeans as a true mystery school, the organization later became corrupted by the Sirians, another ET group responsible for many of today's religions.

The Illuminati has been controlled by the Betelguese faction several times. The Council of Light practices "white magic," a form of mind control and ritual designed to banish darkness, and sanctioned by some members of the spiritual hierarchy. The Council of Light has been heavily polarized against darkness, being the positive pole of duality. Many of the Council's members are beings from higher dimensions who were lured into Earth's drama by Lucifer and his angelic helpers.

As long as there is polarization, there will be pendulum swings. And so the Rigel faction, or "Draconians", infiltrated the Illuminati and swung the balance toward the pole of suppression and oppression of the light. The practice of "black magic" was introduced by the power hungry Rigel faction over the last several centuries, and today, the Illuminati is still controlled by the Rigel faction.

The Illuminati has fragmented into several smaller societies, including the Freemasons, the Rosicrucians, the Knights of Malta, and the international banking community founded by the Rothschilds, Rockefellers and others.

The Confederation

In the 20th century, with the advances in technology leading to the atomic bomb, it became evident that the Illuminati's polarization would lead to the destruction of Earth. As a result, the Confederation of Planets, an intergalactic organization directed by the Godhead, was allowed to intervene. This intervention was allowed not only because there were a small, but sufficient number of souls on Earth who requested assistance, but also because the planet's destruction would have created severe imbalances in neighboring worlds within the solar system. Planetary destruction in this solar system had occurred once before. A planet, often referred to as "Maldek" used to be located between Mars and Jupiter in what is now the asteroid belt.

The Confederation has evolved beyond the dualistic nature of the Orion factions. Confederation members began infiltrating the Illuminati quietly, often agreeing with the decisions made by the current power structure while silently introducing ideas of oneness and unity. This infiltration has been gradually shifting the balance of power away from the Orion factions, although at the time of this writing, the Rigel faction still held about 60% of the power, the Betelguese faction, 20%, and the Confederation, 20%.

Many members of the Illuminati today are not aware of who's who within the organization. There are spies and counter-spies. There are those who "backed in" through being recruited unknowingly. There are those in offshoot groups, such as the DeMolays, who have little knowledge of their real roots. There are many splinter groups, such as the Trilaterals, who have become pillars of government. These include the U.S. National Security Agency (and National Security Council), the Federal Reserve System, and the Central Intelligence Agency.

The Orions Today

Due to interbreeding and soul fragmentation (explained later), the Orions constitute almost 80% of the world's current population (based on the bloodline models shown earlier). The masculine, warrior-like characteristics of the Orion people have become so pervasive and ingrained that most people consider these traits to be "human nature."

The Orion star cluster has evolved significantly since the galactic wars, and most of the civilizations there now vibrate in the higher densities. However, the strong magnetic energies of the Earth have hampered the progress of the Earth-bound Orions and kept them from evolving as fast as their cousins in the constellation of Orion. Much of what the Earth-bound Orions are going through now was completed 100,000 years ago on Betelguese and Rigel. For a long time, emissaries from these stars were given a non-interference directive which limited the help available to Earth.

The help that is available now has come through the Confederation and other galactic organizations that represent hundreds of star systems. Once the Orions on their home planets evolved to a certain degree, they were accepted into the Confederation of Planets, so today, they are assisting along with other organizations within the Confederation.

NOTE: The names given for these galactic groups are for convenience only and are not generally referred to as such by their members. The chart at the end of this chapter shows many of the common names of organizations in the Confederation and the races that make up each group.

The Sirians

You may wonder why it has taken so long for the Earth-bound Orions to evolve out of their warrior-like energies. In addition to the dense magnetic field of Earth, part of the reason can be found by looking at the Sirians.

The Sirians (from the star "Sirius") have been involved with Earth for thousands of years. They were one of the first ET races to interbreed with the Adamic/Pleiadean strain. Like the Pleiadeans, they are descendants of a star in the Lyran system that went supernova many millions of years ago. Unlike the Pleiadeans, who look like humans, the Sirians, in their native state, have more almond-shaped eyes and lighter skin (although nowhere near as light as Type 1 Zeta Reticulins). The Sirians are peaceful now, but had a lot of turmoil in the past. They tried to take over the Earth on numerous occasions because their home planet was horribly polluted from their wars.

Many Sirians were the gods referred to in Earth mythology, since they had extraordinary psychic powers and a messiah complex. They enjoyed power over others, which contributed to their drop in vibration as they interbred. There are stories of how the ancient gods (Sirians) interbred with Nordic people (Orions and Antareans) eventually bringing about the downfall of ancient Egypt and Greece.

The Sirians invaded Earth almost 10,000 years ago, taking over much of Egypt and the holy land. The priest-kings of ancient Egypt were descendants of Atlantis, a civilization destroyed some 25,000 years ago. They reincarnated in Egypt around 11,000 B.C. and received help in building their civilization from the seventh density Pleiadeans. The Great Pyramid was built by the Pleiadeans. The secret knowledge of the Atlantean mystics was re-introduced in Egypt by the Pleiadeans. When the Sirians invaded and interbred, the vibration of the Egyptians dropped to the point where the Pleiadeans had to withdraw their secret knowledge lest the Sirians misuse it to destroy the Earth. I have included some additional information on the pyramids near the end of this chapter.

The Sirians interbred voraciously during the latter period of ancient Egypt. They became the new kings, pharaohs and priests, and later the Malachites and Israelites. William Bramley, in his book "The Gods of Eden", explains how these "gods" enslaved the Egyptian people and encouraged conflict and division within the castes and social systems of that region.

The Sirians figure prominently in Biblical history. Jehovah, the God of Moses, was once a Sirian from the seventh density. This partially explains many of the contradictions of the Old Testament. Throughout the early Bible, Jehovah is portrayed as an angry, jealous God who frequently visits the Israelites and their enemies with plagues, pestilence and all manner of punishment. As the leader of a power-hungry ET race, Jehovah's tyrannical rule of Earth was accomplished through demands of strict obedience to his tenets, best known as the "Ten Commandments."

In "The Gods of Eden", Mr. Bramley postulates that Earth's ET rulers maintained their power by creating division and strife among the tribes and peoples, thereby preventing the kind of unity that would empower the Adamic race sufficiently to rise above the chains of the Illuminati. He goes on to suggest in his book that Adam and Eve were the beginning of a slave race created to mine and harvest the Earth for the Sirians. According to his theory, the reason Adam and Eve were kicked out of the Garden of Eden was because the "tree of knowledge of good and evil" that they partook from would have given them true spiritual knowledge, something the slave drivers (Sirians) could not tolerate. After reading Genesis 3:22 a few times, I am inclined to consider this a real possibility.

(NOTE: This does not invalidate the metaphysical interpretation of the Garden, nor the "fall from grace" stories mentioned in Chapter 13 of this book. As we shall see in later chapters, the concept of original sin goes back much further than the Bible.)

The Sirians were a major factor in the continuing deterioration and corruption of the Illuminati, and in fact, a secret alliance was formed between the Sirians and the Rigel faction. The Orions and Sirians together are referred to in Mr. Bramley's book as the "Custodians." The control of the world's religions by the Custodians has been one of the most carefully guarded secrets of modern times. In addition, it appears that they had a hand in most of the wars that have erupted on Earth since the time of Egypt.

Although the Earth-bound Sirians have been in alliance with the Earth-bound Orions, the Sirians living on their own star system are still visiting Earth. They have evolved significantly since the time of Egypt and are now coming back to Earth primarily through telepathic and trance channeling. Their ships rarely land on Earth, but remain airborne during contact with humans. The craft are luminescent and golden, sometimes triangular, but not opaque, and have been mistaken for swamp gas. Many Sirians are "do-gooders" atoning for their abuses of power in the past, and provide huge volumes of information to their channels.

The Venusians

The Venusians are another race that has a great deal of prominence on the Earth. Almost 0.5% of Earth's current population are descendants or walk-ins from Venus. Although these beings come from our own solar system, many of them are space travellers who only spend an occasional incarnation on Venus or Earth. Venus is a planet of special initiation set up by the Confederation to prepare souls for higher spiritual truths between Earth incarnations. Many souls, including the author, have journeyed frequently to Venus between incarnations.

Venus is a sixth density world of incredible beauty and artistic achievement. Because of its high vibration, it is invisible to third and fourth density sight. Venus is considered to be the planet of love, named after a goddess of great beauty. I have personal remembrance of my lifetimes on Venus and I can assure you everything you've heard is true.

Imagine the most beautiful sunset. Then imagine living in a world where the sky is ablaze with glory all the time. Colors of yellow, gold, orange, pink and red dazzle the sight. Great temples spiral into the sky. Huge gardens with exotic plant life abound. Shimmering streams of liquid light flow along, providing nourishment for all life forms. Sparkling crystal palaces and golden temples await initiates who come to learn the secrets of the universe. These images are remembered by a few, but are seen on Earth only through a visionary artist's canvas. And then there is the music that calls from beyond time and space of a place long forgotten by Earthbound souls - a place where love surrounds and penetrates everything, ending all separation forever.

This is Venus, training center for gods and goddesses and the pinnacle of life in this solar system.

Venus is a way station for beings from all over the galaxy. They are initiated in spiritual teachings there, and many Earth souls have chosen Venus as their first post-ascension lifetime. I have been through at least two ascensions and both times, Venus has been on my itinerary.

Until you evolve into fifth density, you will be unable to behold this paradise directly. For third density Venus is a hot, poisonous wasteland that discourages all who would try taking a shortcut to Heaven.

The key to Venus is love. And it is love that will take you there. Many a Venusian in Earthly embodiment has looked longingly at the brightest star in the evening or morning sky, wondering where those strange feelings are coming from. Perhaps you have a long-lost love on Venus. I do, for my beloved twin flame is a Venusian.

Venusians, as you probably have guessed, are tall, slender, feminine and godly. They have radiant, golden hair and light complexion. They have learned how to materialize into third density using holographic projection, and have done so many times. Often, they incarnate or walk in. Their craft are saucer-shaped and metallic, although the ships can appear in different colors of the rainbow. They are capable of interdimensional time travel and many of them have come here from the future.

The Venusians made a lot of appearances during the atomic testing of the 40's and 50's, contacting George Adamski, George Van Tassel and others. Although these individuals (now deceased) have been heavily discredited by debunkers, they left behind a lot of documentation, photos and technological journals which are available if you know where to look.

The Vegans

The Vegans are similar in appearance to the Sirians, but a bit more feminine. They are also descendants of the Lyrans. Their non-interference doctrine has kept them out of the spotlight, and they have preferred to help from the inner planes through telepathy and channeling. They are a peaceful people who were non-violent in the past, but were often conquered and abused by more aggressive races. They are great artists and their music has influenced Earth through the inspiration of classical composers and now, some New Age artists as well. They have a great devotion to the "Radiant One" and are members of the Confederation.

The Vegans incarnated on Earth throughout the centuries, seeking to instill values of peace and beauty. As star seeds, they grew up, often in hostile environments, and yet retained their quiet, introverted ways. Often, they were viciously persecuted by religious zealots. Today they can be found in the Baha'i faith and other heavily persecuted peoples. The harp and lyre are among the musical instruments brought to Earth by the Vegans.

The Zeta Reticulins

Although the Zeta Reticulins represent only a small percentage of Earth's current inhabitants, their influence is one of the greatest on Earth at the present time. If you include their off-planet presence, their numbers are greater than the Sirians and Vegans, as they have millions of members in spacecraft in the vicinity of Earth. There are three subgroups of Zetas, which, for the sake of convenience, I am going to call ZR-1, ZR-2 and ZR-3, that originate from different civilizations in the Zeta Reticuli star cluster. They are all third and fourth density (physical), but, like humans, have wide variations in their level of consciousness. Because of their physical nature, they constitute the greatest percentage of reported encounters with humans. If you have seen a UFO with the naked eye, the odds are very great that it belonged to the Zeta Reticulins.

NOTE: Not all beings who match the descriptions given below are Zeta Reticulins. This humanoid form can be found in several parts of the galaxy and even in other galaxies.

The Zetas are here for a variety of reasons. These include biological experimentation, harvesting of Earth's natural resources and psychological study of Earthlings. The greatest reason for their presence, however, is interbreeding.

The Zetas' emotions are atrophied, like many of their body parts, from lack of use. They function much like a colony of insects, being very group-oriented and mechanical. While they are considered benevolent, they are not highly spiritually evolved and do not fully understand the "prime directive" of non-interference. They have been involved in abductions and experimentation on humans, supposedly in the name of research and gaining understanding of human emotions. The real reason is that they have serious imbalances in their race that are threatening their existence, and they believe they can save themselves by taking on certain qualities of humans. They are creating a hybrid race by mating with humans in the hope that the new race will retain the group mind while incorporating the emotional nature of humans.

ZR-1s

The first subgroup of Zetas are the ZR-1s. These beings are white, three to four feet tall, have huge craniums with large almond-shaped eyes and small spindly arms and legs. They are the most numerous of the Zetas and their craft can be spotted frequently in the night sky in most parts of the world. The ZR-1s vibrate at third and fourth density. They are technologically advanced and have highly developed powers of telepathy and mental projection. They can project holographic images of themselves that may or may not be visible to humans, although they themselves are very physical.

Their craft are spherical and saucer-shaped, gray or dark gray in color. Their mother ships are cylindrical or cigar-shaped. All of their craft use electromagnetic propulsion systems and have cloaking devices to evade radar and visual sight.

The ZR-1s are often accompanied by tall, blue beings from another star system, along with tall slender grey beings from the star Altair. These three races form what they call "the Triad."

There are well over 20 million ZR-1s on and around the planet.

ZR-2s

The ZR-2s are from another star in the ZR cluster. The ZR-2s are commonly called "greys." They are around four feet tall, are dark gray-brown, and have huge lidless eyes and coarse skin. They have four fingers and toes which are partially webbed. These beings have been in contact with various branches of Earth's government ever since two of their craft crashed in the 1940's. They have been involved in abductions, animal experimentation (cattle mutilations) and genetic manipulation in cooperation with a secret division of the National Security Agency of the U.S. government that is directed by the Illuminati.

The ZR-2s are not as benevolent as the ZR-1s, although some of their members are as evolved spiritually. Mostly, the ZR-2s are here to interbreed and to exploit the Earth and her resources, and have made a deal with certain world governments (primarily the United States) to trade technological secrets for the right to remain here without interference from others. They have secret bases in Groom Lake, Nevada and Dulce, New Mexico, as well as two other sites.

The recent TV movie "Intruders" (based on the book by Budd Hopkins) was an accurate portrayal of Type 2 Zeta abductions. However, the movie failed to mention that fetuses are removed from abductees around the third month of pregnancy and transferred to a special biological environment aboard the spacecraft for continued growth. Over one million Earth women have been abducted for breeding purposes. Abductees are often chosen at an early age and are "programmed" through the use of implants. The programming is designed to not only provide "tracking" and telepathic linkups between the Zetas and abductees, but also to prepare the proper environment for later impregnation. The abductees return to Earth with "missing time," discover their pregnancy, and three months later experience a "mysterious miscarriage" along with another episode of missing time. The Zetas use biological implants to deactivate memory of the abduction experience, but since all soul experience is recorded in the akashic records, abductees often remember what happened by contacting their personal akashic while under hypnosis.

Although the Zetas appear to violate the free will of humans by interfering in their lives, some Earthlings have agreed to the experience on a soul level, and all Earth souls have drawn the experience to them as a reflection of something in their consciousness. If you have been abducted, and your participation is helping save a race of beings from extinction, you may be less inclined to view the Zetas as evil invaders. Instead, you may see their actions as a desperate attempt to survive.

One more note on abductions: Many, if not most, of the abductees are Zetas who have incarnated into human form to experience it first-hand. In this case, the Zetas are merely reclaiming their own members at a time pre-arranged by the souls of the abductors and abductees.

ZR-2 ships are usually grey saucers and triangular scout craft which are seen frequently near their bases. They number close to 100,000. The NSA has prototypes of spacecraft designed from ZR-2 schematics, and ZR-2 technology is currently in use at certain military installations around the world. Certain members of the Illuminati are involved in the ZR-2/human interactions.

For the most part, the ZR-2s, like the Illuminati they deal with, have no intention of respecting the free will of humans. In fact, the Illuminati has enlisted the cooperation of the ZR-2's to help implement their version of a "New World Order" based on control, manipulation and domination (see the next chapter). One of the proposals they have considered is to stage an artificial crisis (something like an "invasion from outer space"), with the friendly men on the white horses (the Illuminati) coming to the rescue to save humanity from the Zetas, thereby gaining the respect of the people. By uniting the world against a common threat from outer space, the Illuminati figures control of world government will be all but certain. In the end, these "partners in crime" are just as likely to turn on each other, especially when it becomes apparent that the Divine Mother has Her own plans for a New World Order. For more on the New World Order, see Chapter 15.

The ZR-3s

The ZR-3s are the least friendly of the ZR races on Earth. They have been at war with the other ZRs for a long time. The ZR-1s and ZR-2s consider them to be an evil force to be banished. They are only allowed to come to Earth as long as the fear and negativity here are sufficiently strong enough to accept their presence. If the mass consciousness of Earth evolves sufficiently to integrate negativity, the ZR-3s will no longer be able to vibrate here because they are a reflection of our own fears.

The ZR-3s have black and red saucer-shaped craft. They are adept at mind control, black magic and psychological manipulation. They tend to play on and magnify the fears of humans, using anger and fear as opportunities to enter into the psychic space of Earth. If you encounter one of their craft, DO NOT under any circumstances approach it or attempt communication. Immediately call forth Divine Protection in whatever way works best for you. Methods of Divine Protection are given in the Appendix.

The ZR-3s shot down some of the ZR-2s' spacecraft over New Mexico in the late 1940's. The crashed saucers were retrieved by the U.S. military which began the long liaison between the ZR-2s and the government. (NOTE: Prior to this crash, the presence of the Zetas on

Earth was confined to a few very discrete encounters between their members and some Earth-bound Orions and Sirians. The true nature and purpose of the Illuminati-Zeta alliance will be discussed further in Chapter 16.

The ZR-3s are lizard-like in appearance, and because of their psychological deception, could conceivably invade Earth in a manner similar to the one portrayed in the TV mini-series "V."

The Pleiadeans

In addition to the Adamic race, there are three other groups of Pleiadeans currently working with our planet. Only one of these groups is visible to third density humans.

Fourth Density Pleiadeans

These are the beings documented by famous Swiss farmer, Billy Meier. They are tall, feminine and peaceful (the men are very feminine as well). They are easily identified by the long hanging earlobes and long silvery hair. Photos of several of them are available, although government harassment may make the photos hard to obtain. Their craft are saucer-shaped, metallic and somewhat complex in design. They use cloaking devices to go in and out of visibility. The mother ships look like huge chandeliers, much like the craft in the movie "Close Encounters of the Third Kind." The most famous of these beings is one known as Semjase (described in detail in the Billy Meier material). Although there have been numerous attempts to discredit Billy Meier and the handful of other Pleiadean contacts, these beings are very real and most of the photos are authentic.

Seventh Density Pleiadeans

These beings are not as well known as the fourth density ones. They have light bodies that are luminescent and humanoid in shape. Because they vibrate at such a high level, they have no bodily features, just a brilliant outline of a humanoid. Unlike celestial beings, you cannot see through them. The light is gold in color.

The seventh density Pleiadeans travel in interdimensional spacecraft that can change shapes and go in and out of third density at will. Although they are rarely visible, I have seen one of their craft, which resembled a green glowing sphere travelling horizontally at tremendous speed.

Some of these beings travel through time. They are explorers and many of them are future incarnations of the original Adamic race that have evolved back into higher dimensions after lowering their vibration to incarnate on Earth. They communicate primarily through telepathy and channeling. There are several prominent channels disseminating their teachings on Earth at the present time.

Twelfth Density Pleiadeans

These are an offshoot of the Founders we spoke of earlier. In addition to the original Founders, which have changed little in the last 100 million years, there are those Pleiadeans who evolved from the legendary Lyran star system back into 12th density. They have all evolved way beyond physical form and appear in spiritual sight only as huge, glowing balls of blue-white luminescence. They look like the seven sisters of the Pleiades cluster in miniature. There are perhaps 100 or so of these magnificent beings in Creation and it is believed that their oversouls are the stars themselves.

The Founders come to Earth periodically during special planetary initiations. They travel through all the dimensions of space and time using pure consciousness as the vehicle. Someday all evolving souls will reach this unlimited state.

Although the Founders are aware of the Brotherhoods of Light and the Spiritual Hierarchy, they are not directly affiliated with these groups. By the time a soul reaches 12th density, the idea of hierarchies and levels is meaningless anyway.

The Arcturians

The Arcturians are another multidimensional group who have visited the Earth many times since the early days. There are two main groups of Arcturians.

Seventh Density Arcturians

The seventh density Arcturians are tall, blue-skinned beings (not to be confused with the Triad) that are invisible to the third density eye. The first time I saw them with my inner eye, they resembled a tree with a multitude of branches made of energy shooting out in all directions. They appeared to be eight to ten feet tall and floating in the ethers. Their ships are also etheric, saucer-shaped and blue, like their skin. They have underground bases on Earth, but due to their etheric vibration, are rarely seen in the physical.

I have spent time in one of the sacred places of the Southwest located virtually right on top of an entry and exit point for their spacecraft. Some people I took there reported the feeling of being inside a spacecraft.

Tenth Density Arcturians

The 10th Density Arcturians are fragments of the original archangels. Like all celestial life forms, they are luminescent, yet clear to opaque, and very large. The closest physical depiction I know of is in the paintings of Gilbert Williams and Aeoliah. The Arcturian system is a multidimensional time portal, also known as a midway station. A midway station is a bridge between the Celestial realms (densities 7 through 9) and the intermediate realms (densities 4 through 6). The station provides an opportunity to acclimate on the way through the dimensional shift.

In addition to the blue-white opaque beings that resemble shimmering crystal light bodies, the Arcturians also have a great winged form. The Pegasus and White Serpent of folklore have their origin in Arcturus. These mighty beings have wingspans of 50 feet or more as they soar through the ethers at tremendous speed. The light emanations from their auric fields are as dazzling as the noonday sun.

These beings have great love for humanity and are members of the Confederation. Their purpose here includes balancing the auric field of the planet and restoring balance to the etheric fields high above the planet.

The Andromedans

The Andromedans originate in the Andromedan star cluster, a system that is actually a separate galaxy and neighbor to the Milky Way. They are light skinned, tall slender beings who resemble in some ways the Zeta Reticulins. The main difference is their height, which is six to seven feet, and their eyes, which are almond shaped but much smaller. Their heads are long and narrow and shaped like an inverted pear. They bear a close resemblance to the Essassani, one of the hybrid races between humans and Zeta Reticuli.

The Andromedans are explorers who noticed this planet due to the nuclear testing going on here. They desire to assist mankind in preventing nuclear holocaust, but they have a messiah-like attitude and have been known to interfere in the free will of humans by trying to save them from themselves.

I am not aware of any connection between the Andromedans and the governments of Earth, although the Andromedans do seem to be interested in certain minerals and rare elements in the Earth. Being fourth density, they require considerable time to traverse the distance between Earth and their home planet, which is more than one million light years away in third dimensional terms, so they are not likely to be a threat to humans. Their craft are cylindrical to cigar-shaped and utilize warp-speed propulsion systems much like the Starship Enterprise on "Star Trek."

The Antareans

The Antareans (from Antares) are, like their red giant star, a race of giants with, believe it or not, reddish skin. They have incarnated on Earth in many different periods, but due to the extreme gravitational and physiological differences between Earth and their planet, they have rarely visited here in their native form or landed directly on the surface of Earth. They have been in contact with a subterranean race of beings which will be discussed later. Their ships, like everything else about them, are huge, computer-like spheres or cylinders reminiscent of something from "2001: A Space Odyssey."

The Antareans have highly developed telepathic and PK abilities, but have found Earth to be hazardous to their psychic health. Many who incarnated here have become trapped in third density and look longingly to the sky for answers to long-lost questions.

Other Races

There are many other ET races incarnated or visiting here from various star systems that I have not already mentioned. Some are guiding Earth only from other realms. A brief summary of some of the other races are as follows:

Deneb - A member of Solar Cross (an intergalactic organization), they provide spiritual guidance through channeling and telepathy.

Altair - A member of the Triad, they are taller than the Zeta Reticulins.

Trantor - Head of government for the councils of light of the Solar Cross.

Aldebaran - A star system whose members provide counsel for the Ashtar Command, another intergalactic group.

Alcyone - A celestial world providing counsel for the Great White Brotherhood (a spiritual order that predates the mystical orders of the Illuminati before its corruption).

Polaris - A 12th density race providing spiritual guidance through telepathy and channeling.

Our Solar System

Our own solar system contains several races in different densities. In addition to Venus and Earth, there is a subterranean fourth density race on Mars, a fifth density race on Jupiter and Saturn, and a number of outposts and alternate life forms on Uranus and Neptune. There is also a hall of records on Pluto. The asteroid belt was originally a planet destroyed by laser and nuclear weaponry. Many of the souls who originally incarnated on this planet migrated to Mars. Our own moon has outposts on the dark side which have been observed by the secret government and NASA missions and, of course, kept from the people. More information on intelligent life in our solar system will be forthcoming in later books.

The Inner Earth

There are many legends about a civilization existing inside the Earth. Actually, there are several subterranean groups. Some of these civilizations were driven underground by disasters on the surface; some came here from other planets and found the interior more to their liking. The three biggest ones are underneath Mount Shasta in Northern California, under the Amazon basin in South America and under the Gobi desert. Their respective names are Telos, Poseidon and Shambhalla. The beings known as Sasquatch (or Bigfoot) originate from inside the Earth. They are descendants of an ET race from Sirius with whom they are still in contact.

All these subterranean cities are fourth density, although they have corresponding fifth density "parallel" cities in another layer of the Earth. These fifth density cities include the "Halls of Amenti" located under the Sphinx in Egypt. Although geologists are busily excavating that area in search of proof that this legendary subterranean world exists, they will never find it, for two reasons: (1) Fifth density is invisible to third density; and (2) the Pleiadeans "locked" the access codes to this underground realm when they departed Earth at the time of ancient Egypt's downfall.

Ascension Chambers

Many of the great monuments of Earth history were built by ETs to serve as ascension chambers. An ascension chamber is a radionics device that steps up the cellular vibration of fourth density humans until the human is able to take on the fifth density light body. Ascension chambers were used as initiation temples by certain ancient societies. Only those who were sufficiently purified could enter the chamber. The two most famous ascension chambers are the Ark of the Covenant, mentioned in the Bible, and the Great Pyramid at Giza. In both cases, humans who were not sufficiently purified attempted to enter the chambers and their bodies were burned up instead of transfigured. As a result, a long list of rituals and sacrifices were invented by those who did not understand the true meaning of purification.

The Pleiadeans were masters of the ascension process, but the Sirians who ruled Egypt and the Holy Land wanted to use the chambers for their own personal gain. Jehovah, the God of Moses, was more interested in having a faithful following than in helping the people understand the true process of ascension. A lot of misconceptions regarding how to achieve ascension originated from the Sirians' misuse of Divine power. Since the Sirians wanted to stay in power, they had an investment in restricting access of the people to advanced technologies. The various sacrifices and rituals outlined in the Old Testament were designed to make spiritual attainment extremely difficult, if not impossible, for the average person of that era. The whole idea of sacrifice was distorted from its original purpose--to purify the soul and give up the old self-image--into a constant battle with guilt and relentless judgment of base desires, all in the name of morality.

The phenomenal amount of gold used in the building of the Ark of the Covenant was designed to be alchemized (transformed into a higher vibrational form) by burning certain materials on the altar. Obviously, the people did not understand the reasons for using precious metals in the construction of religious buildings. Many a civilization has gone broke by giving most of its assets to the altars in the name of sacrifice.

The ascension chambers consist of a mathematically exact structure powered by alchemized metals (usually clear crystalline or white crystalline gold) which set up a resonant EMF inside the chamber. The action of the EMF penetrates the cells of the body causing the RNA/DNA molecules to match the frequency of the EMF. What the ancient mystics did not understand was that in order to properly match frequencies, the ascending human had to have additional strands of RNA/DNA; two strands would not withstand the current generated by the field and the body would disintegrate.

Additional strands of RNA/DNA are generated by light activation codes, a principle described in Chapter 20. Spiritual and physical purification is the only way to consciously generate additional strands of RNA/DNA because any dense materials (such as food toxins, suppressed emotions or negative beliefs) in the body will block the light activation codes from reaching the RNA/DNA.

The Pyramids

The only pyramid in ancient Egypt that ever had any radionic power was the Great Pyramid. Built by the Pleiadeans as a temple of initiation, this pyramid could only be activated when a large crystal in the epicenter (near the King's Chamber) was tuned to the frequency of the capstone (most of which is missing now). Shortly after the pyramid was built and activated, the Sirians came to Earth and took over as the gods of the people. There were many power-hungry individuals who sought to use the pyramid for their own personal gain; therefore, it was deactivated.

The Egyptians who incarnated later in the Dynasty did not know how to reactivate it, so they tried all sorts of magic and alchemy, including mummifying the bodies of the Pharaohs and erecting various altars. Of course, none of this worked because they had lost the knowledge of radionics and light geometry. Many similar pyramids were built at great cost and with much sweat by the Egyptians in the hope of recreating the "magic elixir." But the Pleiadeans did not return to enlighten them because the vibration of the Egyptians had deteriorated too much.

The Spiritual Hierarchy

Although the spiritual hierarchy consists of beings that could technically be called extraterrestrials, I prefer to treat them differently because the spiritual dimensions are part of a very different space-time continuum than the realms of the higher density ETs. One analogy I use is that of an x, y and z axis, where each axis represents a particular time-space continuum. (See Figure 14.1)

In this case, the x-axis is the realm of physical ETs (including human/Adamic), the y-axis pertains to higher-density ETs (up to 12th density Pleiadeans) and the z-axis represents the spiritual hierarchy.

Figure 14.1 - A Three-Axis Model of Intelligent Life in the Universe

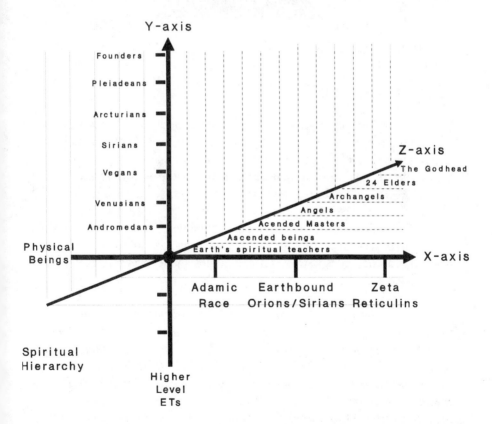

Another way to imagine the relationship between different life forms in the Universe is depicted in Figure 14.2 below. Here, we see physical humans and ETs on the left point of a triangle, higher-density ETs on the right, and spiritual beings on the top.

The advantage of this second model is that it accurately portrays the fact that the spiritual realms are outside the time-space continuum of humans and higher-density ETs.

Figure 14.2 - Another Model of Intelligent Life in the Universe

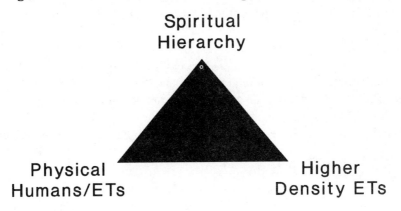

Spiritual
Hierarchy

Physical   Higher
Humans/ETs   Density ETs

Who Are the Spiritual Hierarchy?

There are many great beings working directly with the Godhead who regularly visit Earth. Many of these are well-known angels and archangels. There is much literature on these beings, so my descriptions will be brief. All are original descendants of the Heavenly Father and Divine Mother, which, together with the Christ, form the Trinity of the Godhead.

The following list is by no means complete. There are thousands of beings in service to the Earth at this time that are not mentioned here; deepest gratitude goes to these unseen guides and teachers for making the path easier and clearer.

NOTE: The term "spiritual hierarchy" does not in any way imply that there is an order of value in the spiritual Universe. In other words, "hierarchy" should not imply that one being is "above" another in terms of value. These great beings do not think of themselves as above or below one another. Such concepts belong in the domain of Earthly ego. Rather, the term "hierarchy" simply means that some beings have a greater awareness and higher vibratory level than others, and hence, a greater responsibility to help and guide their Earthly brethren.

One of the main attributes of these life forms is that they have tremendous self-esteem and self-worth. This manifests in the way they look upon their fellow souls as equal to themselves. One of my favorite statements was put forth by the archangels to the people of Earth: "If you valued yourselves as much as we value you, Earth would already be paradise." Not only do these great beings value humans as equal in the grand scheme of things, but they also have great respect and admiration for us. They understand that it is often very difficult to grow and expand in a world dominated by fear, insecurity and guilt, and they consider the Earthly journey to be a challenge no matter what a soul's level of awareness might be. Which brings me to one more saying, this time by a great spiritual teacher in embodiment to one of his disciples: "The only real difference between me and you are your doubts."

Spiritual Beings in Service to Earth

Following is a partial list of the various members of the spiritual hierarchy and their respective densities.

Heavenly Father - The originator of the Universe and generator of all light within it. The Spirit principle of Creation. The Heavenly Father is the oversoul of the Ancient of Days, Yahweh, Enoch, Melchizedek and eight others who are collectively known as the 12 Eternals. The Heavenly Father is called the "Radiant One" by the Brotherhoods of Light.

Divine Mother - The originator of all souls, stars and planets, and the experiencer of all life. The Will principle of Creation. The Mother is equal to the Father as one-third of the Trinity. The Divine Mother is the oversoul of Isis, Kwan Yin, Mother Mary and nine others who form the will counterparts of the 12 Eternals. The 12 Eternals and their will counterparts form the 24 Elders of the Throne spoken of in Revelations and other sacred writings.

The Christ - The balance of the masculine and feminine poles of Creation. The Heart of God, also called the Son of God. The Christ is the oversoul of Sananda who is the oversoul of Jesus.

Ancient of Days - A 12th density presence from the Great Central Sun of the Universe who oversees the Creation. One of the original 24 souls from the First Creation.

Yahweh (YHWH) - A 12th density presence from the Great Central Sun of the Universe who oversees the physical and etheric universes. Yahweh is the oversoul of Jehovah, the God of Moses.

Enoch - A 12th density presence from the Great Central Sun of the Universe who oversees the process of evolution. Enoch is my master oversoul, or the oversoul of my oversoul.

Melchizedek - A 12th density presence from the Great Central Sun of the Universe who originated the Melchizedek Priesthood.

Lord Michael - An 11th density presence from the Great Central Sun of the Milky Way Galaxy. Overseer of the evolutionary process of Earth and many other planets.

Lord Sananda - An 11th density presence who oversees the ascension process (along with Serapis Bey of the angelic order). One of the primary souls from the Christ oversoul.

Sanat Kumara - An 11th density presence from the Great Central Sun of this galaxy. Overseer of Earth, Venus and several other planets.

Babaji - A 10th density being from an alternate universe and an overseer of humanity. Known as Lord Shiva in Eastern religions.

Isis - A primary soul from the Divine Mother who inspired the ancient Egyptians.

Kwan Yin - Another primary soul from the Divine Mother who inspired many of the Eastern religions.

Mother Mary - Another primary soul from the Divine Mother who inspired Christianity. She provided the physical vehicle for Jesus to incarnate on Earth.

Lord Jesus - A physical soul from the Sananda oversoul. After Jesus' death and resurrection, He formed an oversoul consisting of 12 soul fragments who later incarnated on the Earth to carry forward His teachings.

The Seven Archangels - Lord Michael, Uriel, Gabriel, Chamuel, Zadkiel, Jophiel and Raphael. Archangels from the Second Creation overseeing various aspects of spiritual growth on Earth.

Saint Germain - A being from the angelic order assisting in the Aquarian dispensation, another name for the Divine intervention taking place on Earth now.

Ascended Masters - Beings who have graduated from physical embodiment by perfecting the physical form and ascending into the light body.

Ascended Beings - Beings who have reached fifth density, but do not necessarily have complete body mastery.

144,000 - A symbolic number representing those who are currently graduating into the fifth density on Earth. Also can be construed to mean the total body of ascended souls who exist in the realms of the Godhead. In Revelations, those who "walk with God" and are not subject to the "Mark of the Beast."

The Color of God

Since everything in the Universe has a unique vibration and frequency, we can associate particular colors with each being or group of beings. Every soul in Creation has a set of colors and patterns corresponding to the following color rays that emanate from the Source. The following table shows one interpretation of the colors of God.

Table 14.1 - The Twelve Rays of the Godhead

1.	Red	The mechanics of Creation--physical/procreative forces.
2.	Orange	Passion--emotional/sexual energies of the Universe.
3.	Yellow	Intellect--lower mind/ego, God's Logical Mind.
4.	Green	Balance/life force - the primal heart of Creation.
5.	Blue	Conceptual/higher mind - depth and Universal ideas.
6.	Indigo	Etheric, astral, imaginative; fantasy and folklore.
7.	Violet	Subtle/causal realms; ray of purification and cleansing.
8.	Silver	The feminine principle; the Divine Mother.
9.	Gold	The masculine principle; the Heavenly Father.
10.	White/pink	The Christ principle; balance of male and female.
11.	Clear	Transcendental principle; the totality of God.
12.	Black	The void; the unknown.

Figures 14.1 and 14.2 show the organizational structure of the spiritual hierarchy and Confederation of Planets.

Figure 14.3 - The Spiritual Hierarchy

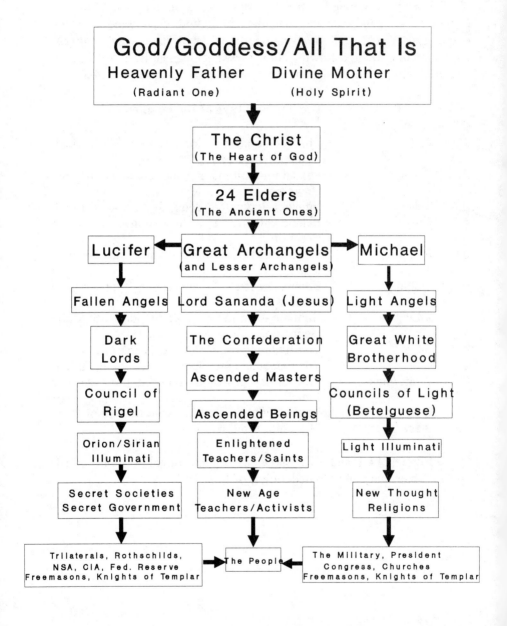

Figure 14.4 - The Confederation of Planets

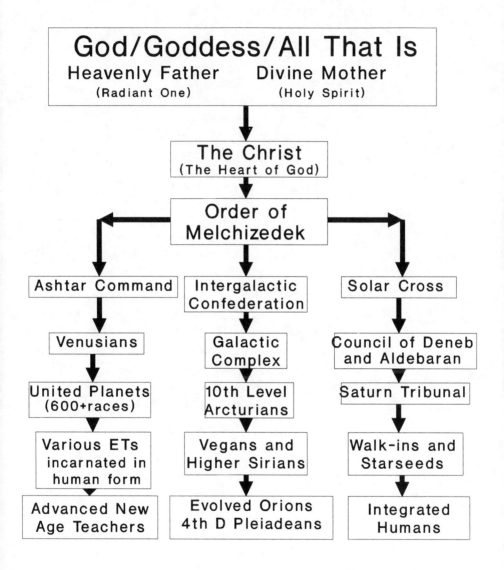

Now that I've taken you to the far reaches of the galaxy and beyond, it's time to come back down to Earth and look at some things a little closer to our everyday lives.

CHAPTER 15
THE NEW WORLD ORDER

Facing the Reflection

By now, I'm sure you're aware that the way to change the world is to change yourself. And you know that what you focus on becomes your reality. So you may be wondering why I've included a chapter that deals with the political and economic situation on the planet.

To be a conscious creator requires that we have the awareness and discernment necessary to recognize the obvious and subtle ways that our thoughts manifest in the outer world. We must be able and willing to dive into the deepest, darkest parts of our reflection to bring healing there. The following sections deal with the possible and probable futures we are creating based on our current beliefs as a society. I encourage you to look objectively and subjectively at this chapter and use it to grow and create in a new way that works for yourself and all of humanity.

The Old World Order

The Old World Order is crumbling. By the time this book goes to print, many of the familiar institutions of the Piscean Age may already be history.

Why is the Old World Order coming to an end? The reasons are many. On the physical level, it is because the world cannot continue on the course it has been on. The old world economy is based on a consumption model. To keep going, it needs ever more consumers, willing to buy an endless list of products and services. To manufacture these products, natural resources are involved. Most of these resources are not being regenerated fast enough to keep up with the demand. If this were the only factor affecting the economy, it would run down by the year 2020 due to shortages of oil, paper, plastic and other basics of the modern manufacturing process.

It is unlikely that this scenario will ever be reached, because a far greater threat to the Old World Order is the backlash of environmental degradation. At the present rate of pollution of air, water and land, much of the Earth will be uninhabitable by the year 2010. Before it reaches this level of crisis, Mother Nature will already be taking her revenge. Even assuming that there are no significant natural disasters, it is a virtual certainty that cancer from ozone depletion, immune system failure from excess carbon dioxide emissions, and genetic mutations from chemical and nuclear waste will wipe out large segments of the population. The massive cost of caring for the sick will bankrupt the economic system in a matter of a few years. My estimation is that up to 50% of the human beings currently residing on Earth may be gone by the year 2010, due to complete immune system failures.

The physical considerations above represent the best possible outcome for the Old World Order based on no natural cataclysms. Actually, the year 1992 saw several volcanic eruptions, major hurricanes and severe climatic abnormalities. Already in 1993, we have seen severe flooding in the Midwest, drought in the Southeast, and other major alterations in the jet stream. Drought, famine and plague caused by these conditions may hasten the demise of the Old World Order.

Regardless of how intense the Earth changes become, the present economic and political world will likely collapse by 1996, long before illness and disease take their toll, and I'm now going to furnish several additional reasons why I believe this will happen.

The Emperor with No Clothes

In case you're not already familiar with the banking system, let me give you a quick lesson in smoke and mirrors. Originally, the currency of the United States was backed by a gold standard. More recently, we have been relying on the Federal Reserve Note, a piece of paper "backed by the full faith of the U.S. government." How much is that piece of paper worth? That depends not only on the whims of the financial markets, but on a number of other factors as well.

It is common knowledge that the banking system only keeps about 5% in hard assets to back its various loans and investments. If only 10% of the depositors were to lose faith in the banks and make a run for their money, the house of cards would topple.

But aren't banks protected by the U.S. government? Yes, up to a point. But the skyrocketing debt incurred by compound interest poses a grave threat to the "faith of the U.S. government." The biggest borrower in the world is Uncle Sam, and the interest payments alone are enough to stagger the imagination. To counteract this runaway debt (which is now more than $6 trillion - that's $6,000,000,000,000.00), the U.S. Treasury prints more money. This increases inflation, which lowers the value of the dollar. The alternative is to refrain from printing money, which dries up the money supply, forcing the economy into recession and/or depression. Typically, the Democrats go the inflationary route and the Republicans the recessionary one.

Although there is a lot of rhetoric about finding solutions to the debt crisis, some simple mathematics tells the real story - the debt situation is completely out of control and no magic wand is going to make it disappear. Long before the value of the dollar disappears under this mountain of debt, the owners of the U.S. (the Japanese) could withdraw their money in favor of something with better value. All Japan has to do to bring everything crashing down is secure enough natural resources from other countries to no longer depend on the U.S. for trade, and then withdraw its funds. The banks would disappear literally overnight. The recent spate of "Japan bashing" only brings this possibility closer. Thus emerges the naked Emperor (the banking system) in full view of the rowdy crowd who have suddenly realized they've been duped.

I have given a compelling reason for the imminent collapse of the Old World Order. But behind the physical conditions lies a deeper, psychological reason. In order to keep the system going, you need to keep the people relatively ignorant. In the past this has been accomplished through the brainwashing of TV and the media. But as the evolutionary process accelerates, more and more people are awakening to the lies and deception of government and the banking system. Even the fundamentalists are seeing the lies and corruption, as evidenced by Pat Robertson's book "The New World Order."

In short, people are getting tired of being "consumption robots." Everyday folks are beginning to question whether one more brand of perfume is really going to bring happiness. Most have lost faith in their political leaders and are no longer willing to support the empty rhetoric. If only 10% of the people were to reduce consumption by 20%, the GNP would decrease 2%. Right now, this would be enough to send the country into a depression.

On a spiritual level, Divine Intervention is playing a major role. As spiritual truths are introduced to the people, they begin to realize what really has value and they are no longer willing to spend their whole lives trying to gain "sex appeal." The outer world is a reflection of the inner, and as the inner changes, the outer must follow suit. The outer world is based on beliefs of scarcity, security and approval-seeking, and as people heal themselves and discard these beliefs, they will no longer give power to the Old World Order.

The Illuminati's New World Order

The Illuminati, seeing the inevitable demise of the Old World Order, have their own idea of a New World Order which they are already in the process of implementing. The basic premise of their Order is to form a One World Government under a One World Banking System. The individual economies of the various nations would be merged under a universal currency controlled by a central computer system. The same folks that brought you the banking system now have in mind a credit system that looks remarkably similar to the "Mark of the Beast."

No, I'm not a fundamentalist preacher and I'm not a raving lunatic. But consider what has already happened. We have a worldwide credit card computer network that can instantly access your accounts from terminals in almost every country in the world. We have a debit card system. We have optical scanners capable of recording all the details of your every purchase. And we have new currency entering circulation with magnetic barcodes imbedded in the paper stock.

These data are fed into a central database which is then analyzed by marketing agencies (I know, I worked for one) to see what's selling and what's not. Right now, if you use a credit card or personal check to buy groceries, it is conceivable that a computer somewhere in Washington could tell you that Mr. Joe Smith, who resides at 345 Riverside Drive in San Francisco bought an 8-ounce tube of Crest toothpaste for $3.49 at 8:02 p.m. on November 15th at the 7-11 store at Market and 35th streets. This same (or a similar) computer can tell you how much money Mr. Smith has in savings and checking, his income for the past seven years, and obviously, what he spends his money on.

If you use a credit card, debit card or have a bank account, rest assured that your finances are not private and are, in fact, available to thousands of companies and individuals. Some supermarkets have done away with check I.D. procedures because they can simply enter your account number from your check directly into a central computer and get a readout while you stand in line at the checkout.

The Illuminati's desire for world control is made easy by the use of consumer databases. They know what you want, when you want it, and even why you want it. They can make marketing decisions that will elicit a certain response from you based on your purchasing patterns. If you become too eccentric in your purchasing, they may notice this. If your income rises unexpectedly, you may suddenly find a host of solicitors on your phone or at your door.

If all this sounds like something out of Revelations, guess what. It's happening now. In fact, I've heard that members of the Illuminati are planning to stage a financial crisis to force everyone onto a credit system. Under this system, goods and services would only be available to those with the proper credit cards. They could even tell you what kind of employment is acceptable; only "approved" institutions would be allowed to issue credit. In other words, if your business or trade does not meet their guidelines, they could refuse to give you a computer account to validate your credit card.

So you think they would never do this? Have you noticed the rash of bills going through Congress lately to outlaw such things as non-prescription vitamins? Or wholistic healing methods?

How will the Illuminati bring down the Old World Order? Here's one possible scenario: Members of the U.S. banking community conspire with Japan to suddenly withdraw their assets, forcing a bank collapse. Officials then inform the people that their money is worthless. But not to worry - Big Daddy to the rescue. Everyone is given a credit card and the banks then determine your credit amount, based on your employment history, etc.

Although all this sounds like paranoia, actually the Illuminati's New World Order is a blessing in disguise. By bringing together the countries of the world into a single, unified presence, the Divine Intervention could be more easily accessible and true unity could result. This would likely be accomplished by some sort of worldwide media event staged to counteract the Illuminati's media events. One possible counter-scenario: Higher Intelligence (in the form of ETs) jam the airwaves (this is really pretty easy to do with existing technology) in a one-world broadcast, instructing people to destroy their credit cards and return to bartering. New technology would then be introduced to ensure an adequate supply of essential goods and services.

Although this kind of intervention from On High would be easy to pull off, such extreme measures are a last resort to protect those who have asked for assistance. Our ET friends would prefer not to intervene in such a direct manner. If too many people thought they would be saved by ETs, they might abdicate personal responsibility for their own lives. This is also one of the reasons why removing people from planetary dangers by evacuating them in spaceships is highly undesirable. If you are waiting to get "beamed up" so you won't have to deal with the mess down here, you may be in for a disappointment. Although there may be a few extreme cases of evacuation, such events would be limited in scope and affect only a small handful of people who would be brought back to Earth a short time later in an area where they would be of greater assistance to humankind.

Most souls on Earth at this time need to be here to gain the valuable lessons and experiences needed and to give assistance to others in crisis. Giving up the ship or abandoning the planet in her time of need is not the highest option for the majority of enlightened souls.

One final note on the subject of Confederation intervention: I have been informed repeatedly over the past 15 years that we will not be allowed to destroy ourselves with nuclear weapons. In fact, our "friends upstairs" have already neutralized our weaponry on four occasions, going back to 1962, when we could have blown ourselves to smithereens.

The Christians' New World Order

There are many references in the Bible to the establishment of a "new Heaven and a new Earth." The New Jerusalem, or Holy City, is prophesied to descend upon the Earth, ushering in a new millennium of peace and prosperity. This is referred to as the Second Coming of Christ. In Revelations, there is a description of a crystal city 1000 miles in length being prepared to receive God's chosen ones.

My personal visions and prophecies support the above information. I have seen the crystal city in my mind, and I firmly believe the 1000 years of peace will become reality on Earth. However, there are a lot of misunderstandings in the Christian community that I would like to address now.

Although some scholars believe the "Rapture" points to a nuclear holocaust, it actually refers to the ascension process, or more accurately, the translation; i.e., that point where the 4th density human enters the 5th density light body. At that point, the body becomes invisible to one remaining in 3rd density, hence "one is taken, one remains."

To be one of the chosen does not mean all you have to do is preach the gospel and wait for Jesus to arrive in a fiery chariot. First of all, the Second Coming is about Christ, not Jesus. The man Jesus is in the process of reuniting with His oversoul, Sananda. When Jesus died and resurrected, His spirit ascended but He left several fragments of His will essence in the Earth, which later incarnated as discrete embodiments.

The 12 disciples symbolically represented 12 different paths to God. When Jesus fragmented, He embodied into 12 different lives simultaneously, each as a discrete soul fragment, to experience a particular spiritual aspect or path. (These are not the same future incarnations as those of the original twelve apostles.) The 12 soul fragments are individuals who have Jesus as their oversoul, and because soul fragmentation is a holographic process, each of these people is, in a sense, Jesus reincarnated. I have met one of these souls and he firmly believes he is Jesus. And I do not believe he is insane.

As an aside, you may be familiar with someone who claims to have been Cleopatra or Athena, or someone else of notoriety. Many great souls in history fragmented in a similar manner to Jesus. So there may actually be several Cleopatras running around in bodies. Of course, not everyone who claims to be an incarnation of royalty is telling the truth. Many souls simply feel identified with a particular energy.

Back to the Christian story: To be one of God's chosen people does not involve having to appease God or meticulously follow every tenet of gospel. Being chosen also does not mean being better or more Divine than someone else. Being chosen simply means choosing to graduate from 4th to 5th density. To do this, you must follow God's laws, not by adhering to a strict list of commandments, but by learning the secrets of translation, transfiguration and ascension.

Unfortunately, most Christians have little or no understanding of what is required to be chosen. If you believe the only path to God is through Jesus and that all others will be damned, I can assure you that you will not be one of the chosen ones. This is not because God doesn't love you, it is because the vibration of judgment will keep you in a lower density.

In a metaphysical sense, the path to God *is* through Christ, because the Christ energies represent the Heart of God--the balance of the male and female polarities, which heals duality. The Second Coming simply means that the Christ energies will return to Earth in the form of souls ending the duality of opposing polarities and becoming One Being. By equating the universal consciousness of the Christ with the man, Jesus, Christians have taken scripture literally and are waiting for a physical Messiah.

A further difficulty with Christian doctrine is the tremendous amount of guilt that permeates most churches. The leaders of the New Right have convinced their followers that to be saved you must travel the straight and narrow. And they would impose their doctrine on the masses by creating strict laws regarding abortion, New Age "Satanic" thinking and the "evils" of secular and scientific methodology. In recent years the U.S. Supreme Court swung toward the Far Right and as a result, existing abortion laws have been challenged. The death penalty has been reinstated in many areas. The absurd part of fundamentalist thinking is that it does not even remotely reflect the true teachings of Jesus. Is state-sanctioned murder (capital punishment) in line with "love thine enemies" and "thou shalt not kill?"

The act of separating out a portion of reality and judging it as "un-Godly" is the basis of Satanic principle. The Christians, and the Moslems too, for that matter, have judged materiality and set it apart as an evil to be overcome. This division within the self manifests outwardly as the "war of righteousness"; the continual battle of good versus evil, the ultimate cause of all wars and human suffering.

Most Christians have a long way to go before they are ready for the Second Coming. To allow Christ to come into awareness requires the ending of judgment and condemnation of other paths to enlightenment. The New World Order of the Far Right would do more than simply put prayer back in the public schools. It would bring back the witch hunts, religious torture and all manner of cruelty. The Divine Mother has had enough of this senseless suffering, and Her New World Order will restore the balance in Creation.

The Divine Mother's New World Order

There is really only one version of the New World Order that can manifest on Mother Earth. And that is Her own version. The Earth is a part of the Divine Mother. She is a conscious, intelligent being who has patiently allowed all manner of parasites to invade Her surface. She asks so little of the creatures She nourishes and nurtures - only that they respect the Earth and each other and refrain from needless destruction. But it seems Her children refuse to listen.

Imagine how you would feel if tiny critters burrowed under your skin and set off explosions there. How would you feel if your protective hair were burned so that these critters could have more room to slaughter each other and consume the dead meat?

I don't need to go on and on about the greenhouse gases, ozone depletion, rape of the rain forest, etc. Suffice it to say that Mother Earth feels Her life being threatened and will take whatever measures are necessary to protect Herself and the beings on Her that wish to live here in harmony with Her.

From Her perspective, it seems sensible to remove the perpetrators and relocate them somewhere else where they can play out their aggressive drama without violating the wills of those who desire peace. Other planets are already being set up to receive incoming souls who wish to continue their warring ways. These planets have agreed to accommodate the souls until they are ready to evolve to a higher understanding.

This is a good time to illustrate the schoolroom analogy. Imagine you live in a small town with a single room schoolhouse. All grades; kindergarten, primary and secondary cram into this single room every day for classes. As the town grows, it becomes increasingly difficult for everyone to get an education. The secondary students are having a hard time understanding algebra; the kindergarten students are disruptive in their lack of attentiveness; advanced students are forced to sit through boring lectures while retarded students feel lost and disoriented.

One day the principal and town council get together and decide to build a new school with several rooms, one for each grade of students. Now the beginners will get special instruction while the more advanced students will get to move ahead. The administrators decide to assign the advanced students to the one-room schoolhouse while the others are bussed to the new building.

Each soul makes the conscious or unconscious choice whether to stay or leave. Although the administration (God) decides which school building (planet) will house which level of students, it is up to each student (soul) to decide which grade is appropriate. For some, this decision is made consciously; for the majority it is unconscious. A soul knows what it can handle, although the mind may not. God does not ask His children to do something that is beyond their capabilities. If you are aware that you volunteered to come to Earth to assist other souls in finding their correct classroom, be assured that you will be given everything you need to fulfill your assignment. You teach by example. For a soul to make a conscious choice requires that mind, heart, will and body be in alignment so they can receive the communication from the Father and Mother. As a volunteer, it is your job to help others align themselves so they can know their own soul paths.

The Mother lives inside each of us. As we reconnect to the Earth, She lets us know exactly what actions are in alignment with Her and which are not. If She needs to remove souls that are destroying Her from a particular area, She will warn those who are in alignment and who are listening to Her and give them specific instructions on where to go and what to do in order to remain on Earth.

If you receive guidance to start a spiritual community and live off the land, go for it. If it is clear guidance, the means (people, resources, etc.) will be drawn to you to accomplish it. If you are guided to move to a large city on an earthquake fault zone, honor this message. You may be needed to assist those in trauma at a later date. As long as you follow the Divine Mother's guidance, you will not be harmed in any way. She does not want you to suffer, and you will not, if you allow Her to direct your Life. She has Infinite Wisdom to steer you clear of all danger and make easy your path. You are a beautiful soul and you deserve to receive the Mother's boundless Love and Compassion.

The Mechanics of the Mother's New World Order

Although the Mother is loving and just, if you oppose Her you will find your life going to hell in a handbasket. This is because you will be fighting the flow of life. The Earth Mother is in the process of raising her vibration into the 5th density. As the Mother rises in vibration, all that is not in alignment with Her will fall away. How will this look in everyday life? For those who don't listen to Her messages, it may start with health problems. If the body is not receiving proper nourishment from the Earth, it decays and dies. Although you can use mind control to force the body to accept toxic food, this is not the optimum path. Soul alignment means giving each part of the Self the most loving and harmonious environment in which to grow and evolve. Foods that used to be acceptable to the body will suddenly (or gradually for some) create a toxic reaction. New allergies may spring up unexpectedly.

These problems are not confined to food. Stressful lifestyles will be less and less tolerable as you raise your vibration. That office job used to feel okay, but now it gives you headaches. That Friday night beer party used to be fun, but now it gives you a stomach ache. Your body needs to be sensitive to hear the Mother's instructions. Denial and addictive behavior dulls the senses and the body starts to rebel. This does not mean you should force yourself to live an ascetic life. If your body wants to party, then party! But you need to discern between addictive urges and genuine desires. How do you feel afterward? Correct action brings a light and expansive, but clear, grounded feeling. If the activities in your life are not bringing this feeling, you are out of balance.

But what about that weekly paycheck? If you are not doing your true work, it will get harder and harder to live from paycheck to paycheck. No amount of money is going to keep your body healthy if you are not listening to the Mother's instructions. If you do not believe you can make a living doing work that is in alignment with your own soul and the Mother's New World Order, then you have negative core beliefs you need to clear out that are keeping you from evolving and fulfilling your true purpose on Earth. If you do not take steps now to clear those beliefs, the Mother may clear them for you by triggering external events that force you to deal with your issues. This is a loving "kick in the pants" to get you moving in the right direction.

If you are willing to clear your own emotional issues and end your denials now, you may not need to experience cataclysmic external events. It is only when you continue to ignore your own internal messages that external disruptions are necessary. At the time of this writing, it appears that approximately 80% of the souls on Earth are not willing to face their own issues and clear their denials. This means these souls are consciously or unconsciously deciding to let the Mother clear these issues for them in the form of Earth changes. Each soul draws to it an outer reflection appropriate for the level of denial present. Those souls who have worked on their issues to some extent will most likely experience less severe outer disruptions than those who have more extensive denials. It is not necessary to learn through pain, but pain can be a very effective teaching and learning device.

The Mother's decision to establish Earth as a school for advanced students was based on the collective request of the light workers who have tried for aeons to get mankind to listen to the simple truths of Creation; and because the Mother has taken enough abuse and wants to rejoin her Heavenly counterpart.

As denials and addictions are cleared, each soul will increase in vibration. The collective will of the people represents a major fragment of the will of the Mother. As the collective will increases in vibration, the Mother increases in vibration as well. The Mother desires to have Her children join Her in fifth density for the grand cosmic reunion of spirit and will. By aligning with the Mother, you raise your individual vibration in tandem with the Mother and eliminate resistance to the new energies coming in from the Father. Discomfort is always some form of resistance to the new energies.

The new energies are represented by the double helix of the ascension flame. The ascending energies emanate from the Mother and enter the body at the base of the spine as Kundalini. This energy rises up the spine and out through the crown chakra at the top of the head, joining the Father energies. At the same time, the Father energies are descending through the crown chakra down the front of the body, continuing out through the base of the spine into the Earth. When you are standing, these double helix energy spirals also use the feet for entry and exit.

Although the energies are continuously moving up and down the spine in both directions, they merge and unify in the heart chakra as love. The merged Mother and Father energies radiate out through the heart to all of Creation as love and compassion.

This love and compassion is essential to the completion of the Divine Plan on Earth. Many souls who are having trouble integrating the new energies will be reaching out for this love. Love is unlimited. The more open your heart, the more this love can come into manifestation. Love is the key to the implementation of the Mother's New World Order.

Figure 15.1 - The Double Helix

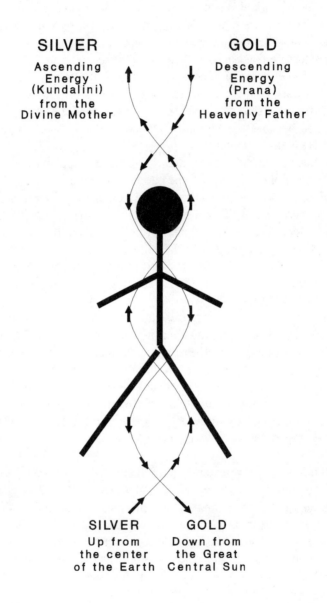

SILVER

Ascending
Energy
(Kundalini)
from the
Divine Mother

GOLD

Descending
Energy
(Prana)
from the
Heavenly Father

SILVER

Up from
the center
of the Earth

GOLD

Down from
the Great
Central Sun

CHAPTER 16
THE DRAMA OF DUALITY

The outer reflections of reality we have looked at thus far are really only manifestations of processes that are going on much deeper below the surface. Until recently, I still had many unanswered questions about the drama on Earth. Even knowing who the major players were didn't explain the purpose of their presence here or why so few individuals had the answers to why things are the way they are on Earth.

Why, for example, do highly intelligent, creative people, such as artists, have such a difficult time financially? Why do people with incredible knowledge and insight lead lonely, poverty-ridden lives? And why is information about spiritual truths and ETs so secretive and difficult to disseminate?

I've come to the conclusion that true spiritual knowledge on Earth has been suppressed and controlled even more extensively than I first realized. To go into this, and to shed light on the above questions, let us first take a new look at who the major players are and their relationship to one another.

Figure 16.1 - Major Players on Earth

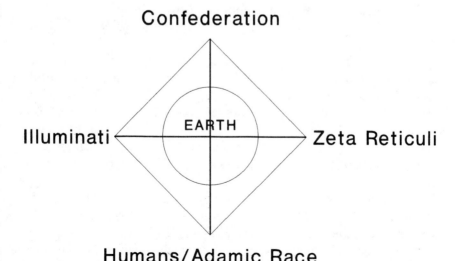

Major Players on Earth

Figure 16.1 shows the groups currently having the greatest influence in the affairs of Earth. I have intentionally positioned each party around, rather than in, the Earth, which implies that essentially all of Earth's inhabitants could be considered "extraterrestrial."

The Confederation

The Confederation, which includes the Godhead and the true spiritual hierarchy, could be likened to a scientist in a laboratory. This individual (male, for convenience) is busy observing various chemical reactions in his latest experiment, and is continually making notes on the progress of the experiment. Such a scientist tries to minimize his influence on the processes involved in order to get unbiased data. In modern physics, scientists are always striving to isolate the observer of a phenomenon because it is well known that an observer tends to affect that which he observes.

How does this apply to the Confederation? In theory, the Confederation has a neutral stance in the affairs of Earth. However, some of its members have an investment in the outcome of various Earth events and therefore influence these events, just like the scientist who has an investment in the success of the experiment will often subtly (or not so subtly) affect its outcome. Even if there is no conscious desire to influence, there will still be a relationship between the observer and the observed. This principle is detailed in quantum mechanics and related fields.

What are the influences of the Confederation? Basically, the other three parties (humans, Zetas and Orions/Sirians) are all in relationship with the Confederation. This occurs not only through external interaction (i.e., members of the Confederation who incarnate on Earth to further their soul experience and to interact with the races of Earth), but also through mental, psychic and spiritual communication with humans, Zetas or Orions/Sirians who are tuned to the frequency of the Godhead.

The teachings of the Confederation involve integration of the various bodies and levels of the self; relinquishment of judgment, guilt and denial; and the fostering of love and compassion for all beings. This is emphasized, while at the same time, individuality and personal freedom is preserved. The spiritual path of the Confederation is an inclusive one, and the aspirant expands his/her consciousness omnidirectionally to include more and more of the Universe. The

Confederation does not promote war, division, separation, or exclusivity. Although the Illuminati considers the Confederation to be an arch-enemy, the Confederation merely sighs, and wonders "when will they ever learn?"

The Illuminati

The Orions and Sirians (which comprise the majority of the Illuminati) are essentially "fallen angels" (i.e., beings originally from the Confederation who dropped in vibration and thus excluded themselves from the Confederation). This occurred because these beings began identifying with that which they were observing, and got caught up in the lower densities of the Earth experiment, thereby forgetting their spiritual selves. Their doctrine is one of separation and division, with an emphasis on ego and personal power.

Although most of the Illuminati claim to be deeply spi al, they are extremely devious and have twisted and distorted the true teachings of the Confederation to their personal benefit. They are responsible for bringing virtually all of Earth's current religions into existence. Although Jesus, Buddha and Mohammed had true spiritual vision, those who institutionalized, and subsequently distorted the teachings, were usually members of the Illuminati. Throughout the last 500,000 years, it has become increasingly difficult for the average person to even tell the difference between the Confederation and the Illuminati. This is because the Illuminati's twists of the truth are often subtle and present an outer integrity, while secretly undermining the work of the Confederation. On the next page are some examples of the differences between Confederation and Illuminati teachings:

Table 16.1 - Comparison between Illuminati and Confederation

Confederation Truth	Illuminati Distortion
The spirit must be free of attachment to material form.	The spirit must deny material form and overcome it.
Seek ye first the kingdom of Heaven, and all things shall be added unto thee.	One must give up one's personal desires and surrender to God.
Enlightenment is everyone's birthright.	One must struggle and toil, and overcome lifetimes of karma to reach enlightenment.
The Universe is neither good nor bad; it simply IS.	God is good; everything not of God is the work of Satan.
One must understand and integrate one's shadow side.	The shadow side must be banished.
Everyone is chosen by God.	Only the elect are chosen.
Material things are part of God.	The material world is an illusion.
Jesus died as a result of his own actions and the actions of others.	Jesus died for our sins.
You are responsible for your own spiritual progress.	Your spiritual progress is determined by God's grace.
You can move beyond karma through learning to love and forgive yourself and others.	Karma is immutable. You must atone for past mistakes. Only God can forgive.

Behind the Illuminati's teachings are the Earth-bound Orions' and Sirians' insatiable quest for power. These gods foster a deep-seated belief that the Universe is ruled by a capricious and whimsical God--an all powerful entity that metes out severe punishment for sins, and demands perfection and obedience. So great is the ingrained fear of God in their followers, and the prospect of burning in hell forever, that some Illuminati members will go to any length to please their God. Many gurus have become outer reflections of this image of God. They have amassed great wealth and power from their disciples while claiming they have a direct line to God, or are receiving the power and energy directly from God.

Why do these gods have this unquenchable craving? It is because they have forgotten their true divinity and must "borrow" power and energy from others to keep going. Deep inside they believe they are separate from the rest of the Universe, and are unwilling to face their own loneliness and despair--feelings they have kept carefully hidden for aeons. Throughout history they have enslaved the human/Adamic race by perpetuating the beliefs shown above. They have sought to entrap souls from the Confederation and convert them to the belief in duality.

These gods of duality would often create a calamity on Earth and then entice Confederation members to come and rescue the struggling souls, thereby becoming embroiled in the disputes and wars. The gods of the Illuminati form alliances with other groups when it is to their advantage to do so. Right now they have an alliance with the Zeta Reticuli. The Zetas need biological and genetic material from Earth to keep going as a species, and the Illuminati needs Zeta technology to maintain its stranglehold on Earth. One of the ways the Illuminati remains in power is by squelching any attempts by other groups to unify and work together for the common good. This is done by fomenting conflicts among the factions of Earth through fragmentation of religions, language barriers and psychological manipulation. By introducing exclusive religions ("mine is the only path to salvation"), various humans will continue to fight which will decrease their power to resist the Illuminati.

This explains why the Illuminati operates with so much secrecy. It is the silent force behind the conflict, similar to the gloating face on the competing scientist when his colleague's experiment goes awry. It is like the saboteur who sneaks into the lab in the middle of the night and destroys the new invention that would have put the competition out of business. By keeping the people ignorant, the Illuminati can continue its abuse of power.

The Zeta Reticulins

The Zetas are caught in the middle of a power struggle between the humans and the Orions/Sirians. They arrived on the scene desperate for help from the humans. If it were not for interference from the Illuminati, the two races would have probably traded biology for technology openly, and would likely have formed an alliance, using their combined strength to rise above the trials and travails of Earth's oppressors.

When it saw the Zeta's technology (which is at least 50 years advanced over human technology), the Illuminati knew it would have to gain control of this technology to keep the humans in line. Thus began a program of secrecy and deceit that involved feeding the Zetas a lot of propaganda about the humans and convincing the Zetas to enter a secret alliance with the Illuminati. This alliance will be temporary. Once the Illuminati has taken everything it needs from the Zetas, it will expose them to the humans as evil invaders from outer space, which will create another division. Now the humans and Zetas will be at war, and the Illuminati will once again watch from the sidelines while pulling the strings. In addition to sending some of its members as the white knights to the rescue, the Illuminati will be able to use a war of this magnitude as an excuse to suspend many liberties and freedoms, thereby increasing Illuminati control over Earth.

If the secrecy surrounding all this were to be exposed, the humans and Zetas would realize they had a common enemy, and they would ask the Confederation for help. The Confederation would respond because it would no longer be in violation of the "prime directive." The response would not be a calling up of arms, but an introduction of true spirituality en masse, utilizing superior technology to reach all corners of the Earth. Hence, the Illuminati would fall.

The Human/Adamic Race

The only way for the humans to be freed from the grip of the Illuminati is for true spiritual teachings to be made available to the masses. The main barrier to this, besides old habitual beliefs, is the fear and guilt instilled in the people by most "Illuminati religions." People have been duped into believing that the gods of religion are the one and only true God, and that if they question the Bible, or Koran, or whatever, that they will be severely punished. The next chapter, "Guilt", will go to the core of the human condition and reveal the reason the Illuminati was able to take over the Earth in the first place. A complete understanding of the next chapter could liberate the soul from the drama of duality, and get humanity back on track.

CHAPTER 17
GUILT

As you can see, I've included a whole chapter on guilt and related subjects. Although many of these ideas were presented briefly in earlier chapters when I talked about the emotional and mental levels of awareness, I'm going into more depth here because I feel having an understanding of guilt is essential to reclaiming our personal power.

Before we get to the nitty gritty, allow me to expound on a few related concepts.

The Two Kinds of Death

In the Western world it is often difficult to describe an experience due to the limitations of language. This is especially apparent when it comes to the subject of death. There are really two kinds of death. One is necessary and desirable as an inevitable part of growth. The other belongs to the realm of guilt and needs to be seen as such.

1.   Death as Transformation

This is the experience of death as an ending of the old in preparation for the new. It is the breaking of continuity leading either to chaos or a new order. There are two experiences of death as transformation: Physical death and ego death.

Physical Death

There are points along a soul's path when physical death may be the highest option. Later, perhaps in another embodiment, the same soul may experience ego death; i.e., death of the personality or sense of self. Both physical death and ego death can be profound spiritual experiences and lead to rapid soul growth, depending on the factors that caused the death.

Ego Death

Usually the more advanced souls will choose ego death to accelerate their growth, because they have already learned as much as possible about physical death, having experienced it so many times. It's true that once a soul completely experiences ego death, he or she may not need to experience physical death anymore.

Death of the ego does not imply that a soul maliciously destroys his/her ego in an attempt to transcend limitation. This is a largely erroneous teaching embraced by those who feel trapped by their egos and are looking for an escape, having found physical death only perpetuates their misery from lifetime to lifetime. True ego death is a willingness to release one's attachment to the image of self and be unconditionally open to the new. Contrary to popular belief, a soul does not necessarily become a vegetable or psychotic after ego death. Mechanical abilities and brain memory may stay intact and even become sharpened. The soul simply doesn't respond to personality issues because, in a sense, he/she no longer has a personality. Even if this soul continues to move the body and speak in ways similar to everyone else, there is no self-consciousness.

While most people who are verbally attacked feel hurt and abused, a soul who experiences ego death may not have a reaction at all to verbal assaults. To this individual, life has become much more significant, and such games are silly and inconsequential.

It is possible to be in a state of continuous ego death, where the self is constantly emptied of its content. Such a soul functions entirely from the higher self perspective, moment-to-moment, with all linear thinking directed by the higher self and utilized only when necessary to accomplish its purposes while in embodiment.

In the truest sense of the word, every soul has an ego. However, the soul who is in a state of continuous ego death has an ego that is dying and being reborn every moment. In other words, such an ego is evolving and mutating constantly to reflect the desires of the higher self.

2.   Death by Stagnation

When the ego becomes crystallized by old beliefs, programs and conditioning, it is no longer evolving. It is then that a soul begins experiencing the other form of death: Stagnation.

Ultimately, death by stagnation will lead to death by transformation. But this can take a very long time and be extremely unpleasant along the way. Death by stagnation involves the gradual withering away of the life force through constant denial, judgment, guilt and separation within the self. A soul caught in stagnation may experience lifetime after lifetime dealing with basic issues and repeating the same patterns over and over.

Stagnation always eventually leads to physical death. Physical death is the spirit's way of trying to free the soul from stagnation, thereby creating death by transformation. Unfortunately, if the will (emotional body) is stagnated, death of the body will not solve the problem, because the same issues will surface again in the next lifetime. Although it may seem to take forever for a soul to break out of stagnation, the worst case scenario is that it will take a few aeons. It is assumed that souls who read this book want to break free of death by stagnation immediately and open themselves to new energies and insights. Understanding guilt is probably the single most important step to breaking free of death by stagnation.

Darkness

While light and dark are two sides of a world of duality, it is necessary to move beyond darkness before you can transcend duality. To dispel darkness, it must be seen for what it is and clearly understood. You do not transcend it by angrily casting it out and refusing to acknowledge its role in the drama of duality. And you do not blindly embrace it either. The marriage of light and dark, yin and yang, alpha and omega, does not occur unless you see what the real darkness is - lack of understanding. It is not the fear, terror, anger, rage, grief, sadness or even shame. These feelings are just responses to the separation. The separation occurred when you judged parts of yourself as not being lovable and denied those parts. You do not end the separation by condemning it, regretting it, wallowing in it or rationalizing it. And you do not dispel it by any form of denial.

There are three aspects to the separation: guilt, judgment and denial. Ultimately these are not evil attributes because they only exist due to a lack of understanding and lack of God presence. In earlier chapters we looked at judgment and denial. Now, let us look at guilt more closely.

Guilt Exposed

The best way to move beyond guilt is to understand all its gross and subtle forms. Let's begin with clarification of definition.

Redefining Guilt

Have you ever wondered why it seems so hard to be free of the limitations of the past? Does it ever seem that you have an endless number of layers of old programming and conditioning that seem to thwart you at every turn and close in on you just when everything is starting to go well? You have the desire for freedom and joy, yet a nameless, faceless something seems to rise up before you blocking the path.

There are some who say shame is much more insidious than guilt. I am not going to debate semantics. If you choose to substitute one for the other, do that if it works for you. Indeed, shame is the most dense of the emotions. And certainly, it arises from an inherent belief in unworthiness. But for our purposes, shame is the emotional component of a phenomenon that has been with all of us since the beginning of time: Guilt.

Guilt is a lack of movement, a lack of essence. Although it appears to move and take over an unsuspecting soul, it can be visualized as a sort of hole in your essence--much like holes in Swiss cheese. Imagine the cheese is your life essence, your soul. Imagine that instead of a static, unmoving block of cheese, it is a vibrating, changing form. Within this movement are holes, or gaps in the essence - areas of absence - that appear to move as well. However, this is much like the wave phenomenon.

If you have two people hold ends of a rope and move their hands up and down, you create a wave which travels from one end of the rope to the other. This wave appears to have velocity and substance, yet by definition, it has no substance. The same is true of guilt. Like the rope, which only has up and down movement, there is only the essence, with its evolving, merging and coalescing form. The holes merely appear to move as the form changes. If the essence vibrates fast enough, it fills the holes and closes the gaps, creating an integrated whole and ending the separation.

Although guilt is ultimately an illusion, it has been given power and belief for so long that it seems to be a dominant force in the Universe. In fact, it seems to be more powerful than God.

How Guilt Originated

Guilt has been with us since the beginning of time. As we said before, God was originally one being - an immense, electromagnetic mass of intelligent energy. This essence became aware of itself and realized it had within it a magnetic part and an electric part. The electric part radiated light and the magnetic part attracted the light into itself and converted it into motion, which became experience. We call the electric part the Father and the magnetic part the Mother.

Because the nature of the Mother is magnetic, she attracted not only the Father's light into her being, but also the presence of the void.

The void is that which is beyond the created Universe. The void, in itself, is nothing, but when it interacts with God essence, it takes on a life of its own. One of the energies that was drawn in from the void was guilt. This presence had no consciousness or intelligence, but as it entered the God essence of the Mother, it cast a shadow on Her and began sucking Her life force into itself, much like a black hole sucks matter into itself.

Like a parasite, guilt worked its way into the Divine Host, wrapping itself around Her like a black cloak. Although Divine Essence is indestructible, it can lose its light if it becomes enshrouded in guilt. Because guilt is a form of unconsciousness, the Mother began to forget She was a part of God. The Father saw the plight of the Mother but did not understand anything outside of His light, and for a long time did not know how to heal the Mother. Eventually, guilt permeated both the Father and Mother and began affecting all of Creation.

Why was guilt able to enter the Godhead? The Mother believed, early in Creation, that She must be unconditionally loving. To Her, unconditional love meant She must take everything into Herself and love it. However, there are some things that are not meant to be taken in as part of the Self, and one of these is guilt. Guilt's true home is out in the void where it can float lifelessly forever in the darkness. When the Mother realized She had taken in guilt, She began to feel unworthy and this is when shame was born.

I do not wish to go further into the story of Original Cause at this time. I have inserted pieces of the story in different parts of this book to stimulate your own exploration. However, I will mention that the best written material I've found on what actually happened at the beginning of Creation is in "Original Cause" I and II from Four Winds Publications in Santa Fe, New Mexico. This set of books is largely fiction, metaphor and allegory. But it is based on the true experience of our Creator and can open the doorway to higher consciousness. Of course, a book is just another tool and, like the book you are now reading, can only point to the truth; it is up to you to take over from there. In the Original Cause books is a truth that virtually all religions and metaphysical groups have overlooked: *The Source, or Godhead, is evolving, growing and learning along with its infinite aspects and parts.* Since we are its aspects and parts, we are a reflection of the totality - a holographic representation of the whole - a microcosm of the macrocosm. Like a wave that radiates outward from an inflection point (the hand moving the rope), what happens in the Godhead radiates outward from the center toward the periphery of the Creation.

Creation evolves like an idea which starts as a rough sketch on a drawing board. In order to get to the finished product, you may have to erase or modify the sketch many times before it begins to make sense. The universe is not perfect. It makes mistakes. Yet it is continually perfecting itself, and so the process itself is perfect. Without guilt, mistakes are simply tools for learning how to perfect the self. With guilt, mistakes become sins, something to be fearful of and shy away from. And so, expansion is suspended, growth is atrophied.

Although evolution never stops, it can be slowed to a crawl if enough guilt is taken in. That is, until the pain becomes unbearable. And that is where separation reaches its maximum. On Earth, this maximum has been reached and guilt must go.

It is time to move on, to evolve beyond guilt. The key is understanding. Not just intellectual understanding, but a deep, inner feeling of true knowing. It is this understanding of guilt that we seek to gain at this time. For this understanding will explain much of what is and has been happening on this planet since the beginning of time.

Understanding Guilt

What are the attributes of guilt? The main quality of guilt is non-acceptance of self, or making the self wrong. This is an absence of love. This unloving, unaccepting presence gave birth to judgment and denial. Guilt began judging parts of the Godhead to be more or less deserving of love and light than other parts. Parts that were considered less deserving were then cast out from the body of God. Because all is God, there are not really any parts that can be destroyed, but they can be denied. Guilt became the judge of what parts of God could stay and what parts would be denied.

Because we emerged in the image and likeness of God, guilt also emerged with us and has continued to feed on our soul essence. The result has been more and more of ourselves being denied over time.

Things went downhill rather fast after our emergence as individual souls. Because guilt judged us as unworthy and wrong, we began to believe we could not receive God's light and love. We had a vague memory of being in the Godhead before guilt entered, and we have spent most of our existence trying to return to that state of innocence. When we began manifesting bodies, we recreated, again and again, our Original Cause, this time using the womb of our physical mothers as our pre-emerged state. We began in a warm, safe, loving space and then were cast out into a cold, judgmental world, helpless to defend ourselves against the onslaught of guilt from the authority figures that interceded throughout our childhood development.

Most of us in this world are still trying to return to the womb. We don't realize that this safe, warm, caring space is within us and is still connected to the Godhead. It is time to awaken to the innocence that has always existed and will always exist. It is time to end judgment and denial that has convinced us that we can never be truly free. And it is time to remember that we are Sons and Daughters of the Most High.

The Role of Guilt on Earth

Earlier, we talked about the Illuminati and its plan for a New World Order. How did the Illuminati come into existence? I don't mean the mechanical process of individuals forming institutions and corporations that control the wealth and resources of the people. That is all after the fact. Certainly, the original idea was to help humanity, through the understanding of the occult sciences, and to form a fraternal brotherhood of light on Earth.

The Orions were reflections of an idea, actors on a stage, with guilt as the director. The corruption of the Illuminati was orchestrated by the belief in unworthiness; the belief in separation. The members became polarized against those whose beliefs differed from theirs. They began to feel they must protect themselves from others. The whole concept that something outside yourself can destroy your well being is one of the cornerstones of guilt.

The present-day Illuminati is a tangible, though largely unconscious, outpicturing of the guilt held in the minds and hearts of each individual in the world. If you look at history, you will see a thread running through every significant era - the rising and falling of civilizations. There have been many civilizations that have risen to a pinnacle of achievement, only to be brought down by corruption and greed. The present civilization is once again at the pinnacle and is just as surely falling prey to corruption and greed as the dozen or so civilizations that preceded it.

The Illuminati is the reflection of guilt within the mass consciousness of the people of Earth. Every time the people have risen up, they have been crushed by the "powers that be." Every time the powers that be have appeared to come into balance with the people, guilt has entered unconsciously and eroded the fabric of society. This was true in Pan, Lemuria and Atlantis, and it is true today.

One of the basic principles of guilt is that one does not deserve to remain happy, blissful, fulfilled or successful. The belief "It's too good to be true" has destroyed the dreams of virtually all souls at one time or another. As it says in the "Ode to Guilt" at the end of this chapter, *"You brought me down when I got too high."* "Too high" means attaining a high state of consciousness without the true understanding necessary to maintain it. If you do not have true understanding, guilt will invade your paradise and turn roses of ecstasy into ashes of despair.

The Mechanics of Guilt's Reflection

Unless you have been living in total ignorance and believing everything you hear and see in the media, you undoubtedly know by now that the Illuminati was responsible for all the major wars and human tragedies of our time.

These are the folks who brought you World War I and II, Hitler and the extermination of the Jews. They brought you Stalin and the blatant oppression of the Russian people. They brought you the banking system, with its cancerous growth: compound interest. These are the ones who brought you the KGB, the CIA, the NSA and the NSC. These dictators, through their puppet agencies of government, brought you the Federal Reserve System and the military industrial complex. They directed the assassination of President John F. Kennedy, Martin Luther King, Jr. and countless others.

If you believe there is no conspiracy, then you must also believe in the tooth fairy and Santa Claus. Who do you think put CIA agent George Bush in the White House? If you don't believe the Illuminati has had the American people by the throat, then I have a bridge to sell you. The Illuminati and its secret government have brought you drugs, drug wars, gang violence, smuggling of arms to support corrupt dictatorships, psychological and germ warfare, chemical and nuclear weapons, coups, revolutions, assassinations, attacks on the U.S. Constitution and Bill of Rights, and on and on and on.

So who is really behind the Illuminati? Not the Orions, not the Sirians, not even Lucifer. It's GUILT, pure and simple!

What guilt hasn't done for government covertly, it has done for religion overtly. Guilt brought you the crucifixion of Jesus. Its influence rewrote the Bible to portray God as vengeful and demanding of obedience. Every Sunday it brings you hell fire and brimstone sermons from a pulpit in a town near you. The whole concept of discipline has been corrupted by guilt. If you don't do this, if you don't do that, etc., etc., etc. Sex with guilt has brought you AIDS and every form of disease. It doesn't matter whether or not you believe there was a conspiracy behind the HIV virus. Whether it was guilt directly that destroyed the immune system, or the Illuminati through the introduction of HIV in vaccines by the World Heath Organization to control the population makes no difference. It still goes back to the central belief that something outside yourself can destroy your Godhood. And this belief originated because of guilt.

The Illuminati will fall. But the only way you and I can be truly free is to move out guilt. The time is at hand.

Journey Beyond the Beyond:
An Ode to Guilt

This is a letter. A very personal letter. When I began writing it, I did not know consciously where it would lead. I only knew I wanted to share it with you because I feel we may be on a very similar journey. I don't know if my journey will resonate with you, but if it does, I hope it makes your path a little easier and a lot more joyful.

In the past, my journey was often dominated by logical and mental understanding, with only occasional glimpses of the truth beyond words and ideas. Today, I will attempt to use words to go beyond words. Words are like a jumping off point to the unknown. There are many ways to step to the edge. One of my favorite is music. I listen to certain melodies that take me to dimensions beyond the beyond. Dimensions of boundless love, where illusions are but shadows with no substance.

My goal in sharing this letter is to remember, with you, what lies behind the veil. To get there, we will go through the primal mist of Creation back to the beginning of time. We will embrace our deepest feelings and yes, we will face the shadow once more. This letter is but one step on the path into the unknown, and a very important one. For unless we clear the cobwebs from our perception, we will not see clearly what lies before us.

In my own experience, I have come face to face with the shadow, which I am calling "guilt." I realize most people think of guilt as a specific feeling amidst a vast array of feelings and thoughts. However, in this letter, guilt pertains to an all-pervading sense of unworthiness, unacceptance and "make-wrong" of myself and Creation - a type of judgment that robs the soul of its life-giving energy.

For aeons, I have allowed this uninvited guest into the holy temple of my being. So this letter will resemble that of a lover explaining to his long-time partner his desire to end the relationship. And in the final conclusion, this will be seen as a true declaration of independence.

Dear Guilt,

We have been together a long time, you and I. Ever since my emergence as an individual soul, you have been there, unseen, guiding my evolution and influencing my decisions. But this will be no more. For now I see you as you are, guilt, in all your insidiousness, in all your disguises. Your words have been clever and convincing, but they ring hollow in my heart. For when I say I want to love all parts of myself, it is you who says I can't. It is you who have caused me to look at the "shadier" sides of myself with repugnance and disdain. You are continuously saying I must strive to be what I am not. And it is you who says I must mold myself according to your image of perfection. But no matter how hard I strive, it is never enough.

Guilt, it is you who have painted a picture of God as one who demands perfection. Your image portrays the Creator as a static, unchanging being sitting in an ivory tower, locked away in cool, rational detachment, beyond the baseness of human feelings and perception. A lofty ideal - with every attempt at reaching it but doomed to failure. For you can always think of something I should have done better, and you never forget my shortcomings.

Yes, it is you, guilt, who seeks to deprive me of the appreciation of the moment - the joyous, awesome, infinite moment, complete with its own natural perfection. In its place, you would substitute the gaudy sparkle of your illusory version of perfection.

Guilt, you have controlled me by fixing my mind forever on the future and assuring me that danger lurks at every turn and that I must escape it by going into the past. You are always comparing the present to the past and telling me to rely on past experience when facing new opportunities. You haven't allowed me to feel good about myself the way I am now, and you have always limited my happiness and pleasure by continuously reminding me of unfinished business.

You gave me the fear of loss and had me hold on for dear life to what I have, never allowing me to let go and open to something new. You gave me impatience with myself and others, telling me that if I don't grab the goodies while I can, I will lose out in the end. You gave me fear of failure and had me attach myself to positive experiences and refuse to look at the negative. You had me rigidly clinging to others for love and acceptance, while underneath my fear of rejection was your certainty that I deserved failure and rejection because of my inherent unworthiness.

You told me enlightenment is but for the few, and that it requires a lot of hard work and sacrifice. You told me sacrifice was a virtue and that if only I put others first in selfless service, somehow I would be favored by God. You had me believing it was selfish to think of myself.

Guilt, you had me create entire lifetimes where I was made wrong by others for my eccentric ways; where I was ridiculed and scorned for speaking my mind. You had me continually seeking the love and approval of others, while at the same time telling me I was not good enough to receive it. And you conveniently withheld the fact that my lack of acceptance from the world was a reflection of my lack of acceptance for myself.

You made my body wrong for its base desires and convinced me I would get lost in its demands, and so I did. You had me judge my physical appearance and the appearance of others. You had me judge my sexuality. You even led me to believe that God was not a sexual being. You made it difficult for me to survive physically because you judged the survival chakra to be less than Divine. You told me I must leave my body behind in order to ascend unto the Father's house. You made me ashamed of my physical vehicle and as a result, I began to get sick and experience aging.

You made my emotions wrong and convinced me I was nothing but a bundle of pain and negativity, and for a time, it seemed to be so. You had me judge my anger, rage, sadness, grief and fear. You taught me to deny my feelings in favor of your image of perfection. You taught me to deny, deny, deny until there was almost nothing left of my emotional body but a few fragments of despair and darkness.

You made my rational mind wrong for always analyzing and clinging to old knowledge, instead of giving it the love and understanding necessary to help it see beyond itself. It is only now that I realize you are not capable of love and understanding, and that is one of the reasons I am ending our relationship.

Guilt, you made my will, my desires and my power wrong,
and told me I shouldn't have free will, I shouldn't have desires,
and that it was wrong to use my power to bring beautiful things
into my life. I believed you and as a result, forgot how to use
90% of my powers. You convinced me I would hurt others if I
exercised my power and free will, and since I believed you, I
often did hurt them.

You gave me many roles to play throughout history. You
cast my role and made me forget I was but the actor on a stage
of my own making. You cast me the part of victim in a hostile
universe, and had me believing it had power over me. When you
tired of this, you cast me as an oppressor, living in the false
contentment that comes from having dominion over the "less
fortunate." You had me live as a martyr, and had me renounce
everything. You taught that poverty was a virtue, and as a
result, those of us who were the most compassionate had the
least amount of resources available to help the planet. You also
cast me as the slayer and the slain, the banisher and the
banished. When I led the church, you had me thrown out when
I got too close to the truth. You extolled the virtues of a kind
and loving God, and in the same breath, assured me I was a
miserable sinner with no hope of salvation.

Guilt, you brought me sorrow when I got too close to joy.
You made me forget when I began to remember. And you always
brought me down to earth when I got too high. You convinced
me that I was too idealistic, that Heaven was only a dream, and
that after my cosmic orgy of freedom would come the bill, due
and payable. And as long as I believed you, the bill always
came, right on time. You had me believing I must work for a
living and that it was not right to enjoy my life if others were
suffering. You led me to believe I was powerless to heal the ills
of the world; that it was wrong to think I could heal the sick and
raise the dead. At the same time, you told me I was not doing
enough to save the planet.

Guilt, I now realize that the most insidious of all the things
you taught me was that the dark stench of death would await me
when my earthly suffering was done. And you almost convinced
me that ascension was not real and that I would be stuck forever
on the wheel of reincarnation. You had me enter into a warm
womb where all my needs were met, than had me cast into a
loud, insensitive world where those with less wisdom than myself
told me what to do. When I was a helpless infant, you had the

world's authorities squash my will and destroy my natural sense of wonder and curiosity. I spent many lifetimes trying to get back to the womb, not realizing that physical birth was but a re-enactment of my emergence as a soul from the Mother of Creation. And you even told me that the Mother aspect of God was a figment of my imagination in a masculine universe. For a long time my soul longed to return to Creation's womb, but now I know that the womb of Creation is within me.

Oh guilt, now I see you for what you are - an empty, cold, dispassionate god who wanders through the void, seeking unsuspecting life to feed your parasitic urges. Although my words are hard, I have no malice towards you, for I know you thrive on anger. I merely see you as you are, and I no longer wish to receive your barren offerings. And so I'm letting you go. In my mind, I see you drifting lifelessly to the edge of my essence and out into the void beyond the manifest universe.

Yes, guilt, our relationship is over, now that I see your game, and it will be but an instant longer that I continue to go through the roles you set for me. For now I desire to bring my brothers and sisters with me to face you. They will see, as I see, that you are really nothing - an Emperor without clothes, without substance, and completely without love. My cosmic family is watching you as you play the last card in your deck of misery on Earth now, the card of Armageddon. And we are calling your bluff. For we have seen your final card and we are not fooled. Although we can hear the wailing and gnashing of teeth of your believers as they await the final deal, we are no longer afraid. For we are leaving your world of darkness. This is our beginning and your end.

And so I return to the task at hand - to reclaim the parts of me you kept hidden from the light, locked away from the sweet taste of freedom. And I embrace my limitlessness and pure innocence which, although long forgotten, was not and can never be completely destroyed.

And in the years to come, the path away from your abode will be lit by the Heavenly Hosts, and there will be no toll takers or bill collectors to plague those who walk through the doorway to freedom. From beyond the hell you made is the sound of ancient melodies, forever new, singing of love beyond our imagining. Each melody stands radiant in its completeness, and as I and my cosmic family align our bodies, emotions, hearts, minds and souls into Oneness, the music descends into our One being and the past drops lightly away into the nothingness from whence it came. And the fear of the unknown turns to excitement and enthusiasm as we embark together on this journey beyond the beyond. Goodbye, guilt!

Signed, your ex: Sal

CHAPTER 18
EARTH CHANGES

The following is a synopsis of my perceptions regarding the Earth changes we can expect between now and the year 2012.

Over the last 20 years, many predictions have been made regarding Earth changes. I have been prophesying for over 15 years, and the overall scenario has changed very little during that time. My prophecies tend to come true almost 100% of the time. However, determining a timeline for events is very tricky. In the lower four dimensions, free will determines when something will take place and how intense the experience will be.

Like many seers, my tendency has been to predict a more rapid rate of change than has actually been experienced by the mass consciousness. This is because visionaries tend to move faster in their own growth than the population at large. Yet the majority of Earth changes are a reflection of the mass consciousness and so those who stubbornly cling to old belief systems will tend to slow down the timetable for change. The present economic system has been propped up year after year by those who refuse to let it be transformed into something that can better serve humanity. Yet much change, particularly in Eastern Europe, has already occurred.

At the time of this writing, many geological changes were already underway. Volcanoes and resulting climactic changes were occurring in many parts of the world. The latest word from the Divine Mother (as channeled through the author) suggests that upheaval on Earth will continue to accelerate through 1996.

Early in this book, I defined several models of reality. I would like to review one of these models now as a precursor to what I am about to say.

From a higher consciousness point of view, "levels" of reality is a meaningless concept; however, on this plane, the concept is helpful in explaining the process of evolution and transformation taking place on Earth. For the sake of simplicity, we will call the three levels relevant to Earth changes the third, fourth and fifth dimensions. The basic laws governing each dimension are as follows:

3rd Dimension: The earth sustains us. We must create a clean environment and ensure adequate distribution of food and water in order to survive.

4th Dimension:	We create our own reality. If we think thoughts of peace, harmony and abundance, that will be the reality we create.
5th Dimension:	We are our brother's/sister's keeper. We are one. We must unite as co-creators of Heaven on Earth.

From a purely third-dimensional perspective, things look pretty bleak. Due to elements of fear, greed and overpopulation, the present economic systems are rapidly depleting Earth's remaining natural resources, and without fourth and fifth-dimensional influences, humans could be nearly extinct by the year 2012, through massive food shortages, disease and cataclysms caused by environmental degradation. Souls choosing to remain in the third dimension would exit Earth and take up residence on another third-dimensional planet.

From a fourth-dimensional perspective, the world is a reflection of our thoughts and beliefs. If we remove all thoughts of fear, greed, scarcity, lack and disease from our minds, we will create a world of peace and plenty. However, the only way to ensure global peace and harmony is for each one of us to heal our minds and think positive.

Because of free will, it is highly unlikely that everyone will go along with this. Consequently, the fourth dimensional world of 2012 could look like Heaven to the positive thinker and hell to the negative thinker. Heaven and hell cannot really coexist, however, because the criteria for creating true Heaven comes from an evolved consciousness; i.e., a fifth-dimensional perspective. The Earth, as a conscious being, has decided to eventually become a fifth-dimensional world. Therefore, those souls creating positive and negative fourth-dimensional worlds may ultimately create a splitting of the present world into two distinct planetary environments - one for those with primarily negative thoughts and one for those who are envisioning peace.

Fourth-dimensional entities often shrug off the downtrodden aspects of society with phrases like "It's their karma, they created it" and will attempt to encase themselves in a bubble of light that excludes other realities. This is a necessary step in the evolution from the third to the fifth dimension, but if we stop here, a likely scenario for the world of 2012 will be small, isolated communities (havens of peace and plenty) living in self-sufficient environments in a world torn apart by the negativity of the masses.

From a fifth-dimensional perspective, we are all one organism, expressing through different bodies and personalities. This means I am the starving child in the third-world country (or the U.S. for that matter), I am the political leader making decisions, I am the common person (whatever that means), etc. Therefore, by integrating (uniting) the various parts of myself, I (we) can evolve into the higher dimensions of peace and unity together.

The fifth-dimensional perspective is where love and compassion are born, and hence, real transformation. The fifth dimension is where the 100th monkey theory takes effect. (Read "The Hundredth Monkey" by Ken Keyes, Jr., Living Love Books.) Each time one individual awakens to his/her loving, compassionate self, it simultaneously affects the entire world in ways we may not even be aware of.

The Hopi prophecy is depicted on a petroglyph which represents the timeline of humanity. The symbols include a line with four human figures standing on it, followed by a junction where steps are shown leading to Heaven, a spiral is shown descending into the Earth and a fifth figure is shown continuing beyond this point on the original line.

The first four figures represent the first four worlds, or major civilizations of the Earth (Pan, Lemuria, Atlantis and the present). The stairs leading to Heaven represent the "chosen ones" who ascend into the fifth dimension at the close of the fourth world (2012 A.D.). The downward spiral represents those who choose to remain in the third dimension by refusing to align with the Mother, thereby perishing with the changes. The fifth figure on the timeline represents the new world and new Earth created by those who evolve into the fourth dimension and remain on the Earth.

As is so eloquently portrayed by the Hopi inscription, an accurate prediction of the future involves looking into the time track for all three of the dimensions and seeing where people are in the dimensional continuum. At present, it appears that approximately 80% of the world population is operating from third-dimensional awareness, 20% from the fourth dimension and less than 1% from the fifth dimension. However, as "A Course In Miracles" states, it only takes one completely enlightened being to change the whole world. In addition, there are many thousands of helpers from higher realms assisting in the evolution of this planet.

Since free will makes it almost impossible to give exact dates for future events, I will not attempt to do so here. However, if the majority of beings on the Earth are evolving into the fourth dimension, it would stand to reason that the fourth-dimensional scenarios would be the most likely to take place. The influence from the fifth dimension could help increase the number of individuals evolving from the third to the fourth dimensions. In fact, by 2012, fully 50% of Earth's population could be living in the fourth dimension.

However, even in the fourth dimension, it is still possible to create negativity, so realistically, half of this 50% could still be living in a world of scarcity and destruction. So what does this all boil down to? Well, the 50% still living in the third dimension would probably leave the Earth (through whatever means), 25% would be living in a hellish world created by their own negative thinking, and 25% would be enjoying peace and plenty. It is also possible that the 25% enjoying life could be cooperating with the 1% co-creating Heaven on Earth from the fifth dimension. So it appears that 20 to 25 percent of the Earth's current population will be part of the New Earth, the Golden Age, the millennium of peace.

I believe in miracles, and I know the Universe is a place of perfection, even in the chaos. And I know that each one of us is capable of evolving beyond "survival consciousness" (the third dimension). I also know we can heal our fears and negative beliefs and create positive ones (fourth dimension) and awaken to our spiritual Self (fifth dimension).

The way to ensure the best possible future is to awaken to our fifth dimensional selves and look upon the Heaven within. To do this, we must stop identifying with third and fourth-dimensional realities. As we have said before, the nature of higher dimensions is that they contain the lower ones. Therefore, if we are identified with the fifth dimension, we have access to all information contained within the third and fourth, but we are viewing it from "on high." In other words, we don't have to give up the things of the lower dimensions, we simply expand our awareness to encompass them, and we keep on expanding until we are no longer identified with them. And there's no limit on how far we can expand!

It is vitally important, if we wish to create Heaven on Earth, that we do not buy into the fear-based realities currently being perpetrated on Earth. The best way to do this is to clear our own issues so we do not attract a negative reflection. However, for those who are just beginning to clear their issues, or for those of us who feel overwhelmed by them at times, I've included some "last resort" methods of psychic protection in the Appendix. As previously mentioned, psychic protection is appropriate under acute circumstances, such as when you are already under psychic attack by negative entities, energy or thought forms. Once you are shielded, then you can focus your attention on clearing your personal issues so you won't need to rely on psychic protection in the future.

A Parable on the Story of Creation

One of the best ways to describe the indescribable is through parable, metaphor and allegory. The following story uses modern day issues to illustrate what might have happened at the beginning of Creation, and what will most likely be happening on Earth in the days to come.

Cosmic Children of Dysfunctional Parents

Not long ago, I could have been burned at the stake for a story like this one. So I'll apologize in advance if I kill any sacred cows, step on any toes, or ruffle any feathers.

I admit to being a little eccentric. In fact, I appreciate those who are willing to be a bit crazy and off-the-wall because it helps me break up old beliefs and thought forms.

Many of us, if not most, were brought up in dysfunctional families. Even if there were no outward signs of distress and no substance or sexual abuse, we were more than likely wounded by our parents' lack of self-esteem and lack of experience raising children. Well, I'm going to suggest that the problem goes back further than a few generations. I think perhaps it goes back to everyone's original parents. No, I'm not talking about Adam and Eve. This goes back long before that. Could it be that the Heavenly Father and Divine Mother themselves were dysfunctional?

Before you write me off and turn the page, consider this: they would have had the most difficult parenting job imaginable. Being the first parents, they wouldn't have had anyone to seek advice from; no role models to follow; no babysitter to take over when they wanted to be alone; and no Dr. Spock how-to manuals. What's worse, according to some Creation stories, the Divine Mother gave birth to every soul in the universe. Now that's a lot of mouths to feed!

So what kind of relationship did our cosmic parents really have? Well, I believe it was rather rocky. My version of the story goes like this:

It seems the Father had His own ideas on how Creation should unfold, and He wasn't a very good listener when the Mother voiced Her opinions. (Sound familiar, ladies?) The Mother's ideas were just as valid as the Father's, but it seemed She had a problem with self-confidence and let the Father have

His way most of the time.

Well, the more the Father dominated things, the more hurt and rejected the Mother felt. She began to doubt Her equality with the Father, and it certainly didn't look like They shared the load equally. He would be out having a good time exploring Creation, while She would be left worrying about the children's needs.

Then one day They had a terrible fight. He wanted everything to be light and happy, but She didn't feel that way, and He accused Her of spoiling the party and being too emotional. He had held His un-Godly feelings in for so long that when they did come out, He lost control and decked the Mother!

Well, She wasn't going to take that kind of abuse, and so She moved out. Unfortunately, many of the children thought it was the Mother's fault that their parents couldn't get along, and they blamed the Mother's emotional nature for creating the problem. So most of the children decided to stay with the Father, and, feeling the need to be super-responsible after all His gallivanting around, He couldn't refuse. So the Mother and Her small entourage moved to a tiny planet far away from the Father where She could live without His domineering influence. This planet eventually became known as Earth.

Meanwhile, the Father raised 90% of the children, and so naturally, they took after Him. Many came to despise the Mother and denied their emotional nature in favor of the Father's cool, rational detachment. They felt they had to control the feminine aspect of themselves, and invented all sorts of rules and procedures for proper self-expression.

Later on, many of the Father's children came to Earth and, with their domineering natures, took over the more feminine race that was evolving there. The Father's children set up civilizations that worshipped law and order and the masculine principle. The Mother retreated into the depths of the planet to escape the cold cruelty of the unbalanced souls who proliferated on Her surface. The Father's children, in their hatred of the Mother, treated Her with little or no respect. They raped Her land, poisoned Her air and water, and imprisoned Her children in rigid, authoritarian schools and churches that were set up to mold them into the Father's image of perfect obedience and intellectual supremacy.

In the meantime, and unbeknownst to the Father's children, the Father Himself was busy mending His ways. Being the first man, He didn't have any men's therapy groups available and no CODA meetings to attend. And so it took awhile for Him to realize the error of His ways. When He finally forgave Himself and the Mother, and reached out for Her, He discovered that She was still angry at Him for the abuse He and His children had heaped on Her and the Earth.

By now, the Father's children had grown quite arrogant and tyrannical, and the Father Himself was becoming displeased at their behavior. While He realized they were a mirror of His own attitudes, He also knew they would have to heal along with Him in order to stay with Him. He appealed to His children to stop abusing the Mother, but most of them wouldn't listen. Finally, the Father and Mother could take no more abuse from the children and told them to either treat Mother Earth with respect, or leave Earth.

By this time, the Mother had regained enough trust in the Father that She decided to respond to His desire to get back together. The separation had caused both of Them much pain and heartbreak.

When the Father had hit the Mother in their fight, the Mother had fallen into the third dimension and become trapped there. The Father had gone to the seventh dimension where His Celestial Heaven was. Now that they were re-uniting, they decided to compromise. He would descend to meet Her, and She would ascend to meet Him, in the fifth dimension.

They sent out invitations to the grand reunion. Souls responded from all over the Universe, but to Their dismay, only a small fraction of Earth's children answered the invitations. The Mother began preparing Her body (the Earth) for this great occasion and instructed Her children to put on their best cosmic finery (light bodies).

The children realized they had a lot of healing to do. They had to forgive their parents and themselves for all the suffering they had experienced as children of dysfunctional parents. They had to embrace both their masculine and feminine sides and balance themselves in love and understanding. And as they did, they began to experience a joy they had never known before, and they filled their hearts with their newfound radiance and went forth to embrace their cosmic parents.

CHAPTER 19
THE GODS OF DENIAL

We have discussed the separation and looked at the root cause of it. Now let us follow it through to its logical conclusion.

Separation seems to be a case where one chooses, from a high level of being, to go from godhood to total darkness and then gradually work one's way back up along a spiral path. Perhaps this is not entirely true, however.

Suppose the pre-separation state, Paradise, the Garden, or whatever you wish to call it, was not true godhood, but only a plateau on the path of learning for an infinitely evolving and expanding God. It is more than just that God isn't finished with us yet. God isn't finished with Himself. Could it be that God is still learning the lesson of denial?

We see this lesson being played out on so many levels, over and over again. Here is an example:

A soul is evolving. As he/she grows in awareness (we will use "he" for now), he gains greater and greater understanding and hence, greater and greater power and creativity. With this awareness comes greater responsibility.

This soul can see that light is expansive and darkness contractive. Because the soul's awareness has become expansive, the soul makes the determination that expansion is more desirable than contraction. He then begins to prefer the light to the darkness. This is all fine and dandy - until the preference becomes a demand; an addiction.

Now the darkness has become unacceptable and the soul seeks to go beyond it. And here is where the problem begins. The soul has become mesmerized by the light and starts to believe he has evolved farther than he actually has. He begins to deny the darkness and believe he has transcended it. He is afraid to admit that he still has unenlightened aspects. So he projects an image of enlightenment and becomes attached to that image, not realizing that he has separated out the darkness and split it off from the rest of him. The darkness goes into denial, where it continues to create unconsciously. Feelings of fear, anger, grief and rage begin to build up inside.

The soul's will, or feeling self, holds more and more of the denied darkness until the feelings become unbearable and must be expressed somehow. But the soul is in a dilemma. He has become attached to his image of enlightenment. He has projected this image out into the world and thus taken responsibility for healing the multitudes. He has become a teacher, a guru, or a great leader, and the people look to him for the truth, expecting to see the embodiment of it in his being.

His will, now feeling desperate, begins to create situations in the outer world designed to reflect back to the soul his unresolved issues. It tries to get his attention by drawing unpleasant situations that bring up "negative" feelings. But the soul believes he shouldn't feel that way, and especially shouldn't express it. After all, he prides himself on being "beyond anger" or "beyond fear." And he doesn't want to let his followers down. So he continues to expand spiritually while his will suffers. Situation after situation occurs that evokes his negative feelings. And time after time he stuffs them.

I'm sure you've heard the expression "the higher they climb, the harder they fall." Well, sooner or later, the feelings catch up with him and the soul snaps. His great power is released in a fury of unresolved emotions and he creates a monumental disaster. Whether it be guru sex scandals, or wars in the Heavens, destruction is the result.

It is my belief that the gods of religion and mythology were souls who had evolved into a state of godhood but had not completed their will (emotional) issues. Finally, they released a torrent of "hell fire and brimstone" down upon the Earth when they could hold back no longer. I believe that God Himself has had to learn this lesson.

The more we evolve, the sooner we catch ourselves on the path of denial, and the less negative buildup there is before the release. Although holocaust still seems possible in the near future of Earth on one level, I do not believe things will be that severe. Why?

We've already done it in the past and each time it has been less destructive than the previous time. Of course, we are talking about the major cycles within the spiral of evolution. Each loop in the spiral is a cosmic cycle of approximately 26,000 years. The destruction of Maldek (the planet that once existed where the asteroid belt is now) happened approximately 520,000 years B.C. (or 20 cycles ago). The destruction of Pan was around 260,000 years ago (or 10 cycles ago). The first Atlantean period ended in destruction around 130,000 years ago (5 cycles). Lemuria was destroyed around 50,000 B.C. (2 cycles ago) and the second Atlantis sank around 23,500 B.C. (1 cycle ago). Each of these events happened at the end of a cosmic cycle, and each was less severe than the previous one.

With Maldek, a planet was blown apart. In Pan, virtually the entire surface of the Earth was made sterile, but the Earth remained intact. Lemuria and Atlantis had numerous survivors. And now, at the end of the current cycle, we appear headed for another shakeup. But I believe up to half of humanity could survive this one.

Of course, there are many variables. The big question is "How much denial is present in the will? How much rage has built up in the Divine Mother? Will She release it in measured doses, or all at once? Our Mother Earth is the collective will of humanity and all life forms on Her. Are enough of us embracing our denied wills to prevent a holocaust?

The Mother is very angry at the abuse She has received. We need to allow Her to express by allowing ourselves to express. We need to lay aside our lofty image of enlightenment and be real about what we really feel. No more pretending we are "beyond it all." We are not, as we are about to find out.

CHAPTER 20
BUILDING YOUR
CRYSTAL LIGHT BODY

I have made many references to the process of ascending into the fifth density light body, so I hope this chapter will clarify many of the questions you might have. This is a rough illustration based on information received directly through my higher self. It is by no means complete, since the complexities of the "master template" are beyond the scope of this book.

From a right-brain perspective, we simply need to be receptive to the incoming energies of the fifth dimension and just allow the process to unfold. However, there do appear to be many distinct steps to this transformation, and different experiences during each step. I have divided these steps into six parts, as follows:

(1)   Purging of old consciousness - integration of Original Cause

(2)   Alignment of the four "lower" bodies (i.e., Body, Emotions, Mind and Heart) with Spirit

(3)   Reception of light activation codes

(4)   Reprogramming of DNA (cellular restructuring) and initializing of the "master template."

(5)   Conversion of carbon-based to silicon-based physiology

(6)   Dimensional/density shift (ascension)

1.   Purging of Old Consciousness - Integration of Original Cause

This is the hardest step, but the most important. That which must be purged can be summed up in three words: judgment, denial and guilt. Contrary to what many "New Agers" would like to believe, virtually all of us are still heavily influenced by this infamous trio. Much of what we have accepted as truth is really a collection of beliefs held in place by judgment, reinforced by guilt and made invisible by denial. This is why I devoted the entirety of Chapter 17 to these conditions.

If you remember back to Chapter 4, we stated a core belief system heavily supported by the New Age: "God is perfect, unchanging love." While this may be part of God, my understanding is that God is also evolving and expanding moment to moment, and that since we were created "in the image and likeness," God is also healing and integrating judgment, denial and guilt. In other words, all of life is a reflection of God.

The cause of all denial is "make-wrong" - i.e., not accepting ourselves unconditionally in the moment. The most heavily denied part of ourselves is the emotional body - we don't accept whatever we're feeling moment to moment. We then either judge the feeling as being un-spiritual, thus reinforcing the denial, or we allow the feeling to express, but then feel guilty for expressing it. Guilt dissipates energy and prevents us from having enough vibration to integrate Original Cause. Integration of Original Cause means understanding, on a feeling level, exactly what took place at the time of our individualization as souls emerging from the Godhead. Until judgment, denial and guilt are understood, everything we think, say, do or believe takes us further into separation from God.

I suggest you re-read Chapters 3, 4 and 17 to reinforce your understanding of Original Cause.

2.   Alignment of the Four Lower Bodies with Spirit

Although we have looked at many systems of thought regarding levels, chakras and bodies, I will speak here of the physical, emotional, mental and heart levels. These correspond to the first four or five levels of awareness, depending on which model you use. (Refer to Chapter 11 if you need a refresher on models.) The term "lower" here does not imply any judgment that any of these levels are less than Spirit.

To review, the physical level corresponds to the first and second chakras (survival and procreative functions). The emotional body pertains to the third chakra (solar plexus), is the seat of the will, and deals with power, intuition, receptivity and desire. The mental body embraces the fifth and sixth chakras and deals with beliefs, ideas, concepts, communication and imagination. The heart level deals with the fourth chakra and represents the collective life experience of the individual soul, as well as the balance point of unconditional love and acceptance.

[AUTHOR'S NOTE: There is a reason why I keep repeating certain concepts periodically.   We need to reprogram our minds to be able to accept the idea of integration, and repetition accelerates this process, so please bear with me.]

The triune nature of God is love, wisdom and power (which corresponds to heart, mind and will).   To be ready to receive the light activation codes (Step 3), these bodies must be aligned with the physical body.   Most spiritually evolved people have aligned the mind and heart levels, but still believe they must deny the body and emotions.   My understanding is that death is a detour on the path of evolution and that we are meant to evolve all of our lower bodies into the higher dimensions.   Complete alignment means that all levels have clear communication with one another and are functioning as a harmonious whole.

3.   Reception of Light Activation Codes

This is the process of drawing light into the cells of the body in preparation for mutation of the genetic structure (Step 4).   Light activation is created automatically when the four lower bodies are aligned.   The process is accelerated by Divine Intervention in the form of assistance from light beings, evolved ETs, angels, etc., and by healing practices such as meditation, bodywork, rebirthing, yoga, visualization, vortexes, sacred sites and group focus.   It is also being accelerated by Harmonic Convergence and 11:11.   The use of pyramids, crystals, Pleiadean disks, multiple-wave oscillators and radionic devices can also help; however, use of these devices before alignment of the four bodies can be dangerous, since the devices may speed up evolution of each body disproportionately (i.e., the bodies in least alignment may not be able to "catch up" to the more evolved ones.)   Further preparation may include purifying the diet and improving exercise.   It is highly recommended that one restrict the intake of alcohol, caffeine, sugar, tobacco and red meat, although each person needs to follow his/her own inner guidance on this.

4.   Reprogramming the DNA and Initializing the Master Template

The master template is the program that prepares the physical body to do the actual atomic conversion prior to ascension (detailed in Step 5 below).   To illustrate this process, I want to recount an experience I had in 1991.   In this visualization, a being of light came to me, and with my permission, inserted a crystalline implant in my solar plexus.   I was informed that within the next several weeks, my body would undergo restructuring and atomic conversion. I then saw, through Universal Mind, a biocomputer program being activated to prepare the body. This program was very complex and included things like how to regulate hormones to counteract rapid environmental changes, and how to adjust digestion and elimination during the conversion process, etc. I was informed that I might begin experiencing strange bodily sensations, and I did have a change in my hearing shortly thereafter.

5.   Conversion of Carbon Atoms to Silicon Atoms

I was informed that the actual conversion from a carbon-based to a silicon-based life form would begin sometime between November 1991 and January 1992, and would complete around the year 2012. My rudimentary understanding of the chemistry involved is as follows (this is over-simplified):

Carbon has two orbits of electrons, with four electrons in the outer shell. Silicon has three orbits of electrons, also with four electrons in the outer shell. To create silicon from carbon, new electrons must be introduced into the atom and original electrons must be "excited" into a new orbit. New electrons will flow into the atoms from the electromagnetic fields of the Universe. As the energies coming into Earth continue to increase in vibration, a "critical mass" will be reached where the EMFs become strong enough to introduce electrons into the atom, thereby exciting the existing ones into the new orbit.

The actual crystallization of the light body takes place as follows: Carbon-based life forms receive oxygen and exhale carbon dioxide (i.e., $C + O_2 = CO_2$). Silicon-based life forms receive oxygen and exhale (or in this case, radiate) silicon dioxide (i.e., $Si + O_2 = SiO_2$). The resulting product, SiO_2, is pure crystal (an equivalent of quartz). Silicon, being a semiconductor, and quartz, being a natural transmitter, are capable of receiving and radiating various electromagnetic frequencies.

6.   Dimensional/Density Shift (Ascension)

As the silicon light body continues to increase in vibration, opening to more cosmic energy (from the fifth dimension), it begins to become luminescent, refracting and reflecting light through its many facets. The auric field around the light body becomes highly charged, creating a mini-vortex or helix. Some visionaries have described this as a spiral of white light, and I recently saw a photo showing a column of this spiralling light ascending through the aura of a person. In "The Keys of Enoch" (J.J. Hurtak, Academy of Future Science) and other writings, the "ascension flame" is described as pyramidal in shape, and as it rises, it becomes compressed into the capstone of the pyramid, eventually merging in a "singularity" (infinitesimal point) at the top of the capstone.

This could be equated to the wormhole phenomenon in physics (the interaction of white holes and black holes). It is believed in the new physics that wormholes are doorways to another dimension, and it would seem to follow that the mini-wormhole created by the ascension flame would translate the physical body into the next dimension as well. It would also seem that the 11:11 doorway (which occurred on January 11, 1992) could be the collective creation of many thousands of individual souls - a giant wormhole, perhaps held in place by those already on the ascension spiral.

In summary, I am reminded that all of life is a reflection. What we see in the world reflects our inner state. So when we see something that triggers fear or anger, we know we have an opportunity to heal and bring into alignment a part of ourselves. The key to ascending into our crystal light bodies is to learn to lovingly accept all parts of ourselves, both within and without. I look forward to sharing ascension with you.

Soul Fragmentation and Physical Immortality

Now I will take a look at two more rather complex subjects regarding the evolution of the soul. There are several phases of soul experience on this planet:

(1)   Emergence from the Godhead

(2)   Separation and descension into the third dimension (Earth)

(3)   Reincarnation and fragmentation

(4)   Spiritual ascension

(5)   Integration and physical immortality

(6)   Physical ascension and evolution to the next spiral of existence

1.   Emergence from the Godhead

In the beginning, there was One being. From within that One, a soul was formed.

Figure 20.1 - Souls in God

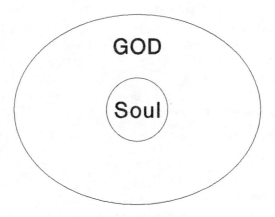

Like a single cell which divides, and divides again, this single soul began creating new beings out of its original essence. Each new soul was a hologram of the original - a piece, and yet, a whole, individual being. Although these souls were divided into individual beings, they were not separated.

Figure 20.2 - Souls Divide

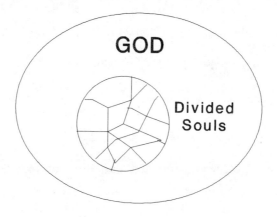

Within each soul was the blueprint for evolution - from a one-dimensional microcosm all the way to a complete, multidimensional universe of its own creation.

2.   Separation

As Creation progressed, these complete, individual souls eventually broke away from each other and fell into unmanifested space. This experience was very traumatic and formed the basis for the separation, or "fall from grace."

Figure 20.3 - Souls Separate

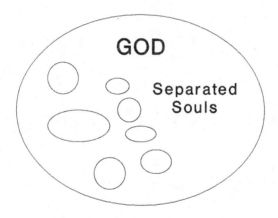

Many of these separated souls began their evolutionary spiral on Earth or similar planets. Within their hologram of the Source, they discovered their essence to be made up of many aspects - a physical form, an emotional vibration, a mental preceptor, and many other "subtle" bodies.

3.   Fragmentation

The trauma of the descent into matter caused these soul aspects to split and shatter, so that by the time they began incarnating on Earth, they were almost completely unconscious. Soon after this, the density and duality inherent in the third dimension caused further fragmentation in their inner being.

Figure 20.4 - Souls Fragment

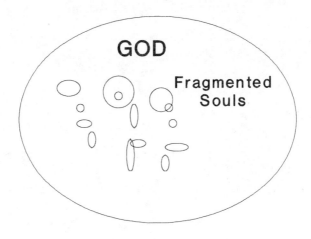

Many soul fragments became identified with the body, and the other parts went into unconsciousness. Because the body was "cut off" from the rest of the soul, it was unable to regenerate itself and eventually began to decay and die. The remaining soul essence then had to create another vehicle for its earthly experience, and thus, reincarnation began.

Figure 20.5 - Souls Reincarnate

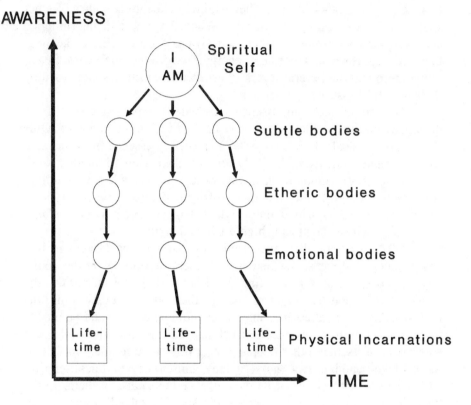

AWARENESS

I AM — Spiritual Self

Subtle bodies

Etheric bodies

Emotional bodies

Life-time Life-time Life-time Physical Incarnations

TIME

For many lifetimes, the soul was unaware of its spiritual nature and spent most of its time between embodiments in the astral dimensions. Eventually, the soul gained enough awareness of its "higher" spiritual nature that it was able to ascend out of the body at death and go to the spiritual realms between incarnations.

4.   Spiritual Ascension and Resulting Fragmentation

During ascension through death, the spirit rises out of the body. However, more is left behind than an empty shell. Although the body decomposes, much of the soul essence that has not evolved sufficiently to ascend along with the spirit remains in the lower density planes of the astral dimension. This essence thus experiences separation and fragmentation from the higher spiritual essence of the ascending soul.

Pieces of this separated essence wander through the astral planes, appearing as ghosts, apparitions, poltergeists, astral entities and various energy forms. In its desire for unity and integration, this essence seeks to attach itself to other incarnate beings, often cohabiting bodies of other souls and intermingling its essence. When persons with intermingled soul essence come to me or other clairvoyants for a reading or healing, they often appear with a mosaic of energies woven into their auric fields. Often there may be several layers of essence from other souls clouding their own true essence.

Not all of the soul essence attached to a person comes from discarnate entities. Often, souls may be "corded" to one another while still in the physical. In other words, a "piece" of essence from one soul has fragmented out from the body and attached itself to another soul. One of the most common ways this occurs is through sexual union. Another is through family bonding. Many people confuse this type of union with higher spiritual union which happens after ascension into Oneness by whole, complete, highly evolved souls.

When a person dies, the essence of that soul may fragment into any number of dimensions (and time frames) depending on the soul's level of consciousness at the time of death. If in the meantime, the essence left behind has attached itself to the bodies of other souls, the reincarnating spiritual essence may enter into a new body and be unable to re-connect with the essence left behind. In this case, the soul could meet parts of itself in other people during this new lifetime. In fact, if the soul has enough awareness, it may consciously or unconsciously attract people with pieces of its own essence embedded in them, in the hope that it can reclaim this essence. If a soul is evolved enough, it can magnetically attract its own essence back from other souls, either when that soul's body dies, or when that soul "cuts the cord" of psychic attachment.

There are many more aspects of soul fragmentation, involving past lives, future lives and other dimensions. This becomes quite complex and hard to understand with the intellect, and so I will not go into it any further right now.

5.   Physical Immortality

It is possible to maintain an eternally youthful body for any length of time - a body that never gets sick and that is immune to environmental degradation. However, to attain this state of immortality, several things must occur. First of all, one must let go of the belief in death. It's amazing to me how many spiritually aware people still believe the body must age and decay. Although I personally may not wish to remain in my present body forever, I certainly want to have a choice about if and when I die. To believe death is inevitable is to buy into a belief system that has incredible power, due to the fact that 99% of Earth's population believes in it.

The truth is, all that is necessary to stop the aging process is to balance the incoming life force (regeneration, or centropy) with the dissipating life force (degeneration, or entropy). Degeneration occurs not only because of the belief in death, but also because of the misalignment of the self through soul fragmentation. To achieve physical immortality, it is necessary to reclaim enough fragments of soul essence to increase the regenerative power sufficiently to offset the dissipation of life force that occurs naturally in the third dimension. This is much like the process of levitation, which requires enough anti-gravity force to balance the natural third-dimensional law of gravity.

How does one reclaim lost soul essence? By bringing the higher spiritual energies more into the body. In other words, being more present in your body. Most of the time, we are scattered around the universe, having left pieces of ourselves in other lifetimes, other dimensions, or in other souls. In a sense, we are quite literally living in the past or future. Psychologically, this is because we are in denial of "what is" in our lives. Most of what has fragmented out of us are parts of ourselves we judged to be undesirable, and we thereby cast them out of our awareness. By removing awareness from the parts of ourselves we didn't like, we withdrew the life force from those areas, and we no longer have enough magnetic energy to keep those parts connected to the whole, thus creating fragmentation. When a lot of the self is denied, eventually the denied parts outweigh the parts receiving acceptance and the dissipation of life force exceeds regeneration, causing decay and death.

When we learn to accept the parts of ourselves we have denied, we create enough magnetic energy to reclaim the parts that have fragmented. When enough aspects of self are reclaimed, the body becomes light enough to transcend the third-dimensional principles. At this point, full ascension is possible.

6.   Ascension into Oneness

Although the details of ascension were explained earlier, there is one more point I want to make. When a soul has become fully integrated and begins to ascend, the original separation at the beginning of Creation is reversed. Individual souls begin to merge into "group souls" or "oversouls," which then merge into "master oversouls," etc. If two parts of a soul have become polarized, they may rejoin as "twin flames."

This chapter has touched on the true nature of the soul, and I hope it stimulated you on your path to wholeness.

CHAPTER 21
A BLUEPRINT FOR THE
21ST CENTURY

Enlightened Living

This chapter explores a possible future for humanity based on the practical application of the ideas in this book. In order to bring about an enlightened society, we must learn to balance the spiritual and material aspects of ourselves. This is often quite difficult because most of us are conditioned to be either spiritual or materialistic.

For example, Western religions teach us to put others first, turn the other cheek, lay up our treasures in Heaven, and sacrifice worldly comforts for the rewards of the hereafter. In Eastern religions, we are taught to give up desire and attachment and just be open, in the moment, to whatever happens. We must surrender to God. "Not my will, but thy Will, be done."

On the other hand, we are encouraged to be more materialistic and to use our creative powers to manifest our heart's desire. We are taught to take back our power from others, be assertive, stay practical and down to Earth, and take care of ourselves instead of always focusing on others. We are told to have goals, objectives and plans for acquiring prosperity, and to "move our feet" instead of waiting for God to do it for us.

Obviously, to live as a spiritual being in the material world, we must have balance between these polarities. To do this, we must heal the denial of desire and emotion present in the spiritual scenario, and the guilt and obsessiveness present in the physical scenario.

In the 21st century, neither the ascetic martyr nor the greedy capitalist will flourish. To live abundantly, we will be asked (by Mother Earth and our own higher selves) to simultaneously do what is good for the whole and what is best for the self. Unless we heal our religious guilt, we will be forever sacrificing ourselves for others. And until we find true inner security, we will continue to clutch and grasp at material objects while squandering our natural resources. The world I've outlined on the following pages arises from a collective consciousness that is centered in the spiritual while focused outwardly on the material. This is only one scenario; for additional ideas, I recommend the novel "2150 A.D." by Thea Alexander.

21st Century Society

The technology exists right now to elevate the standard of living for every person on Earth to the highest level imaginable: superb education, preventative health care, cultural refinement, elegant architecture, a cornucopia of nutritious food, and an opportunity to travel anywhere and everywhere. Add to this a lavish lifestyle of comfort, therapeutic relaxation combined with exciting, creative work and an abundance of social connections. And this is only the beginning. From here, we can evolve beyond the wildest fantasies of science fiction.

The way to bring about this utopian society by the 21st century is not idle dreaming or some impossible formula that will take millions of years to implement. Many of the items mentioned above were present at the height of some of the civilizations of the past. However, humankind was not evolved sufficiently to be able to maintain these high standards. The basic ingredient necessary to provide everyone with an elegant, artistic lifestyle is to create the proper inner environment by making education and personal growth the highest priority in life.

In some parts of the world, this must start with the basics - redistributing and redefining the wealth and resources to provide basic physical items of food, clothing and shelter. It is very difficult to educate those who are starving or dying from disease. Once the simple "creature comforts" are provided, people will be open to real education. Real education teaches about the nature of the self and the relationship of the inner to the outer reality. Everyone's reality is different, but the processes are universal for personal self-mastery. We all must face our fears, cultivate a keen sense of alertness, move out guilt and replace it with a good conscience, suspend judgment in favor of discernment, question our belief systems, and quiet our minds enough to see truth. Through patience and diligence, this can be taught. It requires a strong commitment and a realization that a society is only as good as the consciousness of its constituent parts.

Once education is refined and brought to everyone on Earth, it must be tailored to each individual. Some people learn quickly; others need more time. Programs must recognize this and at the same time stress group cooperation, sharing and feedback. Children will not be taught to mold themselves into an existing society; society must mold itself to the needs of the children. Most children being born today are reincarnating souls with a high degree of mastery from previous lives, or they have descended from higher dimensions to assist in the transformation of the planet. It is important that they have teachers who can recognize their level of soul awareness and remind them of their greatness.

Religions must also be transformed. The Mother's New World Order will see to it that old beliefs die quickly and efficiently. Those who insist on holding on to religious bigotry (defined as "mine is the only way to salvation") and old images of God (as a being who demands obedience and perfection) will not be part of 21st century life on Earth. These people will be unable to sustain the vibration necessary to ascend with the Mother. Other old world institutions will also be history. Banks, insurance companies, and many medical facilities will no longer be needed. Lawyers will decrease in number by more than 90%. Industries tied to old modes of transportation and construction (such as oil and hydrocarbon chemical companies) will be transformed. Over half of the current international corporate structure is involved in some form of managing economic assets. In place of these financial institutions will be an energy exchange system. Each person will give and receive energy units based on his/her real contribution to society. "Real" contribution will be defined as that which enhances the life of one or more people directly or indirectly. With proper distribution of basic resources, each member of the community will begin with material abundance and then add cultural refinements based on his/her level of creative contribution to the whole. No one, no matter how much or how little he/she contributes, will go without basic food, shelter, clothing, education and medical care.

Technology

The next great technological revolution will involve utilization of the electromagnetic field that permeates the physical universe. The power and energy available from this field is millions of times greater than that available from fossil fuels. Proper use of EMFs will create no environmental pollution and will eliminate technologies involving nuclear fission or fusion that create imbalances in the environment.

One form of EMF technology is radionics. Radionics harnesses the electromagnetic currents of the ethers and directs energy to and from a desired location. While radio and TV accomplish this in a rudimentary way, radionics goes far beyond simply beaming signals from here to there. The EMF waves can be concentrated, amplified and shaped in ways that not only transmit wireless power over great distances, but can transcend the limitations of third-dimensional space and time. Radionic devices will replace the more crude forms of electronic power supplies, and coupled with optics, lasers and other modalities that manipulate electrons, will be the basis for automated and computerized technology on a scale approaching that of the human brain in complexity.

There are some good books on EMF and radionics. Tesla, Einstein and others did much research, some of it available for interpretation. The Illuminati has done its best to suppress most of the advances in radionics introduced to the general public. Many of the devices would render petroleum and nuclear power obsolete overnight, thus eliminating dependence on multinational corporations. This would restore power to the people, a concept unpalatable to capitalist and communist regimes.

To help stimulate your own creative process, I will briefly mention a few details of EMF technology. To ensure the protection of those involved in EMF research, I am purposely leaving out certain details. However, there are branches of the Illuminati currently working with these ideas, and some of these technologies are already in use behind closed doors.

One simple energy generator (radionics device) involves construction of a pyramid with a dome enclosed in the base. The dome contains the EMF current and the pyramid directs it into the apex (capstone). A cylindrical core of highly conductive material is then inserted in the center of the dome/pyramid, and a Tesla coil is wrapped around it ascending out through the capstone. DC voltage is then applied to the coil. WARNING: You must be thoroughly familiar with analytical geometry and wave theory to successfully "oscillate" this device, and improper operation can be disastrous.

Another device involves passing a current through superconductive material and beaming the resulting energy into an electromagnetic field, thus partially collapsing the field and bending space and time. This is one of the modes of propelling interdimensional spacecraft of the Confederation. The energy generated by this device creates a "null zone," a sort of EMF vacuum, which then "sucks" the craft into the zone and pops it out into another area of time and space. The size and location of the EMF and the amount of current in the superconducting device determine where and how fast the craft will be propelled and how much time and space will be collapsed. Using this process, a craft can travel to distant stars in a matter of hours or days.

How is this possible? Imagine, for a moment, a piece of paper with two points spaced a few inches apart, Point A and Point B. In third dimensional time and space, the shortest distance between the points is a straight line. Now if you take the paper (which represents 3-D space) and bend it until Point A touches Point B, you have a pictorial representation of the above process.

The superconducting device can be created very easily if you have the right equipment. Superconductors are formed at room temperature by creating a resonant field in the atomic structure of certain elements. To move the craft to a desired location, you must calculate the EMF "signature" of that location and "dial" the superconducting device to that signature. Every planet, star and being in the universe has its own unique signature and can be accessed if you have the proper soul alignment.

Many radionics devices have been under test by scientists and the secret government for years. The Philadelphia Experiment was one example. There are numerous others. The higher ETs would love to share their technology with humanity openly, but unfortunately there are many who would use it to the detriment of others, and so it is carefully concealed. By the year 2000, much of this technology will be out in the open.

Agriculture

In addition to hybrid crops of fruits and vegetables, there are types of microalgae in production today that, properly farmed, can feed up to 10 billion people from just a few thousand acres of ponds. These algae are extremely rich in protein and nutrients and can supply up to 50% of the dietary requirements for humans. The algae reproduce incredibly fast in the right environment. If every country had one algae farm strategically located, distribution would be no problem. Electric vehicles using high-density solar cells would be the primary surface means for transporting the algae. Non-polluting high speed electric trains would carry the algae to every major city within hours of production.

If you are wondering how you would stomach algae, rest assured that, like the many derivatives of soybeans, a variety of tasty, colorful foods could be manufactured from the algae. The replicating device shown on the TV series "Star Trek - the Next Generation" is not that far off, either. Although microalgae can be tasty in their raw form, through genetic manipulation, holography and computer enhancement, this green, slimy food could be made to look and taste like the finest delicacies of modern cuisine.

Housing

Geometric construction (pyramids and geodesic domes) is the way to go. New ultralight, ultrastrong materials made from rare elements and technologically altered common elements would provide superb insulation and comfort. Natural solar materials would provide heating. Ultra low-current lights embodying full spectrometry would replace incandescent and fluorescent bulbs. Computers and robots would do most of the repetitive construction work.

Communications

Communications can be instantaneous, even to distant stars, using EMF signals passed through time warps (the same principle as spacecraft travel). Prior to reaching their destination, the signals are time-reversed to correspond to the time of transmission. Obviously implied here is the ability to send signals into the past or future, a feat which has already been witnessed on Earth by those in contact with civilizations from the past or future.

Social Structure

Basically, political decisions would be made by popularly elected committees of spiritually advanced beings. Each community would have a central meeting place with "council" gatherings on a regular basis. All individual housing units would encircle the communal area. Police would be kept to a minimum - with basic needs met, crime would be almost nonexistent. Education that encourages expression of emotions and teaches listening and speaking skills would make social encounters lively and fulfilling. New forms of entertainment involving virtual reality and holographic visual games would excite the children. Spiritual sexual practices would make artificial birth control methods obsolete. Basic understanding that each person is responsible for his/her own creation would make lawyers a thing of the past; without blame, they would not be needed.

Does all this sound like a pipe dream? Not if the Mother has her way. And I assure you she will. Yes, the phoenix shall rise from the ashes of pain and struggle. Even as I write this, new revelations are coming daily about life on future Earth. Vibrations are accelerating so quickly that even this book could be obsolete by the time it is published. We are only limited by our beliefs. And the time has come to lay our limited beliefs aside and realize we can create paradise.

If I sound idealistic, consider that I am not living in an ivory tower. Actually, I have very little solid evidence of outer security in my life. At the time of this writing, the so-called real world appeared to be crumbling around me, banks were failing, unusual storms were raging on parts of the planet, and the sunset was red from a recent volcano in the Philippines. Even here in Sedona, where the mountain air is still relatively clean and pure, people have been hurting financially, and many have been experiencing immune system disorders and emotional turmoil. By the time you read this, these situations could be a lot more acute...and yet, everything is in Divine Order. I do not claim to be apart from these events, and I do not claim to be anyone special. Information is freely available to anyone willing to receive it from the Universal Mind. So I encourage you to join me in creating the world we all dream of.

CONCLUSION

As I mentioned at the beginning of the book, the information herein is by no means complete. Nor can I guarantee it is 100% accurate. Probably some chapters have touched you, or at least gotten you to think.

Making the changes necessary to live life on the cutting edge is not easy; but the very fact that you are alive at this time in history suggests that on some level you made the choice to "go for it."

To assist you in putting these ideas into practice in your life, you can write the author for a list of classes and events related to the material. Or you can start a study group in your area to discuss the book and the techniques.

I will be traveling and teaching seminars for the next few years, and if you are interested in sponsoring a seminar in your area, let me know. I certainly can't guarantee I will be available to come to your area, but as I've always said, if you desire something strongly enough, you can make it happen.

Regardless of what steps you take next in your life, remember one thing - who you are is always greater than anything you can conceive. I leave you with that to meditate on.

GETTING INVOLVED

There are many of you out there involved in projects designed to bring about the world I've outlined in Chapter 21. If you're not yet sure how you want to participate, you can begin by contacting the author. In addition to the projects mentioned herein, I am engaged in the following programs designed to assist in the transformation of Earth:

(1)   Classes, seminars and lectures

(2)   Books, articles and tapes

(3)   Musical events and recordings

(4)   Psychic and spiritual readings

(5)   Rebirthing and other healing modalities

****

For more information, please contact:

>   Sal Rachele
>   P.O. Box 73
>   Sedona, AZ 86336

APPENDIX A
REBIRTHING

What is Rebirthing?

Rebirthing (or conscious breathing) is a simple, yet powerful method of self-improvement that has been practiced by yogis for thousands of years. In 1974, Leonard Orr developed a "circular" breathing rhythm that often triggered memories of birth and early childhood, hence the name "Rebirthing." A few years later, Jim Leonard (no relation to Leonard Orr) refined the technique and called it "Integrative Rebirthing" and later, "Vivation."*

Rebirthing has been experienced by hundreds of thousands of people, usually in private sessions with an experienced trainer, or in groups or on their own. Some of the benefits they have received include: greater energy and vitality, relaxation and stress reduction, awareness of emotion as "energy-in-motion" (i.e., energy patterns in the body), unconditional acceptance of feelings, strengthening of the immune system, purification of the body and mind through better circulation of oxygen in the blood, and integration of body, mind and spirit.

What is integration and what causes it?

For most of us, birth was a very traumatic event. Recent studies have shown that newborns are highly sensitive to the thoughts and feelings of parents, relatives, doctors, nurses and others in the birthing environment. In addition, in conventional hospitals, the shock of bright lights, separation from mother, and the cutting of the umbilical cord often make the first few breaths feel like a near-death experience. As a result, many of us "shut down" our aliveness by suppressing this traumatic event.

Our experience of birth can give rise to some basic unhealthy beliefs about life in general. For instance, suppose our parents wanted a boy and we were a girl, or our mother was in a lot of pain during birth, or our parent's relationship was rocky, or they felt the new child would be a financial burden, etc. We may create beliefs such as "the world is an unloving place" or "nobody wants me" or "life is a struggle" or "I can never get enough (love, money, etc.)." All this creates a great deal of fear and inhibition.

Fear inhibits breathing. The next time you feel fear, notice how your breath tends to get shallow and erratic. Breathing fully and freely releases the fear, which, according to researchers, has actually become stored in the cells and tissues of the body over the years.

---

* Vivation is the tradename of Jim Leonard and the International Vivation Community.

Conscious breathing need not be painful. Pain is caused by resisting the flow of life energy. If we focus without judgment on the sensation of pain and stop resisting, it simply feels like very intense energy. By shifting our mental context, this energy can be experienced as pleasurable and empowering.

The Five Elements

My approach to Rebirthing combines the basic method, originally taught by Leonard Orr, with the integrative process created by Jim Leonard. Jim's five steps of Integrative Rebirthing are as follows:

1) "Circular" breathing. This is a full, free, relaxed and somewhat rapid breath, with the inhale and exhale connected; this means no pause between them (i.e., inhaleexhaleinhale, etc.) Fear-based breathing is usually short and erratic with a long pause between the inhale and exhale. I guide the breather gently into the circular rhythm and remind him/her to keep the breath connected throughout the session.

2) Deep relaxation. During a session, one often experiences tingling and a feeling of electrical current flowing through the body. In the early days of Rebirthing, this would often escalate into hyperventilation, partial paralysis and tetany - rather painful side effects caused by forcing or holding back on the exhale. I often stress the idea of completely letting go with each exhale, much like a sigh of relief. Even so, a certain amount of tingling and pleasurable energy sensations can be expected. As the session progresses, more life force (prana) enters the body. The tingling is the body's own resistance to the increased flow of energy. If one relaxes into this increased prana, the resistance decreases and the body adjusts more easily.

3) Awareness in detail. Most of our lives we have suppressed uncomfortable feelings, or labeled and judged them. In Rebirthing, we are encouraged to explore feelings as they come up, much like a scientist examines a phenomenon. However, instead of using the intellect to analyze, we let the breath do the work. I often ask clients to "breathe into" an area of the body that is uncomfortable or in pain. This is a way to consciously dislodge suppressed material from the body. In fact, we have learned that suppressed feelings are literally locked into the cells, and the Rebirthing process "liberates" these cells.

4) Integration into ecstasy. Jim Leonard defines this as the ability to shift whatever is happening into a positive context. It is possible to become ecstatically blissful about anything that occurs. Simply

accepting each experience without having expectations is all that is necessary to achieve integration. It is important not to judge your experience. Some clients have reported breathing for an hour with "nothing" happening. Yet I often encourage people to look in a mirror after a session. It is not uncommon for someone to look 10 years younger and have a shiny radiance about them - even if "nothing" happened.

5)   Do whatever you do. This hokey-sounding step was devised for those who are too serious and too worried about doing it right. The important thing is to lighten up, do the five elements, and surrender to the process. If you start to space out and forget to breathe, its okay. I will usually bring you back gently to the process. Letting go is the key to integration, not trying too hard.

What is an individual session like?

During a breathing session, one usually goes through a cycle where levels of fear and suppressed emotions become integrated and the person becomes more comfortable and accepting of the body, emotions and life in general. This can be sudden and dramatic, or a more gradual process spread out over several sessions. Some people report experiencing memories from birth and early childhood. For others, there simply comes a point when the breath becomes easy and natural, and the initial tension and body sensations subside. This is the point of integration.

It usually takes about an hour to complete an "integration cycle." When a cycle is complete, the body relaxes and breathing becomes easy and effortless. The first few sessions take place on dry land while lying on your back. Later, sessions can take place in warm water. Warm water Rebirthing tends to be much more intense than dry land Rebirthing.

For more information about Rebirthing, I recommend "Rebirthing, the Science of Enjoying All of Your Life" by Jim Leonard and Phil Laut (Trinity Publications).

APPENDIX B
PSYCHIC PROTECTION TECHNIQUES

1.   Invocation of Archangel Michael

Visualize a bright blue light descending down through your crown chakra and enveloping your entire body. Imagine yourself encased in a bubble of this blue light extending three or four feet in every direction. Slowly repeat Archangel Michael's name several times with conviction. It may be helpful to have a picture of Michael available to gaze upon. Visualize Michael with your inner eye. See him filling the space around you with his protection. Ask Michael to clear any and all negative vibrations from your psychic space. Ask him to return all energies that are not part of your soul to their rightful places. Thank Michael for his assistance. Repeat the above procedure until you begin to feel a sense of calm.

2.   Invocation of Jesus Christ

Visualize a white light and call on Jesus Christ in the same manner as the Michael invocation.

3.   The Solar Cross

Visualize a brilliant white cross with a circle around it. Place this solar cross around your body. You may want to visualize your arms as the horizontal and your body as the vertical leg of the cross, with the circle around your auric field. Project this image on to any person, place or object that is attacking you psychically. Do not force any entity to accept the cross; just project it into the auric field of the entity and allow the entity to accept or reject it. Keep the cross in your own auric field at all times during this process.

4.   Showing an Entity the Light

Visualize an entity that needs help or is harassing you, and imagine yourself in conversation with that entity. Call forth the Light of God as a bright gold or white light and point the entity in the direction of the light. Tell the entity about the beauty of the light and encourage the entity to investigate the light. Be as loving and gentle as possible, but let the entity know that the light may be able to assist it in its growth.

5.   Cord Cutting

Visualize a person or entity whom you feel is attacking you. Ask your higher self to show you any cords that may be attached between you and the entity. Imagine you have a pair of golden scissors especially for cord cutting. See yourself using the golden scissors to cut any and all cords connecting you to the attacking person or entity. See the cords fall away each time you cut. See the entity drifting slowly away from you. Lovingly bless the entity and wave goodbye to him/her.

6.   Chanting

There are several good chants for protection. I recommend the following (to be repeated over and over):

"I AM THAT I AM"
"I AM LIGHT, LIGHT, LIGHT. I AM LOVE, LOVE, LOVE."
"I AM A BEING OF VIOLET FIRE, I AM THE PURITY GOD
    DESIRES."
"KADOISH, KADOISH, KADOISH, ADONAI SABAYOTH."
"I INVOKE THE POWER AND PRESENCE OF GOD."

7.   Grounding

Visualize a rod of light the diameter of your body extending out through your feet (if you are standing) or out through the bottom of your spine (if you are sitting) and extending into the center of the Earth. Gold is the preferred color, but if you are having extreme difficulty staying in your body, use red. This technique closes your aura and contracts it to within a few inches of your body.

8.   Forcefully Dispelling Entities

CAUTION: This technique should only be used by experienced adepts and teachers, and only when the entity has willfully violated your space.

(1) Stand and face your adversary. (2) Call forth your own God presence through the top of your head. (3) Invoke the Heavenly Father and visualize gold light. (4) Call forth your own Goddess presence through the bottom of your feet and visualize silver light. (5) Extend your hands, one at a time, in the direction of your adversary. (6) Send a beam of white light out through your fingers and direct it into the auric field of your adversary. (7) Make appropriate noises and sonics as you direct the energy. (8) Forcefully sweep the entity out of your auric field with rapid gestures and move him into the light. (9) Vigorously shake out your hands into the Earth and ground yourself.

In the unusual event that this is not sufficient to move the entity out of your space, visualize the solar cross as you make your gestures. If necessary, call forth Archangel Michael to assist you.

APPENDIX C
MEDITATIONS

Meditation Methods

The following are some of the methods used to quiet the conscious mind and allow access to the subconscious. Although all these methods work, some will be more appropriate than others at any given time. The soul has a natural urge to align body, emotions and mind, and if you do not consciously move toward alignment, it will often trigger experiences that move you in that direction. Meditation is a natural method of moving toward alignment.

You can force your mind to become quiet, but this often has serious repercussions. Therefore, I've listed the more forceful techniques for quieting the mind in the "least desirable" section. Consult the Glossary for more complete definitions of these terms.

<u>Most Desirable Techniques</u>

1.   BODY RELAXATION:

Body awareness
    Becoming aware of each area of the body; focusing attention on each part, one at a time. Flexing and tensing body parts, often in concert with the breath.
Rebirthing
    Connected breaths with emphasis on the inhale
Primal breathing
    Rapid breathing with emphasis on the exhale
Kriya breathing
    Measured time intervals between each inhale, pause and exhale
Kundalini breath/breath of fire
    Short, rapid breaths followed by a long breath or pause
Yoga (hatha, Iyengar, raja, kriya, etc.)
    Body postures (asanas), breathing rhythms, chants and meditations
Meditation
    Sitting in lotus posture

2.   MIND RELAXATION:

Alpha-theta induction (see Appendix D)
Hypnosis
    A generic term for deep relaxation through the process of induction (see alpha-theta induction)

Hypnotherapy

Hypnosis led by a therapist with specific therapeutic objectives--often combined with other therapies

Guided meditation

Similar to hypnosis but with no induction process - often involves visualization methods

Silva Mind Control

A two-weekend course in training the mind through meditation and self-hypnosis

Alchemical hypnotherapy/reframing

A technique whereby one regresses to early childhood, mentally re-creates early experiences, and aligns the inner child and other aspects of the self.

Regression

Any technique that takes one back to early childhood or past lives

3.   EMOTIONAL WORK:

Forgiveness

There are many forgiveness techniques, including statement of forgiveness affirmations, listening to tapes of forgiveness affirmations, saying forgiveness affirmations in a mirror, visualizing oneself forgiving another, etc. The "forgiveness diet" involves saying or writing a specific forgiveness affirmation 70 times a day for seven days in a row.

Gratitude

Closely related to self-acceptance, this involves being grateful for everything in life and realizing the perfection of the learning process. One technique involves writing a list of things one is grateful for.

Self-acceptance

Any technique that focuses on accepting and allowing everything moment to moment

Gestalt

Stepping outside the self to view objectively what is happening--can involve dialogue with imaginary characters or with parts of the self

Energetics

Various methods of cathartic release directed by a therapist

Somewhat Desirable Techniques

1.   EXTERNAL STIMULI:

Music

The following pieces of music are recommended for achieving certain meditative states of mind.

Classics   Pachelbel: Canon in D - for joy and transcendence
               Barber: Adagio for Strings - for releasing emotion
               Wagner: Prelude to Lohengrin - contact with angelic realms
               Rachmaninoff: Piano Concerto No. 2 - love and romance
               Gregorian chants - contact with spiritual self

New Age   Jarre: Oxygene - contact with the cosmos
               Lynch: Deep Breakfast - contact with joyful self
               Bernhardt: Atlantis Angelis - contact with etheric self
               Quinn: Open Secret - contact with the soul
               Ernst: Dreamflight III - contact with loving heart
               Rachele: Infinite Peace - meditation and bodywork

Sensory experiences
   Includes isolation tanks, laser light shows, sound and light chambers, etc.
Brain/mind machines
   Goggles, headphones and probes that induce alpha-theta brain waves
Walking in nature
   A tried and true, inexpensive technique that can work wonders for
   stressed-out psyches
Karma yoga
   Conscious work, mindful tasks

2.   REPROGRAMMING:

Affirmations/autosuggestions (see Appendix D)
Creative visualization
   Using the imaging faculty of the mind to create a particular reality
Prayer
   Asking God or the higher self for assistance
Invocation of spirit beings
   Calling forth archangels or spirit guides to assist

3.   CONCENTRATION:

Chanting mantras
   Several examples are given in Appendix B, "Psychic Protection
   Techniques"
Fixing the mind on an idea
Imaging a desired outcome
   A form of visualization
White light meditation
   Another form of visualization
Chakra meditation
   Focusing on each chakra, one at a time

4.   MIND GAMES:

Impossible questions
   Tricking the mind by asking questions that cannot be answered with the
   intellect. Examples: "Who Am I?" "Who is watching this process?"
   "What is between thoughts?"
Negation/negative awareness
   "This is all illusion. I will go beyond it." Seeing the falseness of a
   situation.
Total detachment
   Refusing to identify with anyone or anything

5.   PARTNERS:

Looking meditation
   A process whereby couples sit facing each other and gaze into each
   other's eyes
Tantric exercises
   Sexual or nonsexual energy meditations involving Taoist practices
The withhold process
   A process whereby each partner expresses withheld communications
   while the other partner listens passively (in a form similar to "Something
   I've been withholding from you is... Another thing I've been withholding
   from you is..."
Encounter processes
   Specific questions designed to help partners get to know each other
   better. Examples: "Something I'm feeling right now is..." or
   "Something I like about you is..."
Mirroring
   A communication process whereby one partner mirrors what the other
   has just said. Example: "I heard you say that you're feeling
   vulnerable..."

Least Desirable Techniques

1.   Drugs (hallucinogenic, mind-altering, legal or illegal)
2.   Losing oneself in mind-absorbing activities (TV, etc.)
3.   Sensory deprivation (forcing oneself to go inside)
4.   Forcefully controlling the mind in any way

Involuntary Techniques

Trauma; shock; sudden change

APPENDIX D
A SAMPLE ALPHA-THETA
MEDITATION WITH
AUTOSUGGESTIONS

1.   Self-Hypnosis - Alpha-Theta Basic Induction

NOTE: This exercise requires two people (a hypnotist and patient) or a cassette tape and player. Do not use while driving. Words in brackets are for the convenience of the hypnotist and are not meant to be spoken aloud or into the tape. The autosuggestions given can be combined in various ways for different inductions. The double asterisks (**) indicate a place where the therapist should pause for a few seconds before resuming.

[Part 1 - introductory statements]

In this meditation your body and mind will be relaxed, yet you will remain awake and alert, sensitive to your feelings, aware of your thoughts, and in touch with the sensations in your body. When you are deeply relaxed, your intuitive mind is able to perceive the world in and around you with great clarity. While you are in a peaceful, relaxed state, you will be able to use the control center of your brain to reprogram undesired negative beliefs and integrate burdening emotional experiences from the past. At all times during this meditation, you will be in full control of your mental faculties. You will be able to accept or reject anything I say and you will be able to use the information which is most beneficial to you and humanity. I will be giving you statements designed to increase your awareness and creativity and I will be guiding your breath to help you relax.

[Part 2 - body relaxation and breathing]

Check to see that you are in a comfortable, erect sitting position, feet on the floor, hands resting in your lap, and eyes closed. Take a deep breath, letting the exhale out naturally and connecting it to your inhale. **As you continue to breathe, feel yourself becoming more and more relaxed. **Take another deep breath and as you do, focus your attention on your left foot. **Feel your left foot relaxing. **Now focus on your right foot. Allow it to relax. **You are becoming more peaceful, quiet and aware. **Take three deep breaths and as you do, let your calves loosen up and let any tension drain out gently through the bottom of your feet. **Now, be aware of your thighs. Let them relax. **Focus on the feelings in your buttocks and pelvis. Notice the sensation of sitting and allow your weight to rest naturally in the chair. **Let *a peaceful, warm feeling extend throughout your entire lower body. This state of peace is healthy and beneficial. **Now give your attention to your abdomen. Allow it to let go of any tension. Let your stomach muscles relax and go limp. **You are continuing to listen to my voice and you are awake and aware of what is being said. **Take another breath and as you do, imagine a wave of relaxing, tingling warmth going up your spine, starting with the lower back and continuing to the back of the neck. Let any stiffness in your back go out peacefully. **Allow your chest to relax. Let each exhale be like a sigh of relief for any tension there. **Imagine a warm, radiant glow in the area of your heart. **Imagine a wave of peaceful energy moving through your shoulders, down through your arms, and out through your fingers. Let your shoulders drop naturally. **Ah! It is a wonderful feeling to be deeply relaxed. **Continue to breathe deeply, as you let all tension and tightness out of your neck, the back of your head, the top of your head, your forehead, your eyelids and your face. Let your eyelids rest naturally closed. **Now, let your entire body relax completely. Just let everything go and be completely at ease, completely safe, completely at peace.*

[Pause 10 or 20 seconds]

Relaxing your body and mind is very healthy. This calming and freeing of tension and stress creates more vitality and strength. Whenever you wish to relax and clear your mind, just take a deep breath, close your eyes, and allow your body to relax. Let any sounds or sensations around you add to your peace. Let any thoughts, any resistance, any doubt or fear go by without intruding on your peace. There is no need to try and control whatever is happening. Just notice it and let it be as it is. Accept yourself as you are right now. Let whatever is happening happen. You do not have to do anything. Just allow all concerns from the day, all thoughts of yesterday or tomorrow drift away gently and experience the freedom of being here now, just as you are. You are sensitive to your emotions, to the feelings in your body, and to any images or mental pictures. You are allowing the surface mind to become quiet so that your deeper, intuitive mind can work for you. By quieting your rational, analytical mind, intelligence can see thought as it arises and use it creatively to make your life more rewarding. Every time you enter a deep level of mind, it will be easier to quiet the surface mind and remain there without falling asleep. It is becoming easier and easier for you to breathe fully, freely and naturally. With each breath, you are becoming more awake and aware.

[Deepening process - induction]

Now, I would like you to visualize a 10-story building. **This building represents your consciousness, and the floors represent levels of mind. **Imagine yourself on the 10th floor of the building. This represents surface consciousness. **Now imagine yourself walking to the elevator. **You are pushing the down arrow to go down to the lower floors. **As I count from 10 *down to 1, you will descend one floor at a time. With each descending number, I would like you to visualize being in the elevator going down one floor. We will start on the 10th floor. With each descending number you are entering a deeper, more aware state of mind.* **10 --- 9 --- 8 -- *going down, going deeper --- 7 --- 6 --- 5 --- sounds around you help you go deeper --- 4 --- 3 --- watching the floors go by in your elevator --- 2 --- and 1.* **You are now on the bottom *floor. This floor represents a very deep state of mind, deeper than you have been in a long time.* **The door of the elevator opens now and you walk out. In front of you is a stairway going down into the basement. Begin walking down the stairs.* **Down, down, down...going deeper, deeper than before. [Pause 10 seconds] In front of you now is a long tunnel. At the far end of the tunnel is a light. Begin walking through the tunnel toward the light.* **You are getting *closer to the light.*

[Visualization process - Pause 20 seconds]

You are emerging from the darkness into the light, and you find yourself in a beautiful mountain meadow on a warm sunny day. Everything is alive and you can smell the freshness of the air. You can hear the buzzing of the bees, the sigh of the wind in the nearby trees; you can feel the sun on your body and the earth beneath your feet. As you look around you, you notice the blue of the sky, with a few fleecy white clouds. Take a deep breath and drink it all in. **You *are completely free, completely safe, completely at peace.* **Walk around in the *meadow, noticing the flowers, the grass, the wildlife. Find a comfortable spot in the grass and lie down, basking in the sun. You will remain there until you next hear my voice.*

[Autosuggestions - Pause 60 seconds]

The following statements are designed to help you increase your awareness and improve your creativity.

[General affirmations for when there is no specific topic]

--I am learning to live in greater awareness of myself and others. I use my creative abilities for my benefit and that of humanity.

--When I wish to solve a problem or become more aware of a situation, I will simply relax and allow my higher mind to give me the information I desire.

--Every time I enter a relaxed state, I will find it easier to remain there without falling asleep.

--Every time I enter this state, it will be easier to quiet the rational thought patterns of the surface mind. I find this necessary to gain insight into problems my intellect is unable to solve.

--My energy increases while in this state of mind.

--I am learning to use more of my mind and use it in a more positive way.

--I am able to receive information intuitively that is useful in understanding my life.

[Affirmations for reprogramming the subconscious]

--All positive affirmations penetrate deep into the subconscious mind and are in complete accord with my desire to be the master of my mind. I use these programs to create a happier, more fulfilling and beneficial life for myself and humanity.

--My mind is my humble servant. It allows me to function efficiently and intelligently in the world. It directs my actions in such a way as to bring me what is appropriate for my growth and well being.

--I am now aware of any programs, beliefs, concepts and past experiences that are blocking me from fully expressing my true nature, and I am using only those affirmations which help free me, and help me create what I really want.

--My body and mind are completely relaxed as I breathe and take in the life force. With each day, I find it easier and easier to relax, and my breathing becomes deeper, fuller, easier and more natural.

--I am now letting go of old ideas that no longer serve my interests, and I am open and receptive to new ideas and new opportunities.

--I am in touch with my subconscious mind. I use it to create positive manifestations. All negative thoughts and limiting beliefs are being replaced with positive, life-supporting ones.

--Whenever I wish to contact deeper levels of mind, all I need do is pause, relax, take a deep breath, and be aware of my feelings and impressions. I am then able to see the nature and structure of that which is responsible for my present situation.

--I am now able to easily go deep inside myself and bring all subconscious activity to the surface of my consciousness.

--Any negative, painful emotions that have been suppressed are now free to come to the surface of my consciousness where they can be integrated and expressed in the best possible way.

--I am now able to fully recall all aspects of my birth and early childhood feelings, thoughts and experiences.

--All positive affirmations have immediate results in my life.

--My mind is my humble servant, always directing me to my highest good.

--I am living in the here and now moment. Any attachment to the past, or projection into the future, is now seen clearly and integrated. (Pause)

[Affirmations for clearing old belief systems]

The following statements are designed to help you be more aware of the activity of the subconscious mind and to reprogram undesired negative beliefs into positive, life-supporting ones.

--I am learning to live in greater awareness of myself and others.

--I am learning to use more of my mind and use it in a more positive way.

--Everything I program into my mind is beneficial for myself and others.

--Every time I enter this state of mind it is easier to reprogram the subconscious mind.

--I am reprogramming my biocomputer for positive, life-enhancing results in all my affairs.

--I am being consciously aware at all levels of mind.

--I now perceive accurately the information I need for my growth and self understanding.

--I am freeing myself from beliefs that are no longer beneficial to my everyday experience of life.

--Every day it becomes easier to let go of negative thoughts and beliefs.

--I am now aware of all barriers and blocks to creativity.

--I can easily go deep inside myself and bring subconscious activity to the surface.

--I am letting go of old ideas and letting new and better ones in.

--My positive thoughts are powerful and produce immediate results in my life.

--I now see clearly the whole structure of fear, attachment and pain, and I take immediate steps to integrate these experiences.

--Negative thoughts and beliefs are now being replaced with positive ones.

--All painful experiences and mistakes are opportunities to learn.

--I am now able to fully recall all aspects of my birth and early childhood, and I am taking the appropriate steps to heal any traumas or negative experiences.

--I now see clearly all parental influences and I am releasing any parental programming that is not supportive of my life.

--I am now willing to look at the totality of myself.

--Every day it is easier to let go of the past and be in the present.

--I am aware that I create my own view of the world around me and that the conditions in my life are a reflection of my own consciousness.

--I now take full responsibility for creating my own reality.

--I am penetrating to the core of my being. I can see clearly all aspects of my self-image. I am learning to recognize the difference between who I am and who I think I am.

[Coming out of hypnosis - pause 60 seconds]

Now, I am going to count from 1 to 10. With each ascending number, you will be more wide awake and aware. You will be able to fully recall any and all information received while in a deep state of mind. You will feel refreshed and energetic, revitalized and rested. There will be no ill effects of any kind whatsoever from this meditation. 1 --- 2 --- 3 --- coming out slowly now --- 4 --- 5 --- 6 --- feeling wide awake, fully rested, ready to function in a normal waking state --- 7 --- 8 --- 9 --- and 10. Eyes open. Wide awake. Fully refreshed.

Autosuggestion Sequences and Affirmations

The following autosuggestions are helpful when dealing with specific life issues. They may be added to the autosuggestions in the alpha-theta exercise above, or used in place of them.

Money and Finances

--I love myself no matter how much money I have.

--Every breath I take increases my financial well-being.

--All ignorance, fear and doubt about money is now being brought to the surface of my consciousness and integrated.

--I am learning the appropriate lessons that enable me to act in a manner that ensures my financial success.

--I am now resolving all conflicts regarding money. I am free to enjoy life no matter how much or how little I have.

--I am a free and unlimited being living in the material world.

--Abundance is my true state of being. I now claim it and express it joyously.

--Money helps me express my spirituality in the world.

--I am aware that the manifestation of lack and scarcity in the present economic system is the result of ignorance and limited thinking on the part of those who create and maintain the system. The best way to overcome this is to release all limited concepts within my own consciousness.

--I am responsible for my present financial condition. I am not a victim of the system. If I don't like what I see, I can change my thoughts and personal reality in a way that exerts a positive influence on society.

--It only takes one enlightened being to change the world.

--I forgive everyone, including myself, that has ever hindered my financial well-being.

--I am now living in harmony with money and material things. I focus on financial matters only when appropriate.

--I now realize that money, like everything else, is divine substance.

--All my needs are supplied. I always have what I really need.

--I am one with Infinite Manifestation. I am abundance. I am success.

--People enjoy paying me for doing what I enjoy most.

--I deserve to be prospered for the services I perform.

--I use money in ways that support my growth and the growth of others.

--I deserve to enjoy my money. I spend it wisely. I am generous.

--I now penetrate all barriers, thoughts of lack, and seemingly unfavorable circumstances and allow the unlimited flow of abundance into my life.

--I'm now very clear on what to do to bring in a huge personal fortune.

--I am an open channel. My prosperity flows into the world in the best possible way.

--I have everything I need to be happy.

--I now decree that I am the master of my life, reaping total success and abundance in everything I do.

--I am now freeing myself of all blocks to unlimited wealth.

Relationships and Self-Esteem

--I am willing to accept others as they are without trying to change them.

--I express myself intuitively and spontaneously.

--I am learning to experience others intuitively from the heart.

--The best way to meet the right person is to be the right person.

--All my relationships contain lessons I need to learn. People tend to mirror my feelings about myself, and I choose partners that reflect my consciousness.

--I am freeing myself from relationships that hinder my growth by resolving issues within myself that hinder me.

--I am aware of anyone in my life who is acting out an aspect of myself or who represents a parent or sibling.

--I am able to listen accurately and give my full attention to people who are expressing themselves.

--The best way to help others is to help myself.

--I am gentle and patient with myself. I accept myself even when I appear to fail.

--I approve of myself. I have confidence in my abilities. I follow my intuition.

--I give myself what I want. I am clear on what I want and how to manifest it.

--I love everything about myself. I love myself no matter what. I love myself all the time. I AM LOVE. I AM INNOCENCE!

--I love all parts of myself unconditionally.

--I love myself completely, now and forever.

--I am making all the right connections to manifest my soul's desires.

--I am an unlimited and creative being. I can create anything I want. I now let go of struggle and open to effortless creating.

--I am consciously aware at all levels of being.

--I totally accept myself emotionally, here and now. I am whole and complete.

--I now let go of the ego's defenses and listen to the reality of my heart.

--I now let go of the past and surrender to my real self.

--I create miracles wherever I go, because I AM a miracle.

--I now forgive myself for each and every error or negative thought I ever had about myself, my parents, others, the world or the universe.

--I now forgive myself for every action, event and experience I've ever had.

--I am freeing myself of any parental influences that do not serve my well-being.

--Miracles are an abundant part of my life.

--I deserve to have beautiful, satisfying, loving relationships. I am now drawing open, sincere people into my life.

--I am attracting the kind of relationships best suited for my enjoyment and growth.

--I now receive assistance and cooperation from those beings necessary to bring about my desired results. I am supported and nourished in being myself.

--I don't have to perform or impress people in order to get attention. Being myself enables others to be more open and real in my presence.

--I am an expression of unconditional love, here and now.

--I always receive enough love and support. I am now willing to give myself the pleasure and love I deserve. I am creating a safe environment for others to give to themselves and me.

--I don't need to struggle and strive for love. It is already here because I AM LOVE.

--It's totally OK to feel the way I do. I feel good about expressing my emotions. I am honest and real with people.

--I'm OK no matter what I say or do. I'm OK even when I feel upset, angry, depressed or helpless.

--I am innocent now and I have always been innocent, no matter what happened in the past.

--I now correct all errors and misperceptions about myself and others.

--It's safe for me to open my heart. My openness and defenselessness is my strength.

--I am a beautiful, sensuous and compassionate being.

--I am beautiful, capable and lovable.

--Every day I love myself more and more. My love spreads to include everyone.

--I can love others unconditionally without taking on their energy and issues or making myself responsible for them.

--I don't need approval to be happy. I can be happy just by being myself.

--It doesn't matter what others say or do. I'm OK just the way I am.

--The more I give, the more I receive. I give and receive abundantly now.

--I now have enough time, money, energy, love and wisdom to accomplish all my desires.

--I am good enough.

Sexuality

--I am now willing to move through any barriers of ignorance, fear, guilt or jealousy so my sexuality can assert itself.

--I now express my sexuality in ways that stimulate my spiritual growth.

--I deserve sexual pleasure. I now enjoy a fulfilling sex life.

--It's OK to be a sexual being.

--It's OK to be alone. It's OK to be celibate.

--I am a healthy, sensual and sexual being, and I really enjoy making love and giving myself pleasure.

--I choose sexual partners who support my growth process and add quality to my life.

--I now express sexual feelings openly, honestly and appropriately.

--I'm OK whether I have sex or not. I am clear on what I want sexually.

--It's easy to ask for what I want from my partner. I am capable of giving my partner what he/she wants. I choose a partner who is realistic about what he/she wants.

--I am freeing myself from any and all parental attitudes, beliefs and programs about sex.

--I am now clear on all aspects of birth control, disease and abortion.

--I am a beautiful, capable and knowledgeable lover. I don't have to perform to receive approval.

Health

--I love my body and nourish it with good food and loving thoughts.

--I am now in perfect, radiant physical health.

--I love to express my spiritual nature through my radiant physical vehicle.

--All the cells of my body are daily bathed in the perfection of my divine being.

--I now let go of all limiting beliefs and habit patterns that dissipate energy and cause illness.

--I now use my intelligence to see and end all conflict within myself.

--I am freeing myself of all medical myths that portray illness and death as inevitable. My body is capable of permanent health and well-being.

--All aspects of my diet and lifestyle are now moving into alignment and harmony with my being.

--My built-in body intelligence protects me from harmful substances and environments.

--My body and mind are innocent and reflect my loving heart.

--I'm glad I was born. The universe rejoices at my physical presence.

--I always have everything I need to be happy.

Developing Creativity/Imagination

--I am now developing superior imaginative and creative abilities.

--My imagination is a powerful tool used by memory and intelligence to perceive information and create reality.

--I am learning to recognize when images are arising from memory and when they are coming as psychic impressions.

--I always use imaginative and psychic information in ways that are beneficial for my growth and well-being.

--I always respect the free will of others when I use my psychic and imaginative abilities.

--I am now developing my higher mind and psychic faculties to perceive information my intellect is incapable of perceiving.

--I am using my psychic and creative faculties to bring positive and harmonious things into my life.

Additional Techniques for Triggering an Alpha State

The following techniques are appropriate when you have very little time to meditate or are not in a quiet environment. They are most effective when the mind has already been trained in the standard Alpha-Theta meditations.

General Induction

1. To trigger Alpha, take three deep breaths, counting from three down to one with each breath. Relax the body completely as you do this.

2. Pass the left hand across the forehead to trigger Alpha.
   Pass the right hand across the forehead to recall information.

Problem Solving

1. Write the question or state the problem on a piece of paper and put it under your pillow before going to sleep. Trigger Alpha and say "by morning my question will be answered" or "I will see the solution to my problem." When you wake up, write the first thing that comes to mind on the other side of the piece of paper. Also write down any dreams you can recall. If you are unsuccessful the first day, try this technique for two more days. The answer should come by the third day.

2. Pour a glass of water before going to bed. Trigger Alpha, then state "the answer to my question/problem is in this glass of water." Drink half the water and then go to sleep. When you wake up, repeat the process and drink the other half. The answer should come shortly.

3. When recalling information, mentally project yourself to the time and place where the answer is or was, such as a classroom or library, or another's thoughts. Ask your inner guidance to show you exactly where to look in your mind's eye for the answer/solution.

Energy Meditation

The following meditation is designed to take you into a transcendental or expanded state of consciousness.

[Repeat the standard Alpha-Theta induction before continuing if you desire to get into a deep state of mind.]

You are completely relaxed. Now, be aware of your body. Imagine a pulsing, tingling current of energy moving through your veins, through your cells, through the atoms of your body. Imagine that this energy is very healing, cleansing and purifying. Let it permeate every fiber of your being with its *radiance. Imagine your entire body is immersed in a sea of vibrating, brilliant white and gold light. This light energy surrounds the body in an aura that protects you from all disharmony. Now, allow this aura of brilliant, healing energy to expand and include the space around your body, going out two feet in all directions. Now expand it further - out four feet from your body. Feel it merging and mingling with the people or objects nearby. Continue to expand this healing radiance until it fills the room with warm, vibrant, glowing brilliance. Allow all persons or objects in the room to be cleansed by this light. Now let it expand to include the entire building you are in. And now the entire neighborhood. ...**City...**State...**World...**Solar system... **The galaxy. **And now, the entire universe. **Imagine everything in the universe is now experiencing this soothing, peaceful, healing life-force energy. Let it fill every dark corner of your mind with love, life and vitality. This love and light is within and all around you, and you need only tune into it, feel it and let it shine.*

*   **Whenever you feel the need to heal, or let go of something inharmonious, just fill yourself with this light and love. Let it flow forth freely to illuminate all you come in contact with. You can project it mentally to people in stress or distress and envelop them in its protection.*

*   **Continue to feel this radiance expanding throughout the entire universe.*

*   **Now begin to bring it back into your immediate aura. Shrink it back down to the galaxy, the solar system, the world, the country, the state, the town, the neighborhood, the house and finally, the room. Feel it shrink down to within six inches of your body. Bring your awareness back into your body, back into the place where you are sitting [lying].*

[NOTE: If you used the Alpha-Theta induction to go into a deep state, use the coming out procedures before opening your eyes.]

*   Take a few deep breaths and open your eyes.*

Music Meditation

For this meditation, you need a peaceful, yet deeply spiritual piece of music. I recommend Pachelbel's "Canon in D" or Barber's "Adagio for Strings." Do not begin playing the tape until you are instructed to do so.

*   Find a comfortable position and close your eyes. Take a few deep breaths and let your body and mind relax. In this meditation we will begin with awareness of three primary dimensions of being - body, emotions and mind. Then, as the music begins, we will explore the deeper levels of being.*

*   Let's begin by getting in touch with the body. What is it feeling? Is there any tension? If there is any aspect of the body that does not feel in harmony, let the inharmony go, gently, as if a fog were burning off and being replaced with radiant sunlight. Envision the body as a vibrant, clear channel through which the life force moves unhindered. See it as a healthy instrument of peace, always serving you in the best possible way. Listen to it. Be sensitive*

to its messages. Find out what is going on inside it.

Now be aware of your feelings and emotions. Just let them be as they are. Let them reveal your inner state to you. They are your friends, your means of life expression. Let your feelings always be in harmony with your body and mind.

Be aware of the mind. If there are thoughts, let them come and go, like waves on the sand. See them for what they are - memories of days gone by, yet also the building blocks of future creations. Flow with the movement of consciousness. View it across the vast expanse of the mental universe. Let it reveal itself in all its complexities. Learn to be choicelessly aware. What is going on in this moment? Are you experiencing who you are, or are your images and memories of past experiences painting veils over your awareness? Look at the whole process of thought - the demands you place on life, the desires, pleasures, pursuits, expectations, ideals, hopes, worries, fears. Do not judge, condemn or resist this movement, but simply look; really look. Are you looking and listening choicelessly to reality, or are you limiting the impressions that enter your consciousness? Where is your awareness? Are you hanging on to yesterday? Are you afraid of tomorrow?

**Whatever is taking place, accept the reality you have given it. Can you accept yourself as you are, without trying to be something else? We all have our individuality, our uniqueness, but deep inside are we really separate?

[Begin music softly]

**It's time to go beyond illusions, beyond the endless conflict of desire, beyond the madness of the world, to the heart of your being, to your true essence. Let the music take you to the far shores of time and beyond. Be still, quiet, alert to your real Self. **We have often searched for truth, and occasionally have had glimpses of that unnameable state. You can realize this everlastingly loving state right now. You can be free of identification with the ego. Let go of all those petty concerns. Let go of yesterday and tomorrow. You can now be free to be one with all of life. You can receive true guidance and insight in all your affairs. You can express your emotions creatively and take proper care of your body. You don't need a teacher or guru to show you the way, for life itself is your teacher, and the inner voice is your guru. All you need is the passion, the energy of attention, the flame of awareness, to find out for yourself what is true.

[Music gets louder]

**Let go of the burden. Let go of all that you carry with you into this eternal moment. Let your beliefs, your concerns, your worries, fade into the distant past, which is as dead as last summer's leaves. Be innocent, free, unconditionally open to the new, the creative, the unknown. Let the light of intelligence penetrate the veils of fear and darkness, exposing their nakedness. See that they are really nothing. Look directly into the deepest recesses of

thought and see it dissolve into the emptiness from whence it came. Allow the grace of the divine within to swallow and consume all limitations, liberating your consciousness.

There is an incredible love within and it radiates out into the farthest corners of the world. You never need to feel isolated or separate from love, for you are love.

**Rejoice! You know who you are. You are as you have always been, a complete, pure expression of life. Feel the joy, the love that is not bound by thought, that is not of time, but just IS - complete, free, flowing through and beyond everything. Love has a limitless expression waiting to be shared by all who have wandered far from home. Your function is being fulfilled, you are in control of your destiny, you are no longer guided by unseen forces. You know, deep within you, that all is unfolding in perfection. Let your love flower and flourish as you take a moment to BE - be here now.

**You are free. Free of the pain and turmoil of the world. Free to spread your wings of pure spirit and gently leave behind the rocky road of sorrow and suffering. Wait no longer - the time is now! See the world through eyes of innocence, washed clean, purified, made new, whole, complete. Let the peace within envelop you as you celebrate the fragrance of rebirth. You are free, now and forever.

[Silent music meditation for several minutes]

[Coming out procedures]

10-Step Creative Thought Process

This process is designed to turn inner turmoil and conflict into creative problem-solving.

Begin by picking an area of your life where a conflict or problem exists.

1. Name at least three characteristics of the situation (physical appearances, emotional reactions, etc.)

2. How do you feel about this situation? What is your reaction to it? (describe emotions and body sensations)

3. What are your favorite statements about the problem? What do you tell yourself most frequently?

4. What would you like to see happen? What is your desired outcome?

5. How certain are you of reaching your desired outcome?

6. What do you really want from this situation? What is your ultimate goal?

7. How do you think you will feel if you get what you want?

8. What do you think will be the reaction of others if you get what you want?

9. Considering the above information, what would you say is the main thing holding you back? What is the root cause of the conflict?

10. Turn the core belief(s) in Step 9 into positive affirmations and use them in the Alpha-Theta meditations described earlier. For example, if the core belief identified in Step 9 was "I'm not good enough", you can turn it into "I'm always good enough", or "I love everything about myself."

APPENDIX E
HIGHER SELF TRANSMISSION

The following channeled message was given from the soul, or higher self, of the author in 1989.

We are the collective self of Sal. We are always here, although not always in Sal's conscious mind. We are the "normal" reality; the ego self is the "abnormal" or illusory reality. Actually, the ego is like a grain of sand - a tiny fragment of the entire shoreline - that thinks it is the shore. Yet contained within this fragment is the blueprint (or hologram) of the universe.

We can only be accessed by going deep within this tiny self to its essence. The outer layers of the self are like the frame of a painting - they are a shell which holds the essence. The little self is not the reality contained within the frame. "Like a wave on the ocean, like a ripple in the tide," the ego loses itself in the vastness of that which we are - for we are the timelessness and the void - the beginning and the end. Beyond words...and yet words do point to that which is nameless. We are all this, and more.

All the ego must do is simply be quiet and merge with us - "be" us - and realize the outer drama is just like a movie. The film can be changed whenever we choose, and one can even walk out of the theatre for a breather.

The purpose of this communication is to allow the small self to practice focusing on the larger picture and to integrate the physical and emotional bodies through this focus. Right now the movie includes all the daily details of physical life; considerations about finances, time commitments and the like. The ego tries to peek into the future to determine the outcome of its activities, hoping to attain its goals and desires.

We would say to this wandering self: Be still and know that the truth lives from moment to moment. When outer action is necessary, the self will be guided to say what is appropriate. Worry keeps the ego bound to the drama, failing to see how it sets up its life, failing to see it is but an actor on the stage. It desires to be physically secure on Earth and yet it must accept that being incarnated here has its hazards. There is really no security in the four-dimensional worlds. And so we remind the ego once again that the only security is in God - the creative force of which we are a part.

All that is necessary is complete trust. When resistance to complete trust comes up, there must be a willingness to face it directly and see it for what it is. Specific guidance for the body will be given and heard if the resistance is absent. For resistance clouds the mind with its loud cries and demands for security. The ego must be shown the difference between resistance to what needs to be done and a genuine feeling that something is not appropriate. In all cases, the motive must be seen and understood.

Remember, we are always here, always available to guide you onward. Peace be with you.

APPENDIX F
AUTOBIOGRAPHY OF A SOUL

Although I briefly told my Earth story in the introduction, here is a synopsis of my cosmic autobiography.

I emerged as an individual soul more than 10 million years ago in Earth time, although time has a completely different meaning on the soul level. Although lifetimes are ultimately simultaneous, I will chronicle the more significant ones I have memory of in linear fashion.

I have had approximately 600 "incarnations", although only 38 of these experiences involved being born to Earthly parents. The remainder were a combination of physical incarnations on other worlds and etheric lifetimes in the light body. Astral and etheric experience between embodiments, celestial initiations and parallel lives of soul fragments are not included.

The Earth lives I remember are as follows:

51,000 - 45,000 B.C.   Atlantis I   Priest and temple initiate

In this life, I attained a high degree of spiritual awareness and nearly attained physical immortality. I left Atlantis to reside on another planet in another dimensional frequency.

25,500 - 23,500 B.C.   Atlantis II   Weather controller/scientist

In my second Atlantis incarnation, I regulated the weather for agriculture. Later I attained adeptship. I left Atlantis on a spacecraft with 10-12 others to avoid perishing during the destruction of the mother country. I resettled on another planet.

11,500 - 10,500 B.C.   Egypt I   Temple initiate; sorcerer.

In Egypt, I studied under Thoth, priest-king from ancient Atlantis.

6,500 - 6,300 B.C.   Egypt II   Musician

2,000 - 1,900 B.C.   Greece   Scholar and scientist

1,000 - 500 B.C.	India and Persia	Two lifetimes as a monk and priest
1,100 - 1,150 A.D.	England	Druid, member of royalty
1,200 - 1,300 A.D.	England	Gothic period, incarnated as a woman
1,400 - 1,470 A.D.	Europe	Renaissance period, incarnated as a librarian and record keeper
1,525 - 1,575 A.D.	Rome	Priest at the Vatican
1,600 - 1,640 A.D.	Rome	Choir director; priest; at the Vatican
1,680 - 1,750 A.D.	Europe	Classical composer
1,800 - 1,849 A.D.	France	Soldier in war

There were additional lives as a Middle East Jew, Asian Buddhist, peasant farmer in Central America, Aztec Warrior, Mayan Warrior, Spanish conquistador, two more lives as women and 16 other lifetimes.

Significant ET Lives

100,000+ B.C.	Ruler of planet Esu in constellation of same name
80,000-100,000 B.C.	Lemuria (Earth) - assisted civilization from on high, making frequent trips to Earth in spaceships
10,000 B.C.-1955 A.D.	Three lifetimes on Venus attending the temples and spiritual schools. Ascended from Earth to go to Venus on two occasions. Last lifetime prior to this one was on Venus.

GLOSSARY/INDEX

The following is a combination glossary and index. Immediately following the boldfaced headings are the referenced page numbers. Next are one or more definitions for the word or phrase. In some cases, several definitions are given to clarify the term; in other cases, more than one definition is given because the term actually has more than one meaning within the context of this book. Consult the Bibliography for more information on many of these terms.

11:11 doorway (pp. 249, 251)
    (1) A symbolic door representing the evolution of a group of souls from 4th to 5th density; (2) a spiritual initiation of a group of souls into the higher dimensions, symbolized by ceremonies which took place on July 11 and November 11, 1991, and January 11, 1992.

2001: A Space Odyssey (pp. 191)

2150 A.D. (pp. 259)
    A novel by Thea Alexander dealing with communal/spiritual life in the 22nd century of Earth.

A Course In Miracles (pp. 15, 108, 142, 164, 237)
    (1) A three-volume set of books, allegedly channeled by Jesus, consisting of a text, workbook for students and manual for teachers; (2) a 365-lesson course in how to attain "miracle consciousness."

Absolute truth (pp. 11, 14, 57, 81)
    (1) A theoretical idea representing a truth that never changes and that encompasses all dimensions and levels of reality; (2) that which is perceived with total awareness of everything in Creation.

Abduction (pp. 161, 185-186)
    Methodology used by the Zeta Reticuli to procure human subjects for creating a hybrid race between humans and ETs.

Adamic Race (pp. 172-174, 177-178, 180-181, 188, 194, 219-220)
    (1) The root race of humanity; (2) Name given to the Pleiadeans who began incarnating on Earth millions of years ago.

Adamski, George (pp. 183)
    UFO/Venusian contactee in the 1950's.

Addictions (pp. 1, 27-29, 97, 212-213, 243)
    Behavior patterns whereby one becomes dependent on a substance, person or experience in order to feel validated or in control--such behavior usually masks denied or suppressed emotional pain from early childhood.

Affirmation (pp. 94-95, 276-277, 281-290, 294)
    (1) A positive statement designed to reprogram the subconscious mind; (2) a statement of the truth behind appearances.

AIDS; HIV virus (pp. 40, 228-229)
    One of several diseases which weaken the immune system of humans, thereby leaving them open to numerous secondary infections. Caused by biological experimentation and/or excessive carbon dioxide in Earth's atmosphere.

Akashic records (pp. 68, 84, 86, 100, 136, 138, 144, 170-171, 186)
    (1) Etheric blueprints; i.e., electromagnetically etched imprints that store/record

every movement, thought, emotion or event of a soul in a holographic medium in the etheric plane; (2) the cosmic history of a soul since its emergence from the Godhead.

Alchemical Hypnotherapy (pp. 276) - See Appendix C

Alchemy; alchemized metals (pp. 193-194)
(1) The process of converting common elements into rare ones; (2) the process of creating a resonant field in the atomic structure of a rare element thereby creating a superconductor; i.e., a virtually unlimited energy source.

Alcyone (pp. 192)
A higher-dimensional world that is home to the Confederation of Planets.

Aldebaran (pp. 191)
A star system that is home to the Confederation of Planets.

Allergies (pp. 212)

Alpha and Omega (pp. 147, 223)
(1) The beginning and the end; (2) a term coined in Revelations referring to the timelessness and eternity of the Christ.

Alpha-Theta induction (pp. 275, 277, 279-284, 290-291, 294) - See App. A

Alpha-Theta state (pp. 15)
A relaxed, meditative state of mind whereby the brain generates waves in the alpha and/or theta range.

Altair (pp. 185, 191)
A star system associated with a group of ETs calling themselves the "Triad".

Amplitude (pp. 21-22)
(1) The height of a waveform; (2) the relative strength of a waveform.

Ancient of Days (pp. 197)
A being associated with the spiritual hierarchy as one of the "Elders of the Throne." See "Spiritual Hierarchy"

Ancient pain (pp. 3)
(1) Pain experienced during a soul's initial drop in vibration after emergence from the Godhead; (2) pain that lies deep within a soul that manifests as a longing to return to the pre-separation state.

Andromedans (pp. 190-191)
Beings from the galaxy of Andromeda.

Angel (pp. 2, 17, 80, 124, 126, 146, 157-159, 177-178, 196, 198, 249)
A being of light commonly residing in the celestial realms, usually depicted as a radiant, winged humanoid.

Angelic Realms (pp. 126-127, 145-146, 157-160, 277)
Celestial worlds inhabited by angels--part of the 6th through 8th dimensions. See "Celestial Realms"

Antareans (pp. 181, 191)
Beings from the star system Antares.

Anti-gravity (pp. 257)
Any force which counteracts the effects of gravity.

Aquarian dispensation (pp. 198)
A term coined by the Confederation referring to the Divine intervention taking place on Earth to assist humanity in evolving into the higher densities.

Archangel (pp. 17, 126-127, 147, 149, 157-159, 190, 196-198, 273-274, 277)
A great being of light originating in the heavenly realms, with a universal awareness and presence.

Arcturians (pp. 189-190)
   Beings from the star system Arcturus.
Ark of the Covenant (pp. 193)
   A device created by the Israelites approximately 4000 years ago designed to immortalize the physical body in preparation for ascension--it utilizes resonant field superconductivity to alter the RNA/DNA structure of humans. The Ark was built under the instruction of the Sirians, commanded by Lord Jehovah, and is documented in the Old Testament of the Bible.
Armageddon (pp. 233)
   A battle of light and dark forces referred to in the Bible.
Asanas (pp. 277) - Yoga postures - See Appendix C
Ascended being (pp. 123-124, 198)
   Any soul who has evolved into 5th density.
Ascended master (pp. 123, 198)
   A soul evolved into 5th density that has attained mastery of the physical body.
Ascension (pp. 32, 114, 123, 125-126, 135, 183, 193, 198, 208-209, 213, 233, 247, 249-251, 255-257)
   The process of raising one's cellular vibration from fourth to fifth density, thereby becoming luminescent to fourth density perception and invisible to third density.
Ascension chamber (pp. 193)
   A device designed to assist a soul in evolving from 4th to 5th density, usually consisting of a resonant field superconductor that reprograms the RNA/DNA for silicon-based life (the crystal light body).
Ascension flame (pp. 213, 250-251)
   The double helix consisting of ascending energy (kundalini) and descending energy (God's grace), when raised in vibration sufficiently to create ascension.
Ashtar; Ashtar Command (pp. 191, 201)
   Leader of an intergalactic group of ETs serving the spiritual hierarchy.
Astral body (pp. 134-135, 256)
   An aspect of self that resides in a parallel subdimension of the 4th dimension, commonly accessed between incarnations or during certain dream states.
Astral entities (pp. 256)
   Beings who dwell in the astral realms.
Astral plane; astral worlds (pp. 19, 89, 122-123, 131, 133-136, 138, 153, 157-159, 199, 255-256, 297)
   (1) A subdimension of the 4th dimension consisting of various repositories for thoughts and energy; (2) a fairly dense realm where souls go between physical incarnations.
Athena (pp. 208)
   Venusian goddess, Greek mythological figure, and member of the Confederation.
Atlantis (pp. 178, 181, 227, 237, 244, 277, 297)
   A civilization that existed for thousands of years on a continent that is now submerged beneath the Atlantic Ocean. Atlantis was destroyed by laser and crystal weaponry during warfare between the Orions and Pleiadeans approximately 25,000 years ago--the survivors reincarnated as the Egyptian, Aztec and Maya cultures.
Atom; Atomic (pp. 7-8, 68, 80, 87, 136, 154, 166, 170, 179, 183, 249-250, 262, 290)
   The basic building blocks of elements, consisting of electrons, protons, neutrons, and various other subatomic particles.
Atrophied (pp. 185, 226)
   Withered and stunted from lack of use, as in the Zeta sexual organs.

Attachment (pp. 46, 92-94, 107-108, 136, 218, 222, 256, 259, 273, 283)
Identification with an object, event or experience whereby a soul has an emotional investment in the outcome.

Aura (pp. 20, 51, 121, 124-126, 138-140, 144, 170, 250, 274, 291)
An electromagnetic field surrounding a soul's physical body that contains various information about that soul.

Aura clearing (pp. 77)
A healing technique utilizing movement and/or sound that alters the structure of a soul's auric field, adding or removing energies from the field.

Auric field (pp. 138-140, 170, 190, 250, 256, 273-274) - See "Aura"

Autosuggestion (pp. 21, 277, 279-290)
An affirmation or positive statement given under a state of hypnosis designed to reprogram the subconscious mind.

Awakening (pp. 2, 81, 113, 122, 150, 154, 205, 227, 237-238)
The process of remembering, or expanding awareness to include the higher aspects of self.

Awareness (pp. 3, 11-17, 19, 33-34, 36, 41, 45, 47, 51, 63, 71-76, 84, 94-95, 97-99, 101, 104-105, 108, 116, 120-122, 125, 132, 135, 140, 143, 145-146, 149-153, 156-159, 163, 171, 173, 196-197, 203, 210, 221, 237-238, 243, 248, 255-257, 260, 269-270, 275, 275, 278-286, 290-292, 297)
(1) The ability to know or be conscious of one or more levels of reality; (2) the active agent of intelligence that perceives the truth about a given reality.

Babaji (pp. 198)
A higher-dimensional being known as Lord Shiva in the Hindu religion.

Belief; belief system (pp. 9-12, 25, 33, 36, 38, 41-42, 45-46, 51-53, 55-60, 63, 65, 68-69, 88, 92-97, 103-104, 117, 121-123, 133, 137-138, 194, 203, 205, 212, 218-220, 222, 224, 227-229, 236, 238-239, 244, 247-248, 256-257, 260-261, 264, 269, 279, 282-283, 288-289, 292-294)
(1) A model or construct of reality based on one's past experience; (2) a set of beliefs whereby one draws conclusions about the nature of reality and treats the resulting perceptions as though they were absolute truth.

Betelguese (pp. 177-180)
A star in the Orion cluster and home to the Councils of Light.

Bible quotations/references (pp. 124, 181-182, 193, 197-198, 206, 208, 220, 228)

Big Bang (pp. 163, 166)
A theory of how the Universe began--as an initial explosion from a central core.

Bilocation (pp. 87) - See "Psychic Abilities"

Biocomputer (pp. 20, 29, 67, 250, 283)
(1) The part of the mind that regulates the brain and body functions and carries out instructions from the higher self and Universal Mind; (2) the part of the self that contains all the biological information pertaining to a soul's evolution.

Black hole (pp. 164, 225, 251)
(1) A doorway in space-time linking one dimension to another, or one universe to another; (2) a collapsed star with extreme gravitational force that sucks matter, energy and light into itself.

Black magic (pp. 179, 187)
A form of mind control and manipulation used by the Dark Lords of Rigel.

Bradshaw, John (54)

Brahma, Vishnu & Shiva (pp. 164)
The gods of the Hindu trinity. See "Trinity"

Brain (pp. 7, 9, 15, 19-25, 27, 29, 45, 52, 67, 77, 104, 170, 222, 261, 277, 279)
(1) The physical part of the nervous system that functions as a biocomputer, regulating the various parts of the physical body; (2) the physical aspect of mind.

Brain/mind machines (pp. 277) - See Appendix C

Brain waves (pp. 15, 20-24)
(1) Electromagnetic signals emanating from the brain; (2) beta (14-35 cps), alpha (7-14 cps), theta (4-7 cps) and delta (0-4 cps).

Bramley, William (pp. 181)

Breath of Fire (pp. 275) - See Appendix C

Brotherhoods of Light (pp. 84, 189, 197, 227)
Organizations within the Confederation consisting of beings dedicated to serving the Light of the Radiant One. Some groups have been corrupted by the Illuminati.

Buddha, Guatama (pp. 217)

Bush, George (pp. 228)

Capstone (pp. 194, 251, 262)
(1) The top section of a pyramid containing the "point"; (2) the part of a pyramid where the ascending energies are the most concentrated.

Carbon-based life form (pp. 123, 170, 247, 250)
Life forms residing in 3rd density that use carbon to process physical energy.

Catch-22 (pp. 44)
A military term representing a winless strategy whereby each apparent solution to a problem triggers more problems. See Figure 4.2, "Circle of Fear"

Causal plane (pp. 30, 124, 144, 157, 159-160, 199)
(1) A subdimension similar to the soul plane whereby a soul can view its incarnations and make decisions about its future; (2) a crystal-like realm that controls the "lower" realms of Creation.

Celestial realms (pp. 124, 126, 144-146, 157, 159-160, 188, 190, 192, 241, 297)
(1) 7th, 8th and 9th-dimensional realms where angels, archangels and creator gods dwell; (2) commonly referred to as "heaven".

Central database; consumer database (pp. 206)
(1) Computer data files kept by members of the Illuminati and/or elite business community to keep track of individuals and their political/economic interests; (2) Data used by marketing agencies to determine product trends, sales, etc.

Central Intelligence Agency; CIA (pp. 199, 228)

Centropy (pp. 158, 164, 257)
(1) Opposite of entropy; (2) energy that evolves into a higher and more organized structure over time.

Chakras (pp. 75-77, 140-142, 160, 213, 231, 248, 273, 277)
Centers of energy (vortexes) corresponding to areas of the physical body.

Chakra balancing (pp. 77)
A healing technique utilizing movement and/or sound, similar to aura clearing except that it focuses primarily on the chakras and areas of the aura pertaining to the chakras.

Channel (pp. 25, 88, 182, 189, 285, 291, 295)
(1) One who draws energy from the higher or more subtle realms into the physical realm in a form that can be utilized; (2) one who acts as a conduit for the energy of another life form or entity.

Channeling (pp. 15, 22, 81, 83-86, 182, 184, 189, 191-192, 235, 295)
(1) The act of allowing another life form or entity to channel energy through the physical body; (2) similar to telepathy except that it includes a one-way merging of

energy as well as thought forms.

Chanting (pp. 274-275, 277) - See "Mantra"

Choiceless awareness (pp. 13, 41, 63, 72-73, 98, 149, 292)
> (1) A state of awareness whereby a soul is simultaneously aware of everything in his/her field of perception; (2) awareness of momentary time; (3) being fully in the moment while choosing not to focus on anything in particular.

Chosen ones (pp. 208-209, 237)
> The elect of God, as depicted in the Bible and other teachings--a concept of the Illuminati designed to instill fear and obedience in the populace.

Christ (pp. 2, 140, 147, 157-160, 164-165, 196-201, 208-210, 273)
> (1) The oversoul of Jesus; (2) the balance of the spirit and will polarities of Creation; (3) the Son aspect of the Godhead.

Christ consciousness (pp. 108)
> (1) The higher self in a state of universal awareness; (2) a state of consciousness that emulates the values and principles of Christ.

Christ principle (pp. 108)
> Universal laws of balance between the will (female) and spirit (male) joining in the heart as love.

Christians (pp. 1, 13, 109, 164, 198, 208-210)

Circular breathing (pp. 269-270)
> A breath technique used in Rebirthing whereby one connects the inhale to the exhale in one continuous rhythm.

Clairaudience (pp. 79-80) - See "Psychic Abilities"

Clairsentience (pp. 79-80, 138) - See "Psychic Abilities"

Clairvoyance (pp. 76, 80, 86, 88-89, 137-139, 256) - See "Psychic Abilities"

Cleopatra (pp. 208)

Codependent relationship (pp. 1)
> A relationship based on addictive behaviors, poorly defined personal boundaries, self-sacrifice and emotional dependency.

Collective consciousness (pp. 8, 74-75, 89, 100, 145, 213, 259, 295)
> (1) The composite consciousness of humanity; (2) another name for "mass consciousness"; (3) the totality of all the collective realities of humanity.

Collective will (pp. 213, 245)
> The collective emotional state of the mass consciousness.

Collective reality (pp. 8, 10-11, 132-133, 251)
> A reality, the nature of which is agreed upon by two or more people - examples: death and taxes.

Collective subconscious (pp. 51, 67-68, 74, 89, 100, 132, 136)
> (1) The collective beliefs of humanity; (2) consciousness common to all humanity; (3) the part of the collective consciousness of humanity residing in the subconscious mind of each soul.

Collective unconscious (pp. 67)
> A Jungian term not used in this book, but replaced with "collective subconscious".

Composite beliefs (pp. 10, 51)
> The sum total of all the beliefs of a soul or group of souls.

Conditioning (pp. 12, 25, 33-34, 36-37, 51, 53-56, 60-61, 65, 71, 104, 113, 222, 224)
> The environment in which a person was raised from birth to the present, including all the beliefs and programs taught to him/her about the nature of reality.

Confederation of Planets (pp. 179-180, 182, 184-185, 190, 199-201, 207, 216-220, 262)

An organization of ETs from over 600 star systems directed by the Godhead--their purpose in coming to Earth is to help souls here evolve into higher dimensions.
Congress (pp. 207)
Conscious breathing (pp. 2, 27, 269-270) - See "Rebirthing"
Conscious mind (pp. 9-10, 13, 21, 51, 67-68, 71, 77, 85, 97-99, 104, 116, 121-122, 135, 151, 153-154, 157-159, 169, 171-172, 194, 203, 210-212, 216, 229, 236, 256, 271, 275, 277, 283, 286, 295)
The part of the mind that has conscious awareness.
Consciousness (pp. 2-3, 8, 11-13, 15-18, 20, 32-34, 36, 47, 49, 52, 56, 58, 65, 69, 71-72, 81, 86-87, 98-100, 105, 108, 115-117, 120, 133-137, 139, 143, 145, 151, 153-154, 157-159, 169-173, 184, 186, 189, 216, 222, 225, 228, 235-236, 238, 247-248, 256, 260, 280, 282, 284-286, 290, 292-293)
(1) The aspect of Creation (or the individual life forms in Creation) that possesses the ability to be aware; (2) the movement of intelligence.
Conspiracy (pp. 228-229)
In this book, pertains to covert plans by the Illuminati to squelch attempts by others to unseat its members who are in power.
Cord cutting (pp. 273-274) - See Appendix B
Cording (pp. 136)
A process of psychically bonding, or "hooking" one soul to another, usually through emotional or mental manipulation and control.
Cosmic cycle (pp. 160, 244)
(1) The time it takes the Earth and the local solar system to rotate one time around the local galaxy; (2) a period of approximately 26,200 years.
Cosmic consciousness (pp. 16-17, 105, 115-117, 158)
A state of consciousness whereby a soul is no longer identified with the self and thereby perceives all of Creation from no reference point.
Council of Light (pp. 177-179, 191)
A group of beings from the star system Betelguese in the constellation of Orion.
Counterculture (pp. 1)
A group of people who do not adhere to the normally accepted beliefs of society, such as hippies or skinheads.
Creation (pp. 14, 37, 41, 51, 56-58, 67-68, 75-76, 81, 108, 113, 116, 119, 124-125, 133-134, 136-137, 145, 147, 161, 163-166, 169-170, 172, 189, 197-199, 210, 213, 225-226, 229, 233, 239-240, 251, 253, 257)
The totality of that which has emanated from the Godhead.
Creative imagination (pp. 88-90, 281, 289, 293)
(1) The part of the imagination that creates new realities; (2) the 4th- dimensional aspect of imagination.
Creative visualization (pp. 90, 249, 277)
A technique utilizing the imagination and higher mind designed to bring into manifestation that which is imaged.
Creator gods (pp. 127, 134, 147, 157, 159, 165)
Souls who have evolved to the point of being able to create entire worlds or planes of existence.
Critical mass (pp. 153-154, 250)
(1) The number of souls necessary to shift the balance of power away from an old way of thinking to a new one; (2) a process depicted in " The Hundredth Monkey" by Ken Keyes, Jr. (See Bibliography).
Crystal light body (pp. 123, 190, 247-251)

Another name for the 5th density form of humanity, depicting its silicon "crystalline" structure.

Cult (pp. Preface)
A subsect of religion or fraternity that involves one or more leaders and several followers who blindly adhere to the beliefs of the leader(s).

Custodians (pp. 182)
A name coined by William Bramley in "The Gods of Eden" to denote the Orion/Sirian aspect of the Illuminati.

Dark Lords; dark forces (pp. 177)
A name given to members of the Illuminati originating in the star system Rigel.

Darkness (pp. 59, 108, 165, 177-178, 223, 225, 232, 234-235, 243, 281, 292)
(1) Absence of light; (2) ignorance; (3) the void, or unmanifested space; (4) judgment, guilt and denial.

Death (pp. 11, 31-32, 57, 93, 135-136, 153-154, 164-165, 198, 209, 221-223, 233, 249, 255-257, 269, 289)

Deja vu (pp. 80-81)
(1) Manifestation of a precognitive experience where the original precognition has been forgotten; (2) a feeling that the current experience has happened before, with no rational explanation of how or when it happened before.

DeMolays (pp. 179)
A fraternal organization founded by Jacques DeMolay--the DeMolays are a distant offshoot of the Illuminati.

Deneb (pp. 191)
A star system existing on many higher dimensions--home of the Confederation.

Denial (pp. 45, 49-50, 59, 94, 122, 136, 140, 150, 212-213, 216, 222-223, 226-227, 243-245, 247-248, 257, 259)
(1) The act of repressing an experience, emotion, thought or event; (2) the act of splitting, or fragmenting, the self by casting out undesirable aspects.

Density (pp. 14-18, 30, 32, 119-127, 142, 149-154, 157, 159, 165, 169-171, 173-174, 181-185, 188-195, 197-198, 208-209, 211, 213, 247, 250, 254-255)
A specific vibration that creates a certain life form.

Depression, economic (pp. 1, 204-205)

Desirelessness (pp. 36)
A state of complete acceptance of the present moment where no desire exists within the self.

Detachment (pp. 3, 138, 230, 240, 278)
The act of removing identification of the self with an emotion, event, thought or experience.

Diet for a New America; John Robbins (pp. 28)

Dimension (pp. 3, 7, 9-16, 18, 20, 31-32, 41, 51, 54-55, 57, 62, 68, 73, 77, 79-81, 84, 87, 89, 98-99, 101, 108-111, 115-116, 120-122, 126-127, 129-138, 141-147, 149-154, 156-160, 166, 169, 173, 178, 189-191, 194, 229, 235-238, 241, 247, 250-251, 253-257, 260-262, 291, 295, 297)
A plane of existence whereby a certain set of laws and principles apply.

Discarnate entity (pp. 79-81, 135-136, 256)
A life form not currently possessing a physical body.

Disciple (pp. 197, 208, 218)
(1) One who learns; (2) a follower of a particular spiritual path and/or teacher.

Discipline (pp. 34, 71, 73, 77, 122, 228)
(1) The act of creating an environment conducive to learning; (2) the act of being

focused or concentrated on a particular goal.

Divine Essence (pp. 225)

Soul essence emanating from the Godhead that is present in all things--another name for spirit.

Divine Intervention (pp. 198, 205, 207, 249)

Involvement in the affairs of Earth by members of the spiritual hierarchy or the Godhead directly--this happens only when a sufficient number of souls sincerely request assistance, or when humanity is threatened with extinction.

Divine Mother (pp. 58, 127, 140, 147, 159-160, 164, 169, 172, 187, 196-201, 210, 213, 224-226, 235, 239, 245)

(1) The feminine aspect of God; (2) the magnetic pole of Creation; (3) the will, or emotional aspect of God.

DNA (pp. 29-30, 32, 34, 68, 87, 170, 193-194, 247, 249) - See "RNA/DNA"

Double helix (pp. 213-214)

(1) Two spirals of energy: a descending one from the Heavenly Father, and an ascending one from the Divine Mother; (2) interlocking spirals depicted as the serpent and used today as a symbol in modern medicine and in certain secret societies.

Draconians (pp. 179)

(1) A name sometimes given to the Dark Lords of Rigel; (2) sometimes refers to Type 3 Zeta Reticulins, a race who are lizard-like in appearance.

Duality (pp. 59, 108, 138, 169, 172, 177-178, 209, 215, 219-220, 223, 254)

The existence of polar opposites, such as yin and yang, positive and negative, male and female, etc., existing in the first four dimensions of reality.

Dulce, New Mexico (pp. 186)

Approximate location of an underground Zeta Reticuli hybridization laboratory (place where humans and Zetas are interbred).

Dysfunctional relationship (pp. 46, 110, 239, 241)

Any relationship whereby one or more of the parties are heavily influenced and/or controlled by negative childhood conditioning to the extent that effective communication is difficult and/or impossible.

Earth-bound Orions/Sirians (pp. 180, 182, 187, 218)

Humans incarnate on Earth who originally came from Orion or Sirius. While their home star systems have evolved, these souls are still stuck in the Illuminati programming.

Earth changes (pp. 204, 212-213, 235-238)

Climatical, geological and sociological shifts prophesied to occur over the next 20 years due to the rapid increase in spiritual awareness and vibration of Mother Earth.

Earthquakes (pp. 211)

Eckankar (pp. 146)

A religious movement that utilizes a multidimensional model of the Universe similar to the one depicted in this book.

Economic collapse (pp. 204-207)

Hyperinflation (if more money is printed) or depression (if money supply is controlled) caused by runaway debt and/or mass default on outstanding loans-- rendering paper money worthless.

EEG (pp. 20)

Electro-encephalogram: a device that measures brain waves.

Ego (pp. 17, 41-42, 44-46, 49, 51, 63, 67, 92, 94, 97-98, 115, 122, 124, 143, 157-160, 196, 199, 217, 221-222, 286, 292, 295)

The personality, or third-dimensional self, that perceives itself as separate from the rest of Creation.

Ego death (pp. 221-222)
(1) Complete letting go of the self-image/personality; (2) giving up one's identification with the ego, leading to cosmic consciousness--the ego does not really die, but merely fades into the background.

Einstein, Albert (pp. 119, 154, 262)

Electric (pp. 20, 37, 164, 170, 224-225, 262-263, 270)
(1) The masculine, or yang, pole of Creation; (2) movement of electrons.

Electromagnetic energy (pp. 20, 79-80, 86, 138, 140, 164, 185, 224, 250, 261-263)
Energy possessing both electric and magnetic qualities that commonly makes up the auric field of a person and the ethers of the etheric plane.

Electron (pp. 8, 154, 166, 170, 250, 261)
A negatively charged particle orbiting an atom.

Embodiment (pp. 32, 84, 126, 136, 153, 172, 174, 183, 197-198, 208, 221-222, 244, 255, 297)
A soul's incarnation into a physical body.

EMF (pp. 20, 86, 138-139, 170, 193, 250, 261-262, 264) - Electromagnetic field--see "Electromagnetic energy"

Emotion (pp. 3, 9, 12, 15, 17, 19, 25, 27-29, 31, 33-40, 42-43, 45, 48-49, 51, 53, 56, 60, 62, 72-73, 77-78, 90, 92, 94, 97, 103, 109, 113, 115, 117, 136, 138, 140-142, 157-160, 164, 170, 185, 194, 199, 212, 221, 224, 231, 234, 240, 244, 247-249, 253, 259, 264, 269, 271, 275-277, 279-280, 282, 286-287, 291-293, 295)
(1) Energy-in-motion; (2) a type of feeling involving the movement of the will.

Emotional body (pp. 33-34, 38, 42, 71, 90, 98, 125, 136, 138, 159-160, 223, 232, 248)
(1) The will; (2) the aspect of self that has emotions.

Enlightened relationships (pp. 110-111)
Relationships whereby each party takes complete responsibility for him/herself and communicates openly and honestly with unconditional love and acceptance.

Enlightenment (pp. 2, 12, 17, 59, 73, 85, 108, 110, 147, 149, 154, 157, 159, 194, 207, 210, 218, 231, 237, 243, 245, 259, 285)
(1) Supreme understanding/knowing; (2) awareness without veils or distortions; (3) freedom from beliefs; (4) awareness beyond thought and perception; (5) a state of unconditional love and acceptance for all Creation.

Enoch (pp. 197, 250)
A member of the spiritual hierarchy--one of the Elders of the Throne.

Entity (pp. 22, 41, 62, 84-85, 104, 133, 135, 137-138, 218, 273-274)
Any life form possessing rudimentary or advanced intelligence.

Entropy (pp. 158, 164, 257)
(1) Energy which becomes lower in vibration and less organized over time--the opposite of centropy; (2) the 2nd law of thermodynamics.

Essassani (pp. 190)
A Zeta-human hybrid race.

Eternal Ones (pp. 146, 169, 197)
Great beings of light who have existed in an enlightened state for aeons.

Eternity (pp. 108, 143, 146, 157-159)
(1) A state of timelessness that exists throughout all dimensions; (2) the sum total of all linear and momentary time, as experienced from the fifth dimension and higher.

Etheric plane (pp. 18, 33, 79-80, 123-125, 136, 138-139, 144, 157-160, 170, 189-190, 197, 199, 297)

An invisible realm consisting of electromagnetic energy ("ether") that holds the blueprints of material existence.

Etheric blueprint (pp. 170)

A set of electromagnetic codes that define physical life forms by programming the RNA/DNA molecules. This program is directed by higher intelligence.

Etheric body (pp. 17, 19, 30, 33, 138, 140-142, 170, 277)

The "invisible double", or subtle body that exists in the auric field as electromagnetic energy, also called the "body electric".

ETs (pp. 137, 161, 173-196, 207, 215-220, 249, 263) - See "Extraterrestrials"

Evolution; evolve (pp. 3, 18, 30-32, 36-38, 58, 62, 68, 77, 79, 84-85, 87, 98, 119-121, 123, 125-126, 142-145, 150-151, 153-155, 158, 161, 163-165, 169-172, 174, 178-180, 182-183, 185-189, 197-198, 205, 210, 212, 222, 224-226, 228, 230, 235-238, 240, 243-244, 248-249, 251, 253, 255-256, 260)

(1) The movement of an organism and/or life form from lower to higher densities in an orderly progression; (2) the process of increasing soul experience in the linear dimensions; (3) to increase and expand awareness over time.

Expanded awareness (pp. 13, 16, 49, 149-151, 290-291)

(1) The process of becoming aware of more of the subconscious and superconscious mind while still functioning in the conscious mind; (2) the process of becoming aware of higher dimensions without excluding the more mundane levels of existence.

Experience (pp. 2, 4, 7, 9-14, 16, 19, 22, 25, 30, 33-34, 37-38, 42, 44-46, 48-49, 52-55, 59-63, 67-69, 71, 73, 80-82, 88, 90, 92, 95-98, 102, 104, 109-110, 115-117, 121-122, 124, 126, 133, 135, 142, 147, 151-154, 164-165, 169-171, 186, 197, 207-208, 212, 216, 221-222, 225, 229-231, 235, 239, 241-242, 247-249, 251, 253-254, 256, 269-271, 274-277, 279-280, 282-283, 286-287, 292, 297)

(1) The recording of events in a soul's timeline, both in the mind and in the akashic records; (2) stimulus entering the brain to be stored in memory.

Extraterrestrials (pp. 2, 137, 161, 171, 173-196, 207, 215-220, 249, 263)

(1) Any being or life form that is not born on Earth; (2) members of the Illuminati or Confederation that consider another planet to be their home.

Fall from grace (pp. 3, 169, 182, 253)

(1) Any being or life form that voluntarily chooses to experience a lower density than the one he/she has evolved into; (2) the experience of dropping in vibration, taking on veils, and forgetting the true nature of the self.

Fallen angel (pp. 126, 217)

(1) An angelic being who has voluntarily chosen to descend in vibration to experience the realms of matter and duality; (2) an angelic being who has judged higher densities to be good and lower densities to be bad, i.e., who has followed the teachings of Lucifer.

Far Right; New Right; fundamentalism; ultra-conservatism (pp. 205-206, 209-210)

Father principle (pp. 108)

Federal Reserve System (pp. 179, 228)

A central banking system designed by the Illuminati to control the world's monetary resources.

Feeling (pp. 10, 12, 22, 33-34, 38-39, 41-42, 45-46, 48-49, 52-54, 58, 60-62, 65, 68, 72, 75-76, 80, 97, 102-103, 109-110, 116, 132, 139, 183, 190, 212, 219, 223, 226, 229-231, 240, 243-244, 248, 269-271, 278-280, 282, 284, 286, 288, 291-292, 295)

An intuitive hunch, emotion, bodily sensation, or empathic connection to another life form.

Five Elements, The (pp. 270)
Five steps used in Integrative Rebirthing and Vivation.

Forgiveness (pp. 92, 218, 276, 285, 287)
The release/letting go of grievances against self or other.

Forgiveness diet (pp. 276)
The act of forgiving seventy times seven (as mentioned in the Bible)

Founders (pp. 169, 189)
Great beings of light from the 12th dimension who originated the RNA/DNA codes responsible for the creation of humans and other life forms.

Free will (pp. 30, 56-57, 77-78, 81, 145, 154-155, 186-187, 190, 232, 235-237, 289)
(1) The ability to decide how, where and when to experience a soul lesson; (2) the ability to consciously choose how fast to evolve as a soul and in what order to learn soul lessons; (3) the desire of the will when it is not dominated or controlled by the spirit or trapped by judgment, guilt and denial.

Freedom (pp. 12, 55, 94, 107-109, 115, 147, 157, 216, 218, 220, 223-224, 227, 229, 232, 234, 280-289, 292-293)
(1) A state of consciousness unbound by judgment, guilt and denial, or by conditioning, programming and belief systems; (2) a state of being where one is not bound by time and space but has unlimited access to time and space.

Freemasons (pp. 179)
(1) A fraternal organization founded by the Illuminati--membership includes a large contingent of governmental and political entities; (2) founders of the United States of America.

Frequency (pp. 7, 18, 21, 30, 32, 70, 80, 119, 121, 129, 134, 193-194, 199, 216, 250, 297)
Rate of vibration, such as cycles per second (kilohertz).

Garden of Eden (pp. 169, 181, 243)
(1) A mythological paradise spoken of in Genesis; (2) a pre-separation state of consciousness; (3) Earth during the time of the first humans.

Geodesic dome (pp. 263)
A structure invented by Buckminster Fuller utilizing intersecting geometries and domes--proven to be strong and highly energy efficient.

Gestalt (pp. 276) - See Appendix C

Ghosts; poltergeists; apparitions (pp. 256)

Golden Age; new millennium of peace (pp. 238)
A thousand-year era of peace and enlightenment prophesied in the Book of Revelations and other religious texts.

God (pp. 2, 13, 16-18, 41, 56-59, 68, 81, 93, 105, 108-109, 113-115, 124, 143-144, 146-147, 153, 157-160, 163-167, 170, 172, 181, 193, 197-201, 208-209, 211, 218-220, 223-233, 240, 243-244, 248-249, 252-255, 259, 261, 273-274, 277, 295)
(1) All that is; (2) the originator of the Universe and all its dimensions, densities and levels; (3) the Heavenly Father, generator of all that is.

God worlds (pp. 157)
A term coined by Eckankar pertaining to the higher dimensions where the creator gods and universal gods reside.

Goddess (pp. 17, 163-164, 182, 200-201, 274)
(1) Any feminine being who has attained a state of God consciousness or has demonstrated supreme knowledge of universal laws; (2) the Divine Mother, experiencer of all that is.

Godhead (pp. 17-18, 98, 125, 133, 145-147, 157-160, 163-165, 169, 179, 196, 198-201, 216, 225-227)

(1) The 12th dimension, realm of the trinity of Father-Mother-Christ; (2) anything pertaining to the source or Great Central Sun.

Gods of Eden, The (William Bramley) (pp. 181)

Gratitude (pp. 49, 196, 276)

(1) Joyful acceptance of the present moment; (2) thanksgiving; (3) seeing the perfection of life's lessons, trials and tribulations.

Great Mystery (pp. 17, 127, 147, 157, 159)

(1) The aspect of the Godhead that is unknowable, or remains forever beyond the ability of evolving souls to comprehend; (2) the void, or source from which Creation emanates.

Great Central Sun (pp. 127, 147, 160, 197-198)

The center of the Universe, or point around which all matter and energy revolves.

Great Pyramid (pp. 181, 193-194)

A radionics device built by the Pleiadeans to assist their reincarnated members (the original Egyptians) in returning to their immortalized fifth density form. Most other pyramids are nonworking copies built by humans. See "Ascension Chamber"

Great White Brotherhood (pp. 84, 192)

An organization, formed from the spiritual hierarchy and consisting largely of Confederation members, which has been somewhat corrupted by the influence of the Illuminati.

Groom Lake, Nevada (pp. 186)

Location of a secret base where Zeta Reticuli technology is tested by the Illuminati.

Grounding (pp. 116, 139, 274)

(1) A psychic protection technique that consists of directing one's energy and attention downward into the Earth, thereby shrinking the size of the auric field and preventing unwanted psychic interaction with other life forms; (2) the act of focusing firmly on the material plane of existence.

Guilt (pp. 1, 33, 39, 46, 49, 54, 56, 59, 92-93, 108-109, 140, 193, 197, 209, 216, 220-234, 247-248, 259-260, 288)

(1) The belief that one is unworthy and deserving of punishment; (2) a lifeless essence originating in the void that opposes the life force and lowers the vibration of souls who accept it into their being.

Halls of Amenti (pp. 192)

A fifth-dimensional subterranean world where beings are initiated into the Brotherhoods of Light.

Harmonic Convergence (pp. 249)

An event that took place on August 17 and 18 of 1987 symbolically marking the last segment of the Mayan calendar.

Harmonics; octaves (pp. 119, 129)

Resonant chords or frequencies that are linear or logarithmic multiples of basic frequencies or dimensional constants, such as the speed of light, the speed of light squared, etc.

Healing at a Distance (pp. 76-77) - See "Psychic abilities"

Heart (pp. 14, 17, 40, 75, 94, 108-109, 116, 123, 138, 140-145, 157-160, 164, 197, 199, 209, 211, 213, 227, 230, 234, 242, 247-249, 259, 277, 280, 286-287, 289, 292)

(1) The balance of masculine and feminine energy; (2) the 4th chakra; (3) the Christ, or Son aspect of God; (4) a soul's center of love and compassion.

Heaven (pp. 18, 58, 93, 123-124, 126, 132-133, 142, 144-146, 159-160, 171, 178, 183, 208, 213, 218, 232, 236-238, 241, 244, 259)
Pertaining to the celestial or God realms.

Heavenly Father (pp. 58, 127, 140, 147, 159-160, 164, 172, 196-197, 199, 239, 274)
(1) The masculine aspect of God; (2) the generator of all that is.

Higher frequencies (pp. 119, 121-122, 124)
Pertaining to densities or levels of vibration that have finer (closer together) waveforms, such as ultraviolet, as compared with the visible frequencies.

Higher self; higher mind; higher consciousness (pp. 17, 32, 41, 45, 49, 51, 58, 67, 74-76, 84-85, 98-101, 111, 117, 124, 141-143, 171, 199, 222, 225, 235, 247, 259, 273, 277, 281, 289, 295)
(1) The aspect of self that resides in the higher dimensions and that utilizes the higher consciousness of the superconscious mind; (2) often equated with the soul or the soul's true awareness.

Higher intelligence (pp. 47, 62, 88, 98, 104, 170, 207)
Another name for Universal Mind.

Higher dimensions; higher densities (pp. 11, 45, 51, 57, 62, 75, 81, 84-85, 87, 108-109, 116, 121, 126, 129, 133, 135, 141-142, 144-146, 150-153, 171-172, 178, 180, 188, 194-195, 229, 237-238, 249, 260)
(1) Dimensions that encompass many different planes and subplanes of the Universe. Lower dimensions are contained within higher ones; (2) densities that vibrate at higher frequencies and that create higher-order life forms.

Hippies (pp. 1)
A counterculture prevalent in the 1960's.

Historical consciousness; historical content (pp. 34, 36, 99)
The sum total of a soul's subconscious content, including experience, belief systems, programming and conditioning.

Hitler, Adolf (pp. 228)

Holistic; wholistic healing (pp. 14, 27, 207)
Any system or healing method that strives to integrate and include all the many facets of the self.

Hologram; holographics (pp. 114, 166, 170, 208, 225, 252-253, 263-264, 295)
(1) A microcosmic picture or pattern that contains all the characteristics of the macrocosmic; (2) an image or projection that depicts the higher dimensions from within a three-dimensional or two-dimensional medium.

Holographic projection (pp. 87, 137, 183, 185)
The ability of a soul to project an image of himself/herself to another location in space and time and appear to observers to be the actual embodiment of the soul--a more advanced form of mental projection, this ability utilizes the mind's ability to manipulate and direct light.

Holy Spirit (pp. 164) - See "Trinity"

Hopi Prophecy (pp. 237)
(1) A set of pictographs and petroglyphs representing the rise and fall of civilizations on the Earth; (2) sacred teachings passed among the Elders of the Hopi tribe regarding the coming Earth changes.

Hopkins, Budd (pp. 186)
A UFO/abductions researcher and author of the book "Intruders" from which a TV mini-series was made.

Horizontal time (pp. 73, 81, 98, 101) - See "Linear Time"

Hundredth Monkey, The (pp. 237)
As documented in Ken Keyes book "The Hundredth Monkey", a phenomenon witnessed by scientists studying monkeys on remote Pacific islands and how they evolved their eating and cleaning habits. When a certain percentage of monkeys started washing their food in a new way, the idea spread telepathically throughout the entire species, even on distant islands. The "hundredth" monkey is symbolic of the number needed to reach "critical mass."

Hypnosis (pp. 21-22, 24, 186, 278, 275-276, 279-284)
A deeply relaxed, meditative state that allows access to the subconscious mind for the purpose of reprogramming.

Hypnotherapy (pp. 34, 77, 275)
A methodology that utilizes hypnosis and counseling techniques to enable a subject to contact and reprogram his/her subconscious mind with the help of a therapist.

Illuminati (pp. 178-179, 181-182, 186-187, 192, 205-207, 216-220, 227-229, 262)
A secret society of occult and mystical beings originally brought to Earth by the Pleiadeans, and later involving the Orions, Sirians and Adamic races, initially dedicated to the pursuit and preservation of enlightenment, but recently (within the last few thousand years) corrupted by power- hungry factions with the goal of total domination and control of the world and its resources.

Illusion (pp. 7-8, 12, 15, 42, 47, 108, 115, 150, 218, 224, 229, 278, 2'_
(1) A belief system or method of perception that is inappropriate for understanding the truth behind appearances. For example, "the world is flat"; (2) a perception from a limited frame of reference where something appears to be true to one with a limited awareness, but is, in fact, not true from a more expanded frame of reference.

Imagination (pp. 88-91, 122, 134, 158, 204, 233, 248, 273-274, 276-277, 280, 289-290)
The imaging faculty of the mind whereby reality is created or perceived that exists beyond the physical senses.

Immortality (pp. 15, 30, 58, 251, 256-257, 297)
(1) A state of deathlessness; (2) pertaining to the eternal nature of the soul.

Implant (biological or psychic) (pp. 186, 249)
A device, physical and/or etheric, inserted electronically into a human by certain ET races, designed to: (1) facilitate communication between the human and the ETs, often involving enhancement of psychic abilities and recall of past life memories by the implanted human; (2) used by Zetas to keep track of the thoughts and whereabouts of certain humans for later breeding and/or abductions; (3) also can be used by the Illuminati to block psychic powers or inhibit memory, which is an effective means of keeping evolving souls from becoming too powerful and thereby threatening the Illuminati's control of Earth.

Implantation (pp. 173-174)
Also known as a "walk-in" or "soul transfer", pertains to the entrance of a soul from another world or dimension into the humanoid form of a soul who vacates the body after birth.

Individual reality (pp. 10)
Reality that is uniquely true to one soul (as opposed to collective reality that is shared by more than one soul).

Infinite Intelligence (pp. 13, 68)
Another name for Universal Mind.

Infinity (pp. 2, 69, 131, 158)

(1) Without beginning or end--going forever in all directions; (2) of unlimited magnitude or size.

Infrared (pp. 7)
An area of the frequency spectrum with a lower vibration than the visible.

Initiation (pp. 144, 182-183, 189, 193-194, 297)
(1) A process of ritualizing or ceremoniously depicting a particular lesson or lessons of a soul or group of souls; (2) assistance given by God or enlightened beings to evolving souls to help them master a lesson or lessons; (3) procedures for admittance into a mystical order or secret society.

Inner conflict (pp. 60-65)
A state of being whereby one or more parts of a soul are opposed to another part or parts, thereby creating soul fragmentation.

Integration (pp. 3, 12, 27, 31, 34, 36, 44-45, 48, 95-96, 143, 154, 158, 187, 213, 216, 218, 224, 237, 247-249, 251, 256-257, 269-272, 279, 282-824, 295)
(1) The process of bringing disharmonious parts of a soul into agreement and alignment so they can work together to manifest the soul's desires; (2) perception of the whole instead of the parts of a given reality; (3) in Rebirthing, the stage where the client fully accepts his/her experience and the breath becomes easy and effortless.

Integrative Rebirthing - See "Vivation"

Intellect (pp. 1-2, 12, 16-17, 41, 62, 67, 72-73, 79, 102, 117, 140, 142, 157-160, 199, 241, 256, 270, 278, 281, 289)
The logical, rational aspect of mind used to communicate thoughts, ideas, concepts.

Intelligence (pp. 13, 17, 47-49, 56, 62, 68, 84, 88, 98-100, 102, 104-105, 113, 144, 146-147, 157-159, 161, 170, 192, 195-196, 207, 210, 215, 224-226, 280, 282, 289, 292)
(1) That which directs conscious awareness; (2) consciousness capable of perceiving its higher nature.

Interdimensional (pp. 175, 183, 188, 262)
(1) Capable of travelling between dimensions; (2) encompassing more than one dimension.

Intuition (pp. 19-20, 38, 67, 75-76, 80, 104, 122, 134, 140-142, 154, 157, 171, 248, 279-280, 282, 286)
(1) The ability of the will to perceive a higher order of reality by feeling the essence of that reality; (2) the ability to sense the truth of a given reality using the will, or gut instinct.

Invocation (pp. 77, 140, 273-274, 277)
A process of calling forth a particular being, energy or level of reality, i.e., to draw an entity to oneself for the purpose of rendering assistance.

Isis (pp. 198)
(1) A female member of the spiritual hierarchy; (2) an Egyptian goddess.

Isolation tanks (pp. 277) - See Appendix C

Israelites (pp. 181)
According to the Bible, God's "chosen people"--in reality, beings from Sirius incarnating as humans on Earth under the direction of Jehovah.

Japan (pp. 205, 207)

Jehovah (pp. 181, 193, 197)
A 7th density Sirian, the God of the Old Testament, and a member of the Illuminati. Jehovah's oversoul, Yahweh, is a member of the spiritual hierarchy.

Jesus (pp. 14-15, 86, 197-201, 208-209, 217-218, 228, 273)
An embodiment of the Christ oversoul (during his Biblical incarnation and several

other times)--he is usually called Sananda by the Confederation.

Judgment (pp. 33-34, 36, 38, 41, 45, 48-49, 51, 54, 58-63, 85, 96, 103, 108, 121, 140, 150, 193, 209-210, 216, 222-223, 226-227, 229, 247-248, 260, 270)

(1) The act of separating out aspects of reality and labeling some aspects as more desirable than others; (2) drawing conclusions about a given reality without having all the information necessary to make an accurate assessment; (3) the act of condemning or invalidating another soul or life experience.

Kali (pp. 164)

An Eastern goddess and member of the spiritual hierarchy.

Karma (pp. 14, 32, 93, 97, 108, 137, 143, 158, 218, 236, 277)

(1) Cause and effect, as seen from the fourth dimension; (2) a process whereby a soul sees a reflection of his/her consciousness manifested in the world.

Karma yoga (277)

Kennedy, John F. (pp. 228)

Keys of Enoch, The (J.J. Hurtak) (pp. 250)

KGB (pp. 228)

A secret military and police intelligence agency in Russia similar to the U.S. CIA. Both organizations are controlled by the Illuminati and actually have had secret alliances at times.

King, Martin Luther, Jr. (pp. 228)

Knights of Malta; Knights of Templar (pp. 179)

Organizations founded by the Illuminati and originally engaged in mystical and occult practices.

Knowledge (pp. 12, 16, 30, 67-68, 76-77, 86-87, 95, 100, 104, 108, 116, 142, 146, 154, 161, 164, 166, 172, 179, 181-182, 194, 204, 215, 232, 295)

(1) Soul experience; (2) information stored in memory; (3) knowing based on a soul's present level of evolvement.

Kriya breathing; kriya yoga (pp. 275) - See Appendix C

Kundalini (pp. 19, 38, 80, 213, 275)

Feminine energy ascending up the spine from Mother Earth (base of the spine) to the Heavenly Father (crown chakra).

Kwan Yin (pp. 198)

Another female member of the spiritual hierarchy.

Layers of time (pp. 99)

Time frames that exist in parallel dimensions, similar to the concept of "warp" in Star Trek, roughly analogous to harmonics of the speed of light.

Left/right brain (pp. 20, 247)

Two hemispheres of the brain, whereby the left side usually pertains to logical, analytical functioning, and the right side, intuitive, psychic and imaginative functioning.

Lemuria (pp. 227, 237, 244, 298)

An ancient Pacific continent similar to Atlantis, but more primitive--it was destroyed by the Orions prior to the dawning of Atlantis.

Levels of reality; levels of awareness (pp. 7, 9-11, 13-17, 20, 27, 29-31, 41-42, 52, 57, 68, 77-78, 83-84, 89, 98, 101, 108, 115-116, 122-123, 125-126, 131, 135, 138-139, 146, 149-151, 154, 156-158, 163, 169, 172-174, 189, 216, 221, 235, 243, 248-249, 271, 280, 282-283, 286, 291, 297)

Densities, dimensions or aspects of self--realities that have specific properties unique to each level--a convenient way to categorize the Universe to better understand it.

Levitation (pp. 57, 257)

The ability of a physical being to float in the air by counteracting the force of gravity with electromagnetic forces in the auric field of the body.

Life force (pp. 34, 38, 58, 77, 140-141, 199, 222, 225, 257, 270, 282, 291)
The aspect of intelligence that activates the RNA/DNA blueprints necessary to sustain life.

Light activation codes (pp. 194, 247, 249)
Information from higher intelligence that activates the master template, i.e., energy that activates the RNA/DNA codes, thereby changing one's genetic structure through the process of mutation.

Light body (pp. 17, 123, 151, 157, 170, 188, 190, 193, 198, 208, 241, 247-251, 257, 297)
The physical/etheric form of the 5th density human, invisible to 3rd density sight and luminescent to 4th density - see "Crystal Light Body."

Light spectrum (pp. 7-8, 119-120, 150, 153)
A chart depicting the various frequencies and waveforms of light, including infrared, visible and ultraviolet. The visible part consists of the colors of the rainbow, with red at the lowest frequency and violet at the highest.

Light workers (pp. 213)
Beings who serve the light through commitment to the upliftment of humanity--such as teachers, healers and social workers.

Light year (pp. 8)
The distance light travels in one year in the third-dimensional universe: approximately 5.8 trillion miles, or 10 trillion kilometers.

Limited awareness (pp. 133, 149-151)
Narrowly focused awareness, i.e., selective awareness focused on a specific density or dimension to the exclusion of the others - examples: materialism (denial of spirit) and space cadets (denial of materiality).

Linear time (pp. 41, 73, 81, 98, 101, 166)
Third-dimensional, past, present and future, as measured by the clock, and as depicted as horizontal time on the x-axis of diagrams in this book.

Logical mind (pp. 41, 62, 67, 199) - See "Rational Mind" and "Intellect"

Lords of Light (pp. 177)
Another name for the Councils of Light of Betelguese.

Lotus posture (pp. 275)
A sitting position where the spine is erect and the legs crossed, often used during meditation.

Love (pp. 14, 17-18, 28, 34, 36, 38, 48, 50, 56, 58-59, 65, 85, 88, 93, 95, 105, 107-111, 113, 121, 123, 138, 140, 142-147, 157-160, 164, 166, 182-183, 190, 209, 211, 213, 216, 218, 225-226, 229-234, 237, 242, 248-249, 263, 269, 274, 277, 284, 286-289, 291, 293-294)
(1) The activity of the heart; (2) the fifth dimension; (3) unconditional acceptance and compassion; (4) emanation of the Christ; (5) masculine/feminine balance and integration; (6) the glue that holds the Universe together.

LSD (Lysergic acid diethylamide) (pp. 1)
Hallucinogenic substance used extensively in the 1960's and 1970's--it often triggers expanded awareness.

Lucid dreams (pp. 135)
Dreams in which the dreamer is consciously aware of himself, his astral body, and the unfoldment of the dream.

Lucifer (pp. 177-178, 228)
A being of light that judged darkness as bad and wrong and therefore separated light from darkness, thereby creating duality.

Lucifer Rebellion (pp. 178)
A name for the war that ensued between the Adamic race and the Orions when the Orions invaded Earth over 300,000 years ago.

Lyra; Lyrans (pp. 169, 172, 180, 184, 189)
(1) A paradise world that originated the human life form in this sector of the galaxy over a billion years ago; (2) 12th density beings who dropped in vibration to 7th density over 100 million years ago and who later migrated to the Pleiades.

Machine language; higher-level language (computers) (pp. 170)
(1) An assembly language containing basic instructions to a computer, usually in binary or hexadecimal form; (2) an English-language program, such as BASIC or FORTRAN.

Macrocosm (pp. 225)
Pertaining to the Universe at large.

Magic elixir (pp. 194)
Also called "manna" or "bread of life", an alchemized form of gold in the form of white powder or crystal, capable of raising one's vibration to the point of ascension in one who is sufficiently purified--but deadly to one who is not.

Magnetic (pp. 37, 164, 171-172, 180, 206, 224-225, 256-257)
(1) The feminine pole of Creation; (2) the yin force that attracts the electric energy, i.e., the receptive, passive aspect of God.

Mainframe computer (pp. 20, 67, 206)
A large-scale computer system with mass storage and numerous remote terminals commonly used in large corporations and government offices.

Malachites (pp. 181)
A group of reincarnated Sirians controlled by Jehovah and other gods of the Sirians and Orions.

Maldek (pp. 179, 244)
A planet, originally located in what is now the asteroid belt between Mars and Jupiter, where a race of beings evolved (controlled by the Illuminati), who destroyed themselves and their planet using laser weaponry approximately 500,000 years ago-- these souls later reincarnated on Mars and Earth.

Mansion worlds (pp. 113, 146)
A phrase used in the Bible to denote the God worlds, or higher dimensions.

Mantra (pp. 280)
A repetitive chant used to quiet the mind and/or focus it on spiritual dimensions -See Appendix B.

Mark of the Beast (pp. 198, 206)
An electronically scanned implant (mentioned in Revelations) employed by the Illuminati to procure certain data from humans--prophesied to also act as a type of credit system during the financial collapse of the late 1990's.

Mass consciousness (pp. 11, 136, 161, 169, 187, 227, 235)
(1) The prevailing beliefs and perceptions of society at large; (2) the composite consciousness of humanity; (3) the average intelligence of a common person as determined by a bell curve statistical model.

Master oversoul (pp. 166, 197, 257)
The oversoul of an oversoul.

Master template (pp. 247, 249-250)

A biological program designed to convert a life form from carbon-base to silicon-base, activated by light codes from higher intelligence.

Maya (pp. 133, 298)
(1) Pertaining to the lower four dimensions; (2) illusion; (3) an ancient people (who were descendants of the Atlanteans) who once flourished in Central America.

Meditation (pp. 2, 13, 16, 21-23, 31, 34, 47, 71-73, 77, 115-116, 135, 150, 157-158, 249, 267, 275-284, 290-293, 295)
(1) A method of relaxation and concentration designed to quiet the mind and achieve self-realization; (2) a still mind with no movement of thought.

Meier, Billy (pp. 188)
A Swiss farmer who has been in contact with 4th-dimensional Pleiadeans for many years and has extensive photos, documentation and other evidence.

Melchizedek (pp. 197-198, 200-201)
(1) Priesthood founded by Lord Melchizedek of which Jesus was a member (see Hebrews 6:20-7:21); (2) an order of the spiritual hierarchy that oversees evolution in the lower dimensions.

Memory (pp. 25, 34, 45-46, 48, 52, 55-56, 63, 67, 80, 83, 88, 90, 102, 108, 132, 143, 170, 172-173, 186, 222, 226, 289, 297)
The aspect of mind that stores soul experience for later recall.

Memory by association (pp. 25-26)
A process whereby a current experience triggers a chain of memories--useful for improving recall ability, but can be a hindrance to meditation.

Mental body (pp. 76, 248, 253)
A subtle body that can be projected mentally to any time or space to perceive what is taking place there. It can also be used to holographically project an image of oneself to another location.

Mental plane (pp. 9, 19, 31, 42, 48, 55, 75-76, 131-133, 135-136, 138, 142, 157-159, 221, 248)
The realms of mind, where daydreamers go and where most psychic functioning takes place.

Mental projection (pp. 76-77, 185, 216, 290-291) - See "Psychic abilities"

Metaphysics (pp. 14, 133, 138, 182, 209, 225)
(1) The study of the mind's relationship to the physical universe; (2) principle and application of mind power and creative thought.

Michael, Archangel (Lord Michael) (pp. 198, 273, 275)
A great being of light and member of the spiritual hierarchy who opposes Lucifer and protects beings from negative influence.

Microcosm (pp. 225)
Pertaining to the microscopic world.

Midway station (pp. 190)
A world designed as a bridge between the lower and higher dimensions--a place to acclimate souls on their interdimensional journeys.

Mind control techniques (pp. 13, 76, 177-178, 187, 212)
(1) Processes designed to reprogram the mind to think according to a specific pattern or ideology; (2) experiments conducted by secret branches of government to control the populace.

Mind (pp. 2, 4, 9-10, 13-18, 20, 22, 25-26, 33-34, 36-38, 41, 44-45, 47, 49, 51, 55, 62-63, 67-72, 76-77, 79, 81, 84, 86, 88-92, 98, 100, 103-105, 107-108, 113, 115, 117, 123, 132-135, 137-138, 141, 143, 145-147, 153, 155, 157-160, 164, 166, 170-171, 177-178, 185, 187, 199, 206, 208, 211-212, 227, 230-234, 236, 247, 249-251, 260, 265,

Tiny receptors in the brain that process information and relay it to the nervous
system.

New Jerusalem (pp. 208)

(1) The promised land spoken of in the Bible; (2) a higher-dimensional "city" or
vehicle of light prophesied to descend upon the Earth, ushering in a golden age of
peace and plenty; (3) Earth during the millennium of peace (see Revelations).

New World Order (pp. 161, 187, 203, 205-213, 227, 261)

A one-world governmental system prophesied to replace the current governments of
the world. Three different versions of the New World Order are detailed in this
book.

New Age; New Agers (pp. 150, 184, 209, 247-248, 277)

(1) A catch-all phrase pertaining to the new thought movement, alternative religions,
wholistic health practices, UFO/ET phenomena, psychic, mystical and occult
sciences, and anything else not in the realm of orthodox religion, science and
culture; (2) people who embrace New Age philosophies and methodology.

Nirvana (pp. 133, 157-159)

A state of supreme ecstasy often associated with freedom and enlightenment.

Null zone (pp. 262)

(1) An area of time or space not affected by an EMF and having no electrical
charge; (2) a vacuum in the space-time continuum; (3) a warp in space-time created
by bending the EMF in a given area until the space-time collapses, allowing
interdimensional space and time travel.

Objective Reality (pp. 7-8, 156, 203, 276)

A purely external point of view.

Occult (pp. 178, 227)

(1) Ritual magic, sorcery or mysticism; (2) religion of the paranormal; (3) practices
of witchcraft, paganism or divining methods; (4) the study of sacred sciences, as
taught in secret societies.

Old World Order (pp. 203-205, 207)

The current (circa 1993) system of world governments and societies.

OM (pp. 80)

A Sanskrit chant designed to connect one with the sound current of the Universe.

One World Banking System (pp. 205-206)

A monetary system with a common currency for every country in the world,
controlled by a central bank--a cornerstone of the Illuminati's plans for greater
control of Earth.

One World Government (pp. 205-206)

A central government planned for the entire Earth, to be run by the Illuminati.

One Year Seminar (pp. 3)

A seminar created by Phil Laut and Jim Leonard that meets one day per month and
one night per week for an entire year.

Original Cause (pp. 96, 109, 166, 225-226, 247-248)

(1) The deepest level of causation behind the situation in the world today; (2) the
events and actions behind the original "fall from grace"; (3) a set of books
describing what went on in the Godhead at the beginning of Creation.

Orions (pp. 174, 177-182, 187, 216-219, 227-228)

Beings from the constellation of Orion who came to Earth over half a million years
ago and interbred with the Adamic race to the point of becoming dominant on the
Earth--they comprise nearly 80% of the world's current population.

Other universes (pp. 18, 81, 127, 143, 147, 159-160, 163-166, 197-198, 253)

(1) Parallel space-time continuums that exist simultaneously with the 12-dimensional model given in this book; (2) universes with entirely different laws and principles that co-exist with the known Universe.

Oversoul (pp. 32, 84, 113-114, 125-126, 144-146, 157-160, 166, 171, 189, 197-199, 208, 257)
(1) A collective entity comprised of many individual souls, much like a large branch on a tree with several smaller branches protruding; (2) the 7th density self of a 6th density soul; (3) a higher self common to many Earth-bound souls.

Pan, God of Paradise; The Land of Pan (pp. 59, 227, 237, 244)
(1) A great being of light who founded an ancient civilization on Earth and was later corrupted by Lucifer and taken captive by the dark forces; (2) a name for the original garden paradise of Earth (aka Eden).

Paradise Sons (pp. 127)
Great beings of light who oversee the various celestial heavens.

Paradise Worlds (pp. 18, 147, 159)
Subdimensions or planes of existence in the higher dimensional continuum inhabited by highly evolved beings living in a paradisiacal state.

Parallel dimensions; parallel time frames (pp. 119, 127, 133, 166, 192)
Planes of existence outside the "vertical" dimensional models given in this book, yet existing concurrently with the vertical dimensions--parallel dimensions may be similar in vibration to the lower and middle level dimensions given in this book (example: the astral plane).

Parallel lives (pp. 297)
Simultaneous incarnations occurring in other time frames - See "Simultaneous Lifetimes"

Past lives (pp. 30, 100, 109-110, 170, 256, 276, 297-298)
Previous incarnations of a soul, as viewed from the soul's third-dimensional timeline.

Perception (pp. 8, 12, 15-16, 53, 55, 58, 75-76, 79, 81, 102, 113, 117, 120-121, 129, 150, 154, 229-230, 235)
A soul's viewpoint of a given reality, based on his/her position in space-time, state of consciousness, beliefs, and many other factors.

Permutations (pp. 170-171)
Various arrangements of data or substance forming numerous configurations of reality.

Personal computer; PC (pp. 67)

Philadelphia Experiment (pp. 263)
An experiment conducted in the early 1940's during the first part of World War II in the Philadelphia naval shipyard designed to render attack ships invisible to enemy radar. The test involved large Tesla coils emitting strong EMFs around the hull of ships. The program was partially successful despite loss of life and property.

Physical immortality (pp. 30, 58, 251, 256-257, 297)
The ability to maintain a youthful physical body indefinitely by balancing the centropy (generative) and entropy (degenerative) forces--attained by a handful of yogis and mystics throughout history, including Babaji (of the Hindu mythology), and Elijah, Enoch and Melchizedek in the Bible.

Piscean age (pp. 203)
The most recent cosmic cycle of approximately 2000 years now coming to an end on Earth.

Pleiadean disk (pp. 249)

A small glass disk with gold, silver or copper embedded inside, used to amplify subtle energies and balance the auric field of the body for healing purposes.

Pleiades; Pleiadeans (pp. 169-174, 178, 180-181, 188-189, 191, 193-195)
(1) A constellation of over 100 stars, seven of which are blue-white giants; (2) 12th density Pleiadeans are the creators of the human form over 100 million years ago, and the original inhabitants of Earth in the beginning. There are over a dozen different civilizations of varying densities associated with the Pleiades, three of which are described in this book.

Polaris (pp. 192)
A star system that is home to higher-dimensional ETs.

Polarity bodywork (pp. 27)
A form of healing utilizing the meridians (energy vortexes) of the physical body.

Polarity (pp. 108, 131, 139, 177, 209, 259)
(1) Positive or negative; (2) anything having a dualistic nature or set of positive and negative poles; (3) alignment and/or orientation of the self.

Polarization (pp. 177-179, 227, 257)
(1) The process of dividing from a neutral position to one with positive and negative poles; (2) taking an extreme position on an issue, thereby creating conflict with those having an opposite orientation.

Poseidon (pp. 192)
A fifth-dimensional subterranean city.

Possible reality (pp. 81, 203)
A level of reality created by imagination having the potential for outer manifestation at some point in the future.

Power (pp. 3, 9-11, 14, 21, 33, 37-38, 51, 55, 57, 88, 94-96, 108, 121-123, 134, 136, 141, 146, 164, 178-179, 181-182, 185, 193-194, 205, 217-219, 221, 224, 227, 232, 243-244, 248-249, 257, 259, 261-262, 269-270, 274, 283, 289)
(1) Potential and kinetic energy; (2) the ability to make things happen; (3) the movement of will and desire.

Prana (pp. 77, 270) - See "Life Force"

Prayer (pp. 77, 79)
(1) Asking or requesting of God or the Godhead; (2) a form of meditation whereby the soul is receptive to transmissions from the Godhead.

Precognition; retrocognition (pp. 80-81) - See "Psychic abilities"

Predestiny (pp. 81, 145, 154-155)
(1) The belief that one's future is predetermined by outside forces or by God; (2) the sum total of all possible and probable realities; (3) the giving up of free will to follow another will's predetermined goals.

Primary emotions (pp. 38-39)
Fear, anger, sadness and happiness.

Prime directive (pp. 185)
A word used in science fiction to denote a policy of non-interference in the affairs of an evolving culture or race. The Confederation has used this policy as often as possible in the past.

Probable reality (pp. 203)
A level of reality likely to occur based on a soul's present state of consciousness and his/her creative actions.

Processing (pp. 21, 72, 97, 271)
Any action designed to clear old programs, beliefs and emotional patterns from the subconscious mind.

Program (pp. 29, 34, 36, 53-56, 61-63, 68-69, 71, 103, 134, 170-173, 220, 222, 249-250, 260, 282-284, 288)

(1) A statement one tells oneself about the nature of reality based on past experience. Commonly repeated programs eventually become beliefs; (2) to manipulate someone into believing a certain way; (3) a set of instructions coded into a computer system.

Programming (pp. 12, 25, 33-34, 36, 51-56, 60, 69, 71, 92, 113, 170-173, 186, 224, 247, 284)

(1) The act of directing one's mind to believe in a certain way; (2) a set of instructions or programs given repeatedly to the subconscious mind designed to elicit a particular mode of response in an individual.

Prophecy; prophet (pp. 80, 208, 235, 237)

(1) A report on the possible and probable realities of the future; (2) a warning of potential future disaster designed to alert souls to potentially damaging behaviors and beliefs; (3) one who sees the possible and probable timelines for future events.

Proton (pp. 166)

A positively charged particle in the center of atoms.

Psychic (pp. 2-3, 15, 17, 19-20, 67, 74-89, 104, 122-123, 125, 129, 134, 136, 139-142, 157-160, 171, 181, 187, 191, 216, 238, 256, 268, 273, 277, 289)

(1) Perceiving with the imaginative faculty of the mind in ways not available to the basic physical senses; (2) extra-sensory perception (ESP).

Psychic abilities (pp. 76-88, 171, 181, 216, 238, 289)

Various techniques utilizing the higher mind--defined and described in detail in Chapter 4, including: mental projection, healing at a distance, telepathy, channeling, psychometry, precognition, clairvoyance, clairaudience, clairsentience, PK and TK, teleportation and bilocation.

Psychic healer; psychic healing (pp. 2, 77-79, 268)

One who perceives psychically what is out of balance in a person and utilizes holistic healing methods to resolve the imbalances.

Psychic protection (pp. 238, 273-274, 277)

(1) An invisible force field surrounding the aura of an individual; (2) techniques designed to keep undesirable entities out of one's personal psychic space. See Appendix B.

Psychokinesis; PK (pp. 86) - See "Psychic abilities"

Psychometry (pp. 86-87) - See "Psychic abilities"

Psychological time (pp. 41, 132)

One's sense of time and how it passes. Psychological time is a variable, depending on one's state of consciousness.

Pure essence (pp. 17-18, 51, 113, 124, 143, 157, 160)

(1) Another name for the soul; (2) the soul after stripping away all the layers of the self.

Purification process (pp. 94-97, 113, 125, 140, 143, 158, 193-194, 199, 249, 269, 290, 293)

The process of releasing old beliefs and programs, expressing pent-up emotions, and eliminating toxins from the mind and body for the purpose of renewing the soul.

Pyramid (pp. 181, 193-194, 249-251, 262-263)

(1) A device with four bases ascending equilaterally to a point, thereby creating four triangular sides; (2) a device used to assist souls in the ascension process; (3) a device used to create a dimensional doorway into other worlds.

Quadrinity (pp. 165, 167)
A four-part model of God based on Spirit, Will, Heart and Body--or Father, Mother, Christ and World.

Quantum shift (pp. 3, 123, 143, 153-154)
A sudden change in vibration from one density to another.

Quasars (pp. 164)
Enormous stars thought to be time portals to alternate universes.

Race mind (pp. 51, 67-68, 104)
Another name for the collective consciousness of humanity.

Radiant One (pp. 1, 184, 197)
A name for the Heavenly Father coined by the Confederation.

Radionics (pp. 193-194, 249, 261-263)
The science of subtle energy and its affect on the physical universe. Radionics utilizes EMFs to direct energy for healing purposes, electrical power, warfare, and other applications.

Rapture (pp. 208)
A Christian term referring to the ascension process.

Rational mind (pp. 25-26, 41, 51, 55, 62-63, 81, 84, 90, 98, 143, 158-159, 230, 232, 240, 280-281)
The logical, analytical aspect of mind that thinks in linear time mode.

Reactive mind (pp. 45)
The part of the subconscious that directs the ego to react to outside stimuli.

Reality (pp. 5, 7-11, 13-16, 30, 45, 50, 55-56, 61-62, 67, 71, 88-90, 99, 111, 115-117, 129, 131-133, 136, 144-146, 150, 154, 156, 161, 203, 208-209, 215, 235-236, 260, 277, 284-286, 289, 292, 295)
(1) The context of a set of belief systems and perceptions; (2) relative truth, or the truth as perceived from a particular viewpoint.

Reality construct (pp. 13, 15, 129, 131)
(1) Another name for a model of reality; (2) a set of belief systems that make up a soul's version of reality, i.e., the conclusions one draws about reality based on his/her belief systems.

Rebirthing (pp. 2-3, 27, 77, 249, 268-272, 275)
A conscious breathing technique designed to facilitate one in releasing old emotional patterns from birth and early childhood, while increasing the prana in the body.

Reflection (pp. 9-10, 65, 97, 137, 142, 178, 186-187, 203, 205, 209, 212, 215, 218, 222, 225, 227-228, 231, 235-236, 238, 244, 248, 250-251, 284, 286, 289)
(1) The response from the world to what a soul is giving out; (2) the outer representation of a soul's inner state of consciousness; (3) instant karma.

Reincarnation (pp. 31-32, 99-100, 136, 158, 164, 173, 181, 208, 233, 251, 254-256, 260, 297-298)
The process of a soul entering into a new physical body after leaving a previous one. Time between incarnations can last from a few hours to many centuries.

Religion (pp. 46, 109, 121, 150, 178, 182, 184, 193, 198, 210, 217, 219-220, 225, 228, 244, 259, 261)
Any organized set of beliefs about spiritual reality.

Renaissance (pp. 123, 298)

Repressed emotions (pp. 34, 59, 69)
Emotions that are denied because they are too uncomfortable or undesirable--one is generally not aware of them anymore.

Reprogramming (pp. 10, 30, 122, 247, 249, 277, 279, 282-284)
The ability to alter the programs in the subconscious mind, much in the same way a computer programmer changes lines of code. Reprogramming the mind is often done through hypnotherapy, autosuggestion and affirmation.

Resonant field (pp. 193, 262)
An EMF that sets up an affinity between atoms in an element, causing the atoms to organize themselves in a harmonic pattern, thereby creating a superconducting field around the element.

Resurrection (pp. 198, 208)
(1) The process of reactivating the tissues and organs in a dormant or dead organism, effectively bringing it back to life; (2) to be born again, literally or figuratively; (3) the replacing of old ideas and beliefs with fresh new ones.

Revelation (pp. 95, 264)
A sudden realization about the nature of the Universe.

Revelations (pp. 124, 197-198, 206, 208)
The last book of the New Testament concerning the visions and various prophecies of John the Divine.

Rigel (pp. 177-180, 182)
A star in the constellation of Orion, home of the Dark Lords.

Right Use of Will (pp. 37, 164)
The first book in a series, channeled by Ceanne de Rohan, allegedly from the Godhead, that depicts the quadrinity model of God (see "Quadrinity").

RNA/DNA (pp. 29-30, 32, 34, 68, 87, 170, 193-194, 247, 249)
Complex molecular proteins that, along with genetic codes, form the basis of humanoid life forms.

Robertson, Pat (pp. 205)

Rockefellers (pp. 179)
Members of the international banking community controlled by the Illuminati.

Rosicrucians (pp. 179)
A mystical order affiliated with the Illuminati, but maintaining some independence.

Rothschilds (pp. 179)
Members of the international banking community controlled by the Illuminati.

Saint Germain (pp. 198)
A member of the spiritual hierarchy.

Sananda (pp. 198, 200-201)
The Confederation name for Jesus in His current state of evolution. Sananda is the spiritual leader of a major branch of the Confederation.

Sanat Kumara (pp. 198)
A member of the Confederation.

Santa Cruz, California (pp. 2)

Sasquatch; bigfoot (pp. 192)
A subterranean race of beings in communication with the Sirians.

Satan (pp. 59, 209, 218)
(1) A mythological character representing God's adversary; (2) the aspect of God that denies the darkness and makes it wrong.

Second Coming of Christ (pp. 208-210)
(1) In traditional Christianity, a prophesy involving the return of Jesus to the Earth; (2) in Confederation teachings, the uniting of the Father and Mother principle within each soul, thereby creating Christ consciousness in the heart.

Second Creation (pp. 198)
A term coined in the book "Original Cause" (Four Winds Publications) pertaining to the birth of the great archangels.

Secondary emotions (pp. 38-39)
Emotions that are a combination of primary ones - for example, jealousy is a combination of anger and fear, hurt is a combination of anger and sadness, etc.

Secret government (pp. 186, 192, 220, 228, 263)
A catch-all phrase pertaining to members of the military or secret societies that work quietly within the government but are not under its control--it influences the CIA, NSA, NSC and elite branches of the military.

Secret societies (pp. 178, 181-183)
(1) Mystical and/or fraternal orders which practice some form of occult or magical ritual and/or science; (2) factions of the Illuminati that hold secret rites and initiations; (3) political and/or religious groups that wield considerable power and control over the affairs of Earth.

Sedona, Arizona (pp. 3, 264)
Location of sacred sites, vortexes and numerous spiritual centers.

Selective awareness (pp. 13, 41, 45, 72-73, 101, 149, 157)
The process of focusing or concentrating on one or more specific realities to the exclusion of all others.

Self-acceptance (pp. 12, 54, 98, 121, 178, 226, 231, 257, 276)
The ability to unconditionally love and accept all aspects of the self--a necessary prerequisite to healing.

Self-alignment (pp. 51, 59-60, 77-78, 143, 168, 211-212, 247-249, 251, 263, 277, 289)
A state of integration whereby all parts of the self are working together harmoniously toward a common purpose.

Self-hypnosis (276, 279-284) - See Appendix D

Self-mastery (pp. 87, 123, 150, 198, 260)
(1) A state of enlightenment whereby one is no longer controlled by the ego, or by conflicting aspects of self; (2) supreme knowledge of the various aspects of self.

Semjase (pp. 188)
A feminine Pleiadean contact of Billy Meier.

Separation (pp. 38, 41-42, 44-46, 48-51, 54, 57, 59, 60-63, 65, 85, 92, 104-105, 108, 111, 115, 121, 133, 136, 143, 158, 163-166, 172, 183, 209, 216-217, 219, 222-224, 226-227, 241, 243, 248, 251-253, 256-257, 269, 292-293)
(1) A state of being whereby a soul perceives him/herself to be cut off from the Source of the Universe; (2) a state of identification with the body and/or ego whereby a soul forgets his/her spiritual nature and is unable to perceive the interconnectedness of all things; (3) the emergence of souls from the Godhead and their drop in vibration as they began exploring the outer universe. See also, "Original Cause."

Serapis Bey (pp. 198)
A member of the spiritual hierarchy associated with the ascension process.

Seven Archangels (pp. 198)
Chamuel, Gabriel, Jophiel, Michael, Raphael, Uriel, Zadkiel--members of the spiritual hierarchy.

Shadow side (pp. 3, 85, 218, 229)
(1) The non-integrated part(s) of the self; (2) the aspects of self containing negative emotions and limiting beliefs; (3) the aspects of self that do not have unconditional acceptance.

Shambhalla (pp. 192)
A fifth-dimensional subterranean city located beneath the Gobi desert in Asia.
Shiva (pp. 198)
The Hindu god of purification and destruction of illusion.
Silicon-based life form (pp. 123, 170, 247, 250)
(1) Any form of life that uses a modified form of $Si + O_2 = SiO_2$ as its basic chemical process; (2) a crystalline intelligence vibrating in high 4th or low 5th density.
Silicon Valley, California (pp. 1)
Silva Mind Control (pp. 2, 76, 276)
A mind training course with emphasis on meditation, ESP and psychic functioning, originated by Jose Silva and taught throughout the world.
Silver cord (pp. 135)
An astral energy beam between the astral and physical bodies that enables a soul to come and go between the two bodies.
Simultaneity (pp. 163)
(1) Concurrent realities; (2) awareness of more than one vertical (non-linear) time frame.
Simultaneous lifetimes (pp. 100-101, 150)
(1) Lifetimes of parallel souls, or soul fragments existing concurrently with the primary soul in physical embodiment; (2) aspects of an Earthly soul existing in other dimensions and having a discrete life form in that dimension.
Simultaneous awareness (pp. 126, 149-152, 163)
Another name for "Choiceless awareness."
Singularity (pp. 251)
An infinitesimally small point in time and space representing the exit point of matter from the physical universe into another universe via a white hole, black hole or wormhole.
Sirians (pp. 169, 174, 178, 180-182, 184, 187, 193-194, 216-219, 228)
Beings from the star system Sirius who came to Earth thousands of years ago and became the gods of mythology and the Bible.
Solar Cross (pp. 2, 191, 273-274)
(1) An extraterrestrial organization consisting of several hundred star systems/planets and over a dozen different ET races that work in tandem with the Confederation and the Radiant One (Godhead); (2) a symbol consisting of a perfect cross (plus sign) surrounded by a circle.
Soul (pp. 16-18, 30-33, 41-42, 49, 51, 58, 62, 67-69, 71, 75, 77-78, 81, 83-85, 87, 97-98, 104, 108-110, 113-114, 116, 120-125, 134-136, 142, 149-155, 157-160, 163, 165-166, 169-173, 177, 179, 182-183, 186, 189, 192-193, 196-199, 207-209, 211-213, 216, 219-224, 226, 228, 230, 233-234, 236, 239-241, 243-244, 248, 251-258, 260, 263, 273, 275, 277, 286, 295, 297-298)
(1) The most basic unit of an intelligent being; (2) the core, or essence of being; (3) an individual spark of divinity; (4) a discrete quantum of spirit.
Soul family (pp. 84, 145)
(1) A group of souls that all belong to one oversoul; (2) a group of soul fragments with discrete embodiments that all belong to one soul.
Soul fragmentation (pp. 32, 60, 62, 84, 126, 136, 150, 169, 208, 251-257, 297)
A process whereby parts (aspects) of a soul split off from the primary essence and take on the illusion of separation from the primary soul--usually caused by physical death, emotional denial, or unconscious bonding between souls.

Soul group (pp. 84, 145-146, 169, 257)
Same as "Soul family", a group of individual souls all belonging to the same oversoul.

Soul plane (pp. 143-144, 157, 159)
The dimension of the soul--the realm where a person's true essence dwells.

Soul signature (pp. 125)
A pattern of energy unique to a particular soul--a method of identifying a specific life form, much like fingerprints are used to identify a physical body.

Soul timeline (pp. 32, 144)
A linear-time progression of a soul's various incarnations on Earth and/or on other planets, traced from the soul's emergence from the Godhead, through the present, to any point in the future.

Soul transfer (pp. 83-84)
Also called "walk-in", a process whereby a soul relinquishes control of his/her physical body and allows another soul to take it over. Two embodied souls can trade bodies directly, or, a discarnate entity can take over the departing soul's body, and that departing soul can then become discarnate.

Space brothers (pp. 2)
An archaic term (because many ETs are feminine) often used in the 60's and 70's to denote members of the Confederation.

Spacecraft propulsion systems (pp. 185, 191, 262)

Spaceship; spacecraft (pp. 119, 124, 175, 184, 186-190, 207, 262, 264, 297-298)
(1) If visible, usually refers to craft employed by the Zeta Reticuli, a physical ET race currently visiting Earth; (2) saucer-shaped, cylindrical or triangular craft employed by various ET races--in the Bible, often depicted as clouds or flying wheels.

Space-time continuum (pp. 8, 18, 76, 81, 98-99, 101, 144, 154, 194-195, 262)
(1) Third-dimensional space and time; (2) any dimension having a discrete set of laws and properties of space and time.

Spirit (pp. 17, 37-38, 67, 75, 84, 97, 108-109, 113-114, 116-117, 124, 133, 135-136, 138, 141, 145, 157-160, 163-164, 166, 168, 197, 208, 213, 218, 223, 247-248, 255, 269, 277, 293)
(1) The energy of the Godhead; (2) intelligent energy that permeates all of Creation; (3) the non-individualized aspect of a soul; (4) the Oneness of Creation.

Spirit guides (pp. 80, 84, 277)
Beings from the spiritual realms who assist humanity.

Spiritual (pp. 1-3, 7, 11, 16-17, 30-31, 37, 41, 77, 79, 85, 87, 104, 108, 140-141, 145-146, 150, 163, 166, 178, 182-183, 185-186, 189, 191-201, 205, 208, 215-218, 220-221, 238, 244, 249, 251, 255-257, 259, 264, 268, 277, 285, 288-289, 291, 297-298)
Anything pertaining to the invisible universe which exists throughout infinity.

Spiritual ascension (pp. 251, 255)
The spirit lifting out of the physical body and returning to the heavenly realms at the time of physical death.

Spiritual community (pp. 2, 211, 264)
(1) Any group of people that meet regularly and have common spiritual beliefs; (2) An intentional community consisting of a few to a few hundred individuals, often self-sufficient, who may grow their own food or have their own form of energy and technology, or in some cases, their own form of government similar to a sovereign state.

Spiritual healer; spiritual healing (pp. 77)
(1) Any psychic healer who bases his/her healing on spiritual values and principles; (2) psychic healing based on principles of love, integration and balance.

Spiritual hierarchy (pp. 85, 127, 146, 169, 178, 189, 194, 196-201, 216)
(1) A term used by lower-dimensional entities to help understand how the influence of spiritual beings becomes more and more all-encompassing as they grow and evolve into higher dimensions; (2) a loose-knit organization of highly evolved spiritual beings surrounding the Godhead who have specific leadership functions regarding the spiritual progress of mankind and ETs.

Spiritual immortality (pp. 251, 255)
(1) The spiritual aspect of self that does not experience death; (2) the natural state of the soul.

Stalin, Joseph (pp. 228)

Star seed (pp. 172, 184)
(1) Any soul who does not consider Earth to be his/her primary sphere of evolution; (2) an ET soul who voluntarily decides to incarnate on Earth in order to assist the beings evolving here.

Star system (pp. 169, 172-174, 177, 180, 182, 185)
Any group of one or more stars containing planetary bodies in orbit--in this book, stars with planets containing intelligent life.

Star Trek; Star Trek: The Next Generation (pp. 119, 191, 263)
TV series set 400 years in the future featuring space exploration.

Subatomic (pp. 136, 170)
Smaller/more basic level of Creation than the atomic level. The subatomic level is made up of quarks, neutrinos and other particle-waves.

Subconscious mind (pp. 9-10, 13, 33-34, 36-37, 42, 45-46, 49, 51, 67-69, 71, 74, 78, 84, 89, 100, 104, 132-133, 135-136, 158, 275, 282-284)
(1) The part of the mind "beneath the surface" of consciousness; (2) the repository for suppressed life experience and emotions; (3) the aspect of mind that stores past experiences, i.e., memory; (4) the part of the mind responsible for involuntary functions, such as heartbeat, body temperature, etc.

Subjective Reality (pp. 1, 203)
Awareness of the inner aspects of self, such as emotions, thoughts and belief systems.

Subset (pp. 129)
A group of numbers, objects or worlds existing within a larger group.

Substance addiction (pp. 27-29, 239)
Habitual craving for a drug or food involving physical and/or psychological dependence.

Subterranean cities (pp. 192)
Civilizations existing inside the Earth; i.e., beneath the Earth's surface in hollowed-out areas.

Subtle realms (pp. 9, 79-80, 86, 89, 199, 253)
A catch-all phrase denoting any plane or dimension not readily observable by the ordinary conscious mind.

Superconductor (pp. 164, 262-263)
A device or substance that conducts electricity with virtually no resistance.

Superconscious mind (pp. 45, 67-68, 74, 84, 89, 133)
(1) The aspect of mind connected directly to Universal Mind and having a broad overview of reality; (2) the "higher self" or all-knowing aspect of self; (3) the part

of the mind that receives input and decides whether to make it conscious (send it to the conscious mind) or suppress it (send it to the subconscious mind).

Supernova (pp. 169, 180)
A gaseous explosion within a star, capable of consuming planets within its solar system.

Suppressed emotions (pp. 33-34, 36-40, 45, 49, 59, 69, 78, 94, 194, 269-271, 282)
Negative emotions in the subconscious mind, also stored in the cells of the physical body, that the soul decided were too uncomfortable to experience consciously, or were inappropriate to express at the time they were originally experienced.

Synapses (pp. 20)
Miniature "highways" or "fiber optic" networks that carry nerve impulses from one part of the brain to another, much in the same way that wires carry electric signals in an appliance.

Ta'i Chi (pp. 27)
A form of passive martial arts consisting of slow, rhythmical body movements, breath and concentration, similar to ritualized dance.

Tantra (pp. 38, 278)
A form of yoga involving the prana, life force energy, and the kundalini, and often accessed and explored through sexual union and related practices.

Tao (pp. 127, 147, 157, 159, 278)
An Eastern name pertaining to the Great Mystery, the Source, or the unknown.

Tarot (pp. 2)
An ancient science of divination, utilizing a set of cards which depict archetypes, or primary aspects of life, used by psychics as a medium for readings.

Telekinesis; TK (pp. 86) - See "Psychic abilities"
Telepathy (pp. 81-82, 182, 184-186, 189, 191-192) - See "Psychic abilities"
Teleportation (pp. 87) - See "Psychic abilities"
Telos (pp. 192)
A fifth-dimensional subterranean city underneath Mt. Shasta in Northern California.

Terraform (pp. 170-171)
To genetically engineer a planetary environment to make it suitable for human habitation (through the introduction of certain gases, plant life, etc.).

Tesla, Nikola (pp. 262)
Tesla coil (pp. 262)
A device created by Nikola Tesla that utilizes metallic coils that induce an EMF, thereby generating usable energy which can be converted into electricity.

Theory of Relativity (pp. 154)
A theory of the Universe developed by Albert Einstein.

Third-dimensional reality (pp. 15, 32, 51, 57-58, 121, 131, 151-152, 236)
A catch-all phrase meaning "normal" or "everyday" reality on Earth.

Third eye (pp. 76)
Another name for the 6th chakra, located in the lower middle of the forehead behind the pineal gland--center of clairvoyant vision and imagination.

Thought (pp. 12, 14, 18, 21, 31, 41, 44-49, 51-53, 55, 60-63, 65, 67-68, 71-72, 81, 86, 90, 101-102, 104, 107-108, 115, 117, 122-123, 131-134, 136-139, 142-143, 147, 203, 229, 236, 238-239, 248, 269, 278-283, 285, 287, 289-290, 292-293)
(1) Movement of consciousness; (2) mental energy; (3) the primary activity of the conscious mind.

Timelessness (pp. 17, 115-116, 132, 143-145, 147, 155, 157-159, 295)
(1) Pertaining to the dimensions beyond time and space; (2) eternal newness; (3) a

state of deep meditation beyond thought.

Time portal (pp. 190)

(1) An interdimensional vortex occurring naturally or artificially that acts as a link between different time frames and/or dimensions; (2) an area where time and space are warped--provides an entry/exit door for beings from other time frames and dimensions.

Trance channeling; trance medium (pp. 21-22, 83, 85, 135, 182)

(1) A state of deep meditation whereby a soul's personality (ego) temporarily vacates the body and the soul's higher self, an entity, or another energy comes through the body. Trance channeling is similar to a soul transfer except that channeling is temporary; (2) another name for a trance channel.

Transcend (pp. 44, 47, 55, 98, 135, 140, 155, 199, 222-223, 243, 257, 261, 277, 290)

(1) To go beyond limitation; (2) to expand awareness until it encompasses the higher dimensions.

Transfiguration (pp. 193, 209)

A form of genetic transmutation whereby the physical form of a soul is radically altered prior to ascension by infusing it with light activation codes, often causing the body to shine and shimmer--described in the Bible as "clothed in white raiment."

Transformation (pp. 3, 58, 221-223, 235, 237, 247, 260-261, 268)

(1) A sudden shift away from an old way of being or thinking; (2) the result of a quantum shift from one density to the next.

Translation (pp. 208-209, 251)

The process of disappearing into light during ascension, or more accurately, the point at which the physical body becomes invisible to 3rd density sight.

Transmission (pp. 2, 83, 264, 295)

(1) Sending of energy or a message through a trance medium, i.e., channeling; (2) the sending of a telepathic message to a receiver; (3) a great outpouring of energy directed into a specific realm or world.

Transmutation (pp. 140)

(1) The ability to consciously mutate the cellular structure of the body through opening to receive light activation codes or higher energy transmissions; (2) any mutation that results in a density shift for a life form; (3) the act of transcending an old belief system or thought form by releasing and integrating suppressed emotional energy at the cellular level (resulting in permanent physical, emotional and mental change).

Trantor (pp. 191)

Spiritual headquarters of the Solar Cross, a galactic organization working with the Confederation.

Trilaterals (pp. 179)

A large organization of governmental and political leaders linked to the Illuminati. Only a small percentage of its members are aware of their ties to the Orion/Sirian complex.

Trinity (pp. 163-167, 196-197)

(1) The triune nature of God as Father, Son and Holy Spirit; (2) any three-part model of the Godhead, such as Father-Mother-Christ, or Brahma-Vishnu-Shiva.

Truth (pp. 1-2, 7, 9, 11, 13-15, 47, 57, 65, 81, 116, 125, 129, 133, 161, 182, 205, 209, 213, 215, 217-218, 225, 229, 232, 243, 247, 257, 260, 292, 295)

(1) That which is actually so about a given reality; (2) the sum total of all relative viewpoints regarding a given reality; (3) a 12th-dimensional perception of reality.

Twin flame (pp. 125-126, 145, 183, 257)

(1) The original counterpart to an emerged soul; i.e., the "other half" of an oversoul that has fragmented into two individual souls; (2) the will (female) counterpart of spirit (male), or vice versa. Each individual soul in Creation has only one twin flame. A related term, "soul mate" is not discussed in this book. "Soul mates" (also known as "parallel souls") are souls with similar evolutionary patterns. Soul mates often come together throughout many lifetimes to work out karma and enhance each other's spiritual growth. Each individual soul in Creation has many soul mates.

UFO; Unidentified Flying Object (pp. 184)

Pertains to any aerial phenomena or craft with unknown origins and/or occupants. Most UFOs are either secret government/military experimental craft (approximately 30%) or spaceships operated by the Zeta Reticuli (approximately 60%). A few (less than 1%) are 4th- dimensional Pleiadean or Venusian craft. Approximately 10% of reported UFOs consist of the planet Venus at low altitude, meteors, weather balloons, missiles, or swamp gas.

Ultraviolet (pp. 7)

Frequencies to the right of violet on the light spectrum, i.e., higher frequencies in the invisible spectrum.

Unconditional love (pp. 107, 123, 225, 248, 286-288)

Love for its own sake, not contingent upon any internal or external conditions.

Unconscious (pp. 21-22, 36, 67, 80, 137, 172, 211-212, 225, 227, 243, 254, 256)

(1) Having no awareness; (2) the part of the self beyond or beneath the conscious awareness that is inaccessible in one's present state of consciousness (not to be confused with subconscious, which is a specific part of the mind accessible at any time).

Unitarian (pp. 1)

A non-denominational, non-Christian religion that stresses individual freedom within commonality, social welfare, and intellectual exploration for both atheists and believers--founded in Boston in the 18th century.

Universal awareness (pp. 17, 116, 159, 209)

Awareness of the Universe as a whole--similar to cosmic consciousness.

Universal gods (pp. 17, 127, 157, 159)

Highly evolved beings capable of creating entire universes.

Universal law (pp. 15-16, 55-56, 131, 158)

(1) Natural principles pertaining to specific dimensions or planes of existence that are consistent within those dimensions or planes; (2) Absolute truths about the Universe and how it functions.

Universal mind (pp. 68, 89, 98, 100, 104-105, 170, 250, 265)

(1) The mind of God; (2) universal intelligence existing in all levels and dimensions and having awareness of same.

Universal mind computer (pp. 68)

The aspect of Universal Mind that functions like a computer, with mathematical precision, governing all mechanical laws of the Universe, such as electromagnetism. Also contains the Akashic records and etheric blueprints of all life.

Universe (pp. 2, 7-11, 15-17, 19-20, 25, 54, 57-58, 68, 76, 80-81, 83, 87, 113-114, 117, 119-122, 124, 127, 131-132, 138-139, 143, 146-147, 149, 157-160, 163, 165-167, 169, 183, 195-197, 199, 216, 218-219, 224-226, 232-233, 238-239, 241, 250, 257, 261, 263, 287, 289, 291-292, 295)

If capitalized, means "all that is"--if lower case, refers to a complete system of dimensions, densities and levels of awareness.

Unknowable (pp. 17, 147, 157-159)
(1) The part of the Universe that will always remain incomprehensible, even to a highly advanced soul; (2) that which cannot be known, no matter how lofty the perception, or high the dimensional awareness.

Unknown (pp. 2, 17-18, 55, 63, 93, 127, 147, 157-159, 163, 199, 229, 234, 292)
The part of the Universe that is not yet comprehensible, but may become so later in a soul's evolution.

Urantia (pp. 177)
An ancient name of Earth given during the "Luciferian rebellion" which occurred over 300,000 years ago.

Utopia (pp. 260)

Van Tassel, George (pp. 183)
Scientist and UFO researcher in the 50's at Giant Rock in the Mojave Desert of Southern California. Venusian contactee.

Vegans (pp. 169, 174, 184)
Beings from the star system Vega.

Veils (pp. 81, 178, 229, 292)
Barriers to awareness voluntarily or involuntarily assumed by a soul prior to incarnation on Earth, causing the soul to forget his/her past lives and/or origins.

Venusians (pp. 174, 182-183, 192, 198, 298)
6th density beings from the etheric realms of Venus--capable of travelling through time and appearing in the physical.

Vertical time (pp. 101)
Another name for momentary time.

Vibration (pp. 27, 32, 63, 80, 85, 119, 121-123, 126-127, 133-134, 142, 169-172, 178, 181-182, 188-189, 193-194, 199, 209, 211-213, 217, 248, 250, 253, 261, 264, 273, 291)
(1) Frequency of movement; (2) movement of energy in a life form or object; (3) energy "signature" given off by an entity, object or thought form; (4) a way of measuring the level of awareness of an entity.

Virtual reality (pp. 170, 264)
(1) An artificial reality made to look like the larger reality in which it is contained; (2) a computer-simulated model of reality that allows the viewer to materially participate, such as the "Holodeck" in Star Trek, or a flight simulator for aircraft pilot training.

Visionaries (pp. 123, 126, 144, 183, 235, 250)
(1) Souls who are able to see beyond the third-dimensional timeline; (2) prophets and idealists who foresee great advances in the future of humanity and are working to bring about the necessary changes to manifest that future.

Visions (pp. 90, 95, 123-124, 142, 208, 217, 236, 299)
Clairvoyant images pertaining to higher dimensions.

Vivation (pp. 269)
A tradename for a process, created by Jim Leonard and the International Vivation Community, similar to Integrative Rebirthing - see "Rebirthing".

Void (pp. 17-18, 96, 127, 147, 157-160, 165, 199, 225, 233, 295)
(1) The part of the Universe containing no life forms or detectable vibrations; (2) the unmanifested part of the Godhead; (3) that which is beyond the Godhead.

Vortex (pp. 140, 249-250)
An area of concentrated EMFs corresponding to the intersection points of flux lines in the Earth's EMF. A vortex can occur naturally along the grid lines of the planet, or can be created artificially through radionics and spiritual practices.

Walk-in (pp. 84, 172-174, 182) - See "Soul transfer" and "Implantation"

Warp factor (pp. 119)
A science fiction term pertaining to harmonics of the speed of light.

White hole (pp. 164)
The opposite of a black hole, an area in third-dimensional time and space where matter and energy from a parallel universe enters the physical universe.

White magic (pp. 178)
The use of occult rituals to achieve positive, life-enhancing results.

Will (pp. 11, 17, 30, 33, 36-38, 56-57, 72, 75-78, 81, 84, 108, 134-136, 141, 145, 154-155, 157-159, 164, 169, 186-188, 190, 197, 208, 210-211, 213, 223, 232, 235-237, 243-245, 248-249, 259, 274, 289)
(1) Emotional desire coupled with power; (2) the feminine pole of Creation, or experiencer of life; (3) another name for the emotional body.

Will fragments (pp. 134, 136)
Parts of an un-integrated will that are split off from the parent part. See "Cording" and "Soul Fragmentation"

World Health Organization (pp. 229)

World War I and II (pp. 228)

Wormhole (pp. 251)
A bridge between two universes connecting a black hole and white hole. The black hole is like the entrance to the wormhole, and the white hole, the exit.

Yahweh; YHWH (pp. 164)
A member of the spiritual hierarchy and the oversoul of Jehovah, the God of Moses.

Yang (pp. 164, 223)
The masculine, or positive pole of Creation.

Yin (pp. 164, 223)
The feminine, or negative pole of Creation.

Yoga (pp. 2, 27, 249, 275, 277)
A series of sciences involving the relationship between body, mind and spirit, often consisting of meditation, body postures, breathing and philosophy - examples include Raja Yoga, Hatha Yoga, Iyengar Yoga and Tantra Yoga.

Zeta Reticulins (pp. 174, 180, 184-188, 190-191, 216, 219-220)
Third and fourth density beings from the star system Zeta Reticuli who are interbreeding with humans in an effort to save their race from extinction. They have atrophied emotions and an inability to reproduce without outside help.

BIBLIOGRAPHY

2150 A.D.
Thea Alexander, Macro Books, Tempe, AZ.

A Course In Miracles
Foundation for Inner Peace, Tiburon, CA.

Actualizations
Stewart Emery, Dolphin Books, Garden City, NY.

As a Man Thinketh
James Allen, DeVorss & Co., Marina Del Rey, CA.

Autobiography of a Yogi
Paramahansa Yogananda, Self-Realization Fellowship, Los Angeles, CA.

Bashar, Blueprint for Change
Darryl Anka, New Solutions Publishing, Simi Valley, CA.

Diet for a New America
John Robbins, Stillpoint Publishing, Walpole, NH.

Ecstasy is a New Frequency
Chris Griscom, Bear & Company, Santa Fe, NM.

El An Ra, The Healing of Orion
Solara, Star-Borne Unlimited, Charlottesville, VA.

Flight of the Eagle
J. Krishnamurti, Harper & Row, New York, NY.

Genesis Revisited
Zecharia Sitchin, Avon Books, New York, NY.

I Deserve Love
Sondra Ray, Les Femmes Publishing, Millbrae, CA.

Journey of the Heart
John Welwood, Ph.D., HarperCollins, San Francisco, CA.

Krishnamurti's Notebook
J. Krishnamurti, Harper & Row, New York, NY.

Man Triumphant
Annalee Skarin, DeVorss & Co., Marina del Rey, CA.

Maps to Ecstasy
Gabrielle Roth, New World Library, San Rafael, CA.

Physical Immortality
Leonard Orr, I Am Alive Now, Chico, CA.

Rebirthing: The Science of Enjoying All of Your Life
Jim Leonard & Phil Laut, Trinity Publications, Hollywood, CA.

Right Use of Will (Vol. I), Original Cause (Vol. II & III), Earth Spell (Vol. IV), Heart Song (Vol. V)
Ceanne de Rohan, Four Winds Publications, Santa Fe, NM.
Spiritual Economics
Eric Butterworth, Unity Press, Unity Village, MO.
The Flame of Attention
J. Krishnamurti, Harper & Row, New York, NY.
The Gods of Eden
William Bramley, Avon Books, New York, NY.
The Hundredth Monkey
Ken Keyes, Jr., Vision Books, Coos Bay, OR.
The Keys of Enoch
J.J. Hurtak, Academy of Future Science, Los Gatos, CA.
The Life and Teachings of the Masters of the Far East
Baird Spalding, DeVorss & Co., Marina Del Rey, CA.
The Prism of Lyra
Lyssa Royal, Royal Priest Research, Scottsdale, AZ.
The Road Less Traveled
M. Scott Peck, Simon & Schuster, New York, NY.
The Silva Mind Control Method
Jose Silva, Silva Mind Control International, Inc., Laredo, TX.
Way of the Peaceful Warrior
Dan Millman, H.J. Kramer, Tiburon, CA.
Ye Are Gods
Annalee Skarin, DeVorss & Co., Marina Del Rey, CA.